Reclaiming Democracy

Joerg Forbrig and Pavol Demeš, Editors

RECLAIMING DEMOCRACY

Civil Society and Electoral Change
in Central and Eastern Europe

G|M|F The German Marshall Fund
of the United States
STRENGTHENING TRANSATLANTIC COOPERATION

ERSTE Foundation

Published by

The German Marshall Fund of the United States

1744 R St. N.W.

Washington, DC 20009

Cataloging-in-Publication Data

Forbrig, Joerg, and Pavol Demeš (eds.)

Reclaiming Democracy. Civil Society and Electoral Change
in Central and Eastern Europe

p. cm.

ISBN 978 – 80 – 969639 – 0 – 4
(paperback)

Printed in the Slovak Republic

LIST OF CONTENTS

PREFACE

Václav Havel

The epochal social changes that took place in Central and Eastern Europe in the 1980s and 1990s opened an avenue for millions of Europeans to live a dignified life in liberty and democracy after decades under communism. Free elections, human rights, civic liberties, the rule of law, as well as economic transformation and an independent foreign policy were high on the agenda of all newly formed democratic governments.

Yet while the formal establishment of democracy typically took only a matter of days, weeks or, at most, months, real democracy did not emerge easily. It is, indeed, an ongoing process, one that has not been completed even now. New generations, without the burdensome experience of life under totalitarianism, are only now emerging into adulthood. These new generations are only gradually moving into positions in the decision making process in their countries. The situation in countries that overcame communist dictatorship, and the various problems and obstacles they experience on their way to democracy, is called postcommunism.

For long decades under communist rule, private property was not permitted, having been forcibly nationalized in dramatic circumstances after World War II. Similarly, public office was accessible only to those linked to the governing ideology. Thus, the communist regime effectively destroyed the legacies of the older political and entrepreneurial classes, after generations that had developed a sense of responsibility for private property and respect for the rule of law.

Hence, for the democratic governments newly formed after 1989, the renewal of a state firmly rooted in the rule of law and the enactment of an economic transformation process based on privatization were standard, but nevertheless, complicated tasks. The massive redistribution of property not only corrected some of the previous excesses, it also created tempting opportunities for a variety of economic adventurers. While new governments struggled to ensure the functioning of basic constitutional principles and the integration of their countries with the international community, the former nomenclatura used their experience, resources and contacts to their own advantage. They adapted to the new situation very quickly, taking positions in politics and the economy, justice and law enforcement, and the media, all the while retaining the networks they had inherited from the past. Strong social pressure for swift change meant that legislation was prepared and approved without sufficient time for testing it out in practice. As a result, economic transformation often took place in uncertain and imperfect legal circumstances.

Postcommunism, with its exaggerated emphasis on the power of the economy, politics, law enforcement, justice and the media, can be seen, to some extent, as echoing the communist period. Newly formed mafias have often enough simply replaced the old communist authorities, not uncommonly brandishing nationalist flags and slogans. The patience of people has been enormous, but is not without limits. Fortunately, the ethos of the anti-communist revolutions of 1989 and 1990, the natural self-organization of civil society and the international context made a return to totalitarianism impossible. Sooner or later, the situation in various postcommunist countries ripened into civic protest against the new abuses of power. But, in each country this development took a different path and, therefore, one should not equate developments in Slovakia with those in Serbia or Georgia.

I am delighted that this book is dedicated to the role of civil society in rising up against postcommunism. In my opinion, it is an injustice that these revolutions have not received their due share of attention, but have often remained in the shadow of those that preceded them in 1989 and 1990.

Washington, January 2007

INTRODUCTION

Joerg Forbrig and Pavol Demeš

Slovakia, September 1998: Parliamentary elections see the governing coalition of Prime Minister Vladimír Mečiar, criticized domestically and internationally for his backsliding on democracy and isolationist policies, challenged by an alliance of opposition parties stressing their democratic and European aspirations. An energetic and polarized political campaign is accompanied by a broad effort of civil society groups to provide voters with information about the elections, to encourage their participation and to monitor the electoral process. A neck-and-neck race ensues. Eventually, 84 percent of voters turn out, and in an electoral competition deemed fair by the international community, the populist-nationalist Mečiar government is replaced by a democratic coalition government, under Prime Minister Mikuláš Dzurinda.

Croatia, January 2000: Parliamentary elections take place, ousting the Croatian Democratic Union of the recently deceased President Franjo Tuđman, whose nationalist and semi-authoritarian politics dominated the country since independence in 1990. In a civic coalition for free and fair elections, nongovernmental organizations rally voters for democratic change, provide election-related information and motivate citizens to cast their votes *en masse*. 75 percent of voters turn out on the day. In parallel, long-divided democratic opposition parties form two coalitions that win the elections and take office under Prime Minister Ivica Račan.

Serbia, September 2000: Through early presidential elections, nationalist strongman Slobodan Milošević attempts to prolong his rule, but is successfully challenged by Vojislav Koštunica, candidate of the newly united Democratic Opposition of Serbia. A broad civil society coalition provides voter information, calls on citizens to go to the polls and ensures election monitoring, while a youth resistance movement campaigns against Milošević's quasi-dictatorship and demands democratic change. After the ballot is clearly manipulated in Milošević's favor, protests break out and hundreds of thousands take to the streets, eventually forcing Milošević to resign and bringing the democratic opposition to power under President Koštunica, a result confirmed by a landslide victory in parliamentary elections two months later.

Georgia, November 2003: The "For a New Georgia" bloc of incumbent President Eduard Shevardnadze, whose ten-year rule has increasingly led Georgia into political, social and economic crisis, is declared victorious in parliamentary elections. Suspicions of massive electoral fraud abound and are substantiated by independent election monitors. Over the days following the ballot, the political opposition, civil society and youth groups stage increasingly powerful street protests that reach their height when protesters peacefully interrupt the opening session of the new parliament. As a result of what soon comes to be known as the Rose Revolution, Shevardnadze resigns and new elections are held for both the parliament and the presidency. The democratic opposition under Mikheil Saakashvili wins overwhelming victories and Saakashvili is confirmed as president.

Ukraine, November 2004: Presidential elections are held to determine Leonid Kuchma's successor. Kuchma's presidency has led Ukraine increasingly away from democracy. His designated successor, Viktor Yanukovych, is challenged by Viktor Yushchenko, the joint candidate of the united democratic opposition. To ensure a democratic electoral process, civil society groups carry out various campaigns to provide information, encourage a high turnout and monitor the electoral process, while youth groups publicly demand political change. The official result of the run-off gives Yanukovych a clear lead, but is contested by election monitors who provide evidence of massive manipulations of the ballot. In response, the democratic opposition and civil society groups mount month-long protests that bring hundreds of thousands onto the streets of Kyiv. Under the pressure of the Orange Revolution, the Supreme Court eventually orders repeat elections. Viktor Yushchenko becomes the new president.

Reclaiming Democracy through Elections

The sequence of events that has swept through Central and Eastern Europe in recent years is remarkable. What initially seemed to be individual incidents of democratic re-adjustment in Slovakia and Croatia expanded into a series of spectacular political transformations in countries as diverse as Serbia, Georgia and Ukraine. A pattern emerged that has been variously labeled "color revolutions", "transitions from postcommunism" or "electoral breakthroughs". Some observers have gone further and have framed these developments as a "fourth wave of democracy".[1] And, while observers may differ in the terminology they employ, the details of their analyses and in their overall assessments of the events, they typically agree on a number of characteristics common to these recent democratic changes and the situations in the countries where they took place.

First and foremost, all these countries underwent initial democratic reform in the early 1990s. Once communism had collapsed, they established the basic institutions of democracy and held competitive elections. Constitutions were drafted, enshrining fundamental civil and political liberties, and first moves were made towards the development of the rule of law and an independent judiciary. Political parties

---

1 See, among many others, Michael McFaul, "Transitions from Postcommunism", Journal of Democracy, vol. 16, no. 3 (July 2005), pp. 5-19.; and "The Fourth Wave of Democracy and Dictatorship: Compromise and Noncooperative Transitions in the Postcommunist World," World Politics, vol. 54, no. 2 (January 2002), pp. 212-244.

emerged and reflected social pluralism and differing views, as did rapidly developing civil society structures and independent media. Market principles were introduced and privatization started to transform the economy. Thus, embarking on multiple political, economic and social transitions, hopes were high that Slovakia and Croatia, Serbia, Georgia and Ukraine, along with their other neighbors in Central and Eastern Europe, would quickly come to resemble western liberal democracies and integrate with European and international structures.

These expectations were soon frustrated, however. War broke out in the former Yugoslavia and shattered democratic hopes. Reforms stalled in Slovakia, Georgia and Ukraine, and within a few years many moves towards democracy were reversed. Although they were brought to office in free and fair elections, the governments of Mečiar, Tuđman, Milošević, Shevardnadze and Kuchma began to disregard democratic principles and to manipulate fledgling institutions in order to consolidate their power. Over time, executive pressure was systematically broadened to affect any realm that could ensure democratic checks and balances, from political opponents, parties and institutions, to the independent media and civil society organizations. All manner of state resources, from legal changes to administrative procedures to security apparatuses, were employed to silence dissent, while corrupt privatization practices served to solidify the economic *status quo* in favor of the ruling elites. Within a few years, democracy had become a *façade*, a veil for political regimes that were increasingly authoritarian in nature.

Although dubious in their democratic credentials, leaders in the five countries still felt the need to justify and legitimize their actions before the public. For this purpose, one mechanism was strong nationalist rhetoric, arguing that newly independent countries needed to consolidate and fend off domestic and foreign threats, for which a strong center of power, rather than dispersed democratic politics, were required. This reasoning resonated with many, as all these countries had only just emerged from the larger and multi-ethnic Czechoslovakia, Yugoslavia and Soviet Union, and provided a considerable social foundation for non-democratic politics in the five countries, although one that could be expected to weaken over time, as statehood was less and less in question.

Elections were regularly held in the five countries, in order to draw legitimacy from within and international acceptance from without, and even regularly confirmed the support base within society for the "strong leadership" approach. But, while Mečiar and Milošević, Tuđman and Shevardnadze had originally come to office through free and fair elections, they grew increasingly uncertain of the support they could muster in society and started to manipulate subsequent ballots, using biased coverage in government-controlled media, changed election laws to sideline the political opposition and, ultimately, fully-fledged electoral fraud.

But, despite their increasingly far-reaching and aggressive attempts to control power, political leaders in the five countries never managed to fully subdue their societies. Several realms remained outside the control of the state, embodying important "islands of democracy". These included a political opposition that, while often divided, remained present and visible in both national and local politics. Elements of independent, usually commercial, media existed that could, at least in part, counter the propaganda of state-controlled broadcasters and newspapers. Parts of the business community came to see rampant corruption and cronyism as liabilities and readied resources for political change. Civil society groups became increasingly vocal in addressing democratic deficits in their countries. Segments of society, especially the younger, urban and educated among them, grew more and more critical of the social situation in their countries, domestic politics and their international isolation.

In the five countries, the temptation of incumbent governments to grab for power, their need for legitimacy and the survival of democratic pockets within in their societies, were cross-pressures that resulted in settings that can be characterized as both authoritarian and democratic. Analysts have described such regimes variously as "semi-autocratic" or "neo-authoritarian" and as "illiberal" or "phony" democracies.[2] This hybrid nature, however, encapsulated the central weakness of these regimes, as authoritarianism and democracy are essentially irreconcilable. The hybridity of these regimes eventually led to their downfall through elections, the most democratic of means.

What ensued in the five countries was a very similar sequence of events. A semi-autocratic government prepared for elections in order to gain renewed legitimacy, yet was challenged by declining public support and a united opposition that successfully portrayed the elections as a referendum on the principal *status quo* in the country. Through independent media, and supported by civil society activities aimed at voter information and mobilization, this fundamental choice was addressed to the public at large, resulting in an above-average turnout, especially among classical change voters, such as younger, urban and educated people. Defensive government attempts to manipulate the elections in its favor were either limited by the presence of independent election monitors, as in Slovakia and Croatia, or disclosed to the voting public, which came onto the streets *en masse* to protest election fraud, as in Serbia, Georgia and Ukraine. Democratic challengers ultimately prevailed over semi-autocratic incumbents and took office.

---

2 Analyses and characterizations along these lines have been proposed by, among others, Fareed Zakaria, "The Rise of Illiberal Democracy", Foreign Affairs, vol. 76, no. 6 (November-December 1997), pp. 22-43; and Lucan A. Way, "The Sources and Dynamics of Competitive Authoritarianism in Ukraine", Journal of Communist Studies and Transition Politics, vol. 20, no. 1 (March 2004), pp. 143-161.

Yet, in order for this scenario to succeed and to return hybrid regimes to a more democratic path of development, as witnessed in the five countries, a number of conditions had to be present. Crucially, these included an unpopular incumbent leader and government, a united opposition, independent election monitoring, at least some independent media and sources of objective information and a potential for mass mobilization. Other factors, such as splits within the security apparatus, the availability of local resources and foreign support and pressure or incentives from the international community, were also observed.[3]

The Contributions to this Book

An important factor affecting the constellation for change was the involvement of civil society. Be it through election monitoring or the supply of independent information, get-out-the-vote activities or the mobilization of citizens in protest against rigged elections, nongovernmental organizations, foundations, youth groups and many other civic initiatives engaged in pre-election projects and campaigns and made a notable contribution to reclaiming democracy. It is for this reason that this book is dedicated to a more detailed account and analysis of civil society's role in effecting democratic change in Slovakia, Croatia, Serbia, Georgia and Ukraine in recent years.

The first part of the book provides a panorama of the civil society efforts, pre-election campaigns and civic movements that emerged in the five countries. It brings together case studies from the five countries, contributed by key activists, themselves involved in the civic projects described and who, therefore, are in a position to share unique and intimate knowledge of the development, approach and effects of civil society activities before and during the critical elections. These insider accounts place an emphasis on authenticity, rather than on scholarly analysis, and in their focus on specific groups and campaigns, they should be seen as representative of the broader range of civil society actions that contributed to democratic change in the countries concerned.

The case study series is opened by Martin Bútora, who examines the Civic Campaign OK '98 that took place in Slovakia. In response to the growing neo-authoritarianism of successive governments under Vladimír Mečiar, and in parallel to coalition-building on the part of the democratic opposition, civil society joined forces and launched this nonpartisan campaign in the run-up to the 1998 parliamentary elections. As a country-wide concerted action with a focus on informing citizens about the elections, encouraging them to vote and providing for civic oversight of the election process,

---

3 See Valerie J. Bunce and Sharon L. Wolchik, "Favorable Conditions and Electoral Revolutions", Journal of Democracy, vol. 17, no. 4 (October 2006), pp. 5-18.; Michael McFaul, "Transitions from Postcommunism", Journal of Democracy, vol. 16, no. 3 (July 2005), pp. 5-19.

this project not only helped to return Slovakia to democracy, but it set an important example, soon to be followed by civic activists in other postcommunist countries.

Among the first to draw on the Slovak experience were civil society groups in Croatia, as is detailed by Sharon Fisher and Biljana Bijelić in their chapter on the GLAS 99 campaign. Political and social discontent with President Tuđman had grown to such an extent that democratic change seemed possible through the parliamentary elections in January 2000. If such change did eventually materialize, this also owed to civil society taking a stronger role in changing the public discourse, and launching an election-related information and mobilization effort focusing on a few key target groups, including young voters, women and pensioners. In so doing, GLAS 99 helped to overcome the culture of fear that kept voices of dissent from speaking out against the political and social injustices of Croatia's semi-autocratic regime.

Developments in Slovakia and Croatia, and the role of civic campaigns pressing for democratic elections, inspired similar efforts by civil society in Serbia, as Jelica Minić and Miljenko Dereta lay out in their chapter. In Serbia, the IZLAZ 2000 (Exit 2000) campaign presented the September 2000 presidential elections as a potential exit from the domestic crisis and international isolation that country experienced under the Milošević regime. However, the nature of that regime, incomparably more determined to cling to power than the leadership in Slovakia and Croatia, required additional and novel forms of civic action for change. Chief among these was the youth movement OTPOR (Resistance) whose more radical anti-Milošević campaign was an important complement to the more moderate and positive appeal of IZLAZ 2000. Jointly, these and several other civic initiatives succeeded in mobilizing hundreds of thousands of Serbian citizens to protest obvious election fraud, eventually forcing Milošević to resign and give way to a democratically elected government.

This more radical pattern of civic engagement was replicated by Georgian civil society, and especially the youth group KMARA (Enough!), which drew much inspiration from OTPOR in Serbia. Giorgi Meladze and Giorgi Kandelaki illustrate how effectively this relatively small youth movement, in cooperation with a few established nongovernmental organizations, challenged the regime of Eduard Shevardnadze. At times bold, at times funny, but always strictly nonviolent in its resistance, KMARA paved the way for the mass protests that ensued within days of the rigged parliamentary elections in November 2003 and resulted in the installation of a democratically elected government. With this Rose Revolution, as the authors point out, successful civic action for electoral change also made its entry into the post-Soviet space.

Ukraine is the subject of the last case study in the series. One of the driving forces of the spectacular Orange Revolution was, according to Iryna Chupryna, Vladyslav Kaskiv and Yevhen Zolotariov, the Civic Campaign PORA (It's Time!), an information and mobilization program launched prior to the presidential elections in 2004 and involving numerous civic groups and volunteers across Ukraine. Besides its sheer scale and visibility during the democratic breakthrough in Ukraine, an interesting aspect of PORA is that it combined the two forms of election-related civic campaigning observed in the other countries. One of its wings, yellow PORA, pursued a more moderate campaign aimed to ensure free and fair elections through information, get-out-the-vote and monitoring activities, as did OK '98, GLAS 99 and IZLAZ 2000. At the same time, another wing called black PORA espoused more radical demands and openly advocated the ouster of the neo-authoritarian government of President Kuchma, much like OTPOR in Serbia and KMARA in Georgia.

What emerges from these case studies is a fascinating story of citizens engaging in defense of their democratic rights, with a force that often took those in power by complete surprise. While there are many parallels between these five cases of change, the case studies also demonstrate the nuances that often remain hidden behind broader categories such as "color revolutions" that have been applied to recent democratic change in Central and Eastern Europe. In order to trace such differences and similarities more systematically, the second part of this book provides a set of comparative perspectives on electoral breakthroughs in the five countries. At the same time, such comparisons also help to place the observed civil society component in the broader political, social, economic and international context, and thus, to appreciate the relative significance of a broader set of factors that contributed to democratic change in postcommunist countries.

In his contribution, Vitali Silitski demonstrates that a central factor determining the chances for, course and outcome of electoral change was the nature of the semi-authoritarian regime in question. The degree of its consolidation of power and control over society, the existence or absence of any competing leadership and the use of identity politics led to very different scenarios of electoral change, which took the form of transformative elections in Slovakia and Croatia, but electoral revolutions in Serbia, Georgia and Ukraine. This regime factor is of particular relevance for the prospect of further electoral change in postcommunist Europe, which has rapidly decreased in the last years as remaining semi-authoritarian regimes have hardened and systematically narrowed the space for any remaining agents that may potentially become carriers of democratic change in their countries.

This specificity of individual countries and their variously non-democratic regimes relates closely to the strategies and resources employed by civil society in pressing for democratic change, as Pavol Demeš and Joerg Forbrig point out in the next chapter. A few overarching principles for civic campaigns pressing for electoral change do exist, including nonpartisanship and nonviolence, and have been at the core of an active transfer of experience among countries undergoing electoral breakthroughs. At the same time, no universal recipe exists for civil society efforts to assert democracy, a misconception shared by many, be they well or ill-intentioned. Instead, strategies and resources need to be commensurate with the very specific circumstances of individual countries, thus, demanding a high degree of flexibility and creativity among all pursuing and assisting democratic change.

One of the few constants across instances of electoral breakthrough has been the critical importance of young people. In their contribution, Valerie Bunce and Sharon Wolchik maintain that youth figured prominently as both subjects and objects of recent electoral change from Slovakia to Ukraine, although differing in form and extent across the countries. For democratic parties, first-time voters embodied an important reservoir of support, as did youth volunteering for NGOs and civic campaigns, and wherever protests ensued, young people were typically at the forefront of civil disobedience. However, and while in the short-run this upsurge in youth participation contributed much to achieving democratic breakthroughs through elections, the longer-term effects are less certain, as many young people quickly retreated into their private lives and discontinued their public involvement.

By comparison, much less obvious has been the influence of the economy on democratic change. In his chapter, Robin Shepherd surveys the broad parameters of economic development in the five postcommunist countries prior to electoral breakthroughs. His analysis points out that actual economic dynamics, growth and inflation, income and unemployment, make for very mixed effects, suggesting no clear causal links, although it is possible to find specific examples of economic influence. More subtly, perceptions and beliefs held by the broad public on socio-economic issues, such as corruption, affected the legitimacy of semi-autocrats. More overtly, private business played a role in electoral breakthroughs, not least through commercial broadcasters countering the propaganda of state-controlled media. These examples indicate that economic influences on democratization have been intertwined with a broader set of social and political factors.

These various determinants of electoral change are the subject of the chapter by Taras Kuzio. His systematic account describes factors leading to change including a competitive authoritarian state that allows space for a democratic opposition, "return to Europe" civic nationalism that assists in civil society mobilization, a preceding political crisis, a pro-democratic capital city, unpopular ruling elites, a charismatic candidate supported by a united opposition, youth politics, regionalism and foreign intervention. While these factors largely had to be in place for electoral breakthroughs to occur, whether or not democracy has consolidated in a given country has depended on several further conditions, including the ability of new governments to come to terms with the most recent past, divisions among democrats, the return of political parties affiliated with the previous semi-authoritarian regime and manifest progress with democratic reforms. These and other difficulties have marked the aftermath of democratic breakthroughs in the five countries and have given rise to concern. Such critical assessments must not overlook the progress made towards liberal democracy, more rapid in some of the countries while more gradual in others, yet in all cases successful to date in averting backsliding into semi-authoritarianism.

The overall positive record of recent electoral breakthroughs in Central and Eastern Europe, however, provokes the question of continued democratic change in the region and further afield. As Ivan Krastev argues in his more critical outlook concluding this book, the observed pattern of re-instating democracy through elections does not necessarily provide a model applicable to other postcommunist countries. The hardening and sophistication of remaining authoritarian regimes in Eastern Europe, mounting backlashes against democracy assistance, the rising populist threat to liberalism and the weakening of the European Union's soft power place powerful obstacles in the way of continued democratic change.

Acknowledgements

This book and its editors are indebted to many for their support. In the first place, all contributors deserve a special thank you. We would especially like to thank those who, as civic activists, found themselves in the unusual position of being authors, while all those used to writing professionally have had to muster unusual patience for this book to appear. We are also grateful to all those who kindly provided photographic material and illustrations. At the German Marshall Fund of the United States, Craig Kennedy and Phil Henderson supported this project from the very beginning, while Helena Mudríková helped with her usual calm and care. At Erste Foundation in Vienna, Austria, we were fortunate to find generous and gracious partners in Boris Marte, Knut Neumayer and their colleagues, and we hope that this book marks the beginning of a long and fruitful cooperative relationship. We would further like to thank our copy editor Yael Ohana at Frankly Speaking in Bratislava, Slovakia, who has been most flexible, skilful and patient, as well as Lucia Lörinczová and her creative team at Feriva in Bratislava, Slovakia, for ensuring the timely and quality production of this book. Most importantly, however, this book owes thanks to all those who helped to bring about the democratic changes described. It is to the courageous citizens of Slovakia, Croatia, Serbia, Georgia and Ukraine that we dedicate this book.

PART I: CASES

OK '98: A CAMPAIGN OF SLOVAK NGOS FOR FREE AND FAIR ELECTIONS

Martin Bútora

The number of civic campaigns undertaken by Slovak civil society is one of the most remarkable characteristics of the sector's recent history. Slovak nongovernmental organizations earned considerable public reputation in the struggle against the non-democratic practices of Prime Minister Vladimír Mečiar and his government. With the parliamentary elections in September 1998, this struggle came to a head. A consolidated platform of NGOs launched the civic campaign known as OK '98 (full name: *Občianska kampaň '98*) to increase citizens' awareness about the elections, to encourage them to vote and to guarantee a fair ballot through independent civic supervision. The campaign helped to mobilize the electorate and contributed to the record 84 percent turnout. Dozens of NGOs organized educational projects, cultural events, concerts, discussion forums and issued publications, video-clips and films. Hundreds of volunteers across the country attracted thousands of concerned citizens to election-related events.

The 1998 election was a milestone for Slovak citizens. It was a turning point in their struggle to determine the character of their state. After years of deviation towards illiberal democracy and isolation, Slovak voters clearly expressed the wish to live in a country respectful of the principles of democracy and the rule of law, integrated into Europe, recognized internationally and with real prospects for economic prosperity. With the help of OK '98, Slovak citizens ousted the semi-authoritarian Mečiar government and paved the way for Slovakia's rapid democratic and economic reform and full Euroatlantic integration.

Since then, NGOs have remained active and visible in public life, aiming at building a responsible citizenry, providing services, preserving diversity, testing social innovations, controlling those in power, promoting democratic governance and critically reflecting the country's social, political and economic problems. In so doing, civil society organizations have regularly concluded broader alliances and joint campaigns, such as, for example, the nationwide campaign launched in 2000 to ensure the enactment of a better Freedom of Information Act (supported by over 120 NGOs associating over 100,000 members). And, in spite of a certain disenchantment with politics, part of the civic sector was active prior to the 2002 elections, critical for Slovakia's Euroatlantic integration aspirations, following the example and good practice of OK '98.

Authoritarian Temptations:
Slovakia under Vladimír Mečiar

The Velvet Revolution of 1989 ushered in hopes for a new era of democracy, economic prosperity and Euroatlantic integration for Czechoslovakia. However, the usual course of democratic transitions, involving a founding election to confirm change, democratic institutionalization and consolidation[1], was complicated by the country's break-up at the end of 1992. While the peaceful dissolution of Czechoslovakia was rightly named the "Velvet Divorce", citizens regarded it with ambivalence and mixed feelings. Doubts abounded, notably regarding the legitimacy of the decision, as it was made without a referendum, and regarding the democratic convictions of the winners of the June 1992 elections, most notably, of Vladimír Mečiar, leader of *Hnutie za demokratické Slovensko* (Movement for a Democratic Slovakia, henceforth, HZDS), who ran Slovakia almost uninterruptedly from those elections until October 1998.

Mečiar's policy of national populism was not the only complicating factor for Slovakia's development, however. For Slovakia, nation-state building was demanding. The Czech part of the former common state, which had a history of statehood, democratic traditions, ethnic homogeneity and, in 1992, a stronger economy, was better able to cope with the many challenges brought about by independence. The new Slovak Republic faced the tasks of building democracy and the rule of law on the basis of relatively weak democratic traditions and with political elites that were highly polarized, at the same time as having to develop a new societal and cultural identity. The creation of a competent state bureaucracy, establishing new institutions (often from scratch) and strengthening the infrastructure of civil society had to be achieved. A market economy had to be rebuilt, rendered difficult by Slovakia's history of delayed modernization, characterized by strict economic regulation and the dominance of heavy industry and the manufacture of arms, typical of state socialism. While the social engineering of communist rule enabled the state to increase the standard of living and provide education and employment, it also advanced the idea that progress is possible without freedom and that it can be achieved even when human and civil rights are curtailed. Forty years of life under the guardianship of the socialist welfare state made many Slovaks believe that the drastic rise in unemployment that took place after the fall of communism was too high a price to pay for freedom.

An unscrupulous politician with autocratic inclinations, Mečiar built his popularity and power with promises that he would solve the country's problems if only allowed to rule as uncontested leader. After the early elections in 1994, he created a parliamentary alliance with the radical rightist nationalist *Slovenská národná strana* (the Slovak National Party, henceforth SNS) and the extreme anti-reform

---

1 See Soňa Szomolányi and John A. Gould (eds.), Slovakia: Problems of Democratic Consolidation and the Struggle for the Rules of the Game (Slovak Political Science Association and Friedrich Ebert Stiftung, Bratislava, 1997).

leftist *Združenie robotníkov Slovenska* (the Alliance of the Workers of Slovakia, henceforth ZRS). This special amalgam of authoritarian politics embraced both prewar traditionalist nationalist populism and postwar socialist collectivism. Slovakia slid into semi-authoritarianism, starting with the "night of the long knives" (November 3-4, 1994) during which the newly elected majority in the Slovak parliament seized control of key institutions, ranging from the National Property Fund to the Supreme Inspection Office to the Prosecutor General, excluding the political opposition from any important position in the parliament.

Strong criticism from the European Union and the United States of the "tyranny of the majority" developing in Slovakia did not dissuade Mečiar. Disrespect for and open confrontation with President Michal Kováč, repeated violations of the constitution, obstruction of the referendum on direct presidential elections held in May 1997, rising interventionism by the center at the expense of local self-government and the exclusion of the parliamentary opposition from oversight of the intelligence services, public media and the privatization process, all served to undermine democratic checks and balances. As a result, the state administration became politicized, the government openly interfered with state-run television and radio, the sizeable Hungarian minority was ostracized and the privatization process turned clientelist. Concern also spread about ties between organized crime and the government, exemplified by the suspected participation of the secret services in the kidnapping of President Kováč's son and the subsequent murder of a police officer involved in the investigation.

This anti-democratic style of governance, soon dubbed "Mečiarism",[2] left its imprint on political culture in Slovakia. "Winner takes all" majoritarianism, unwillingness to seek consensus, disrespect for minority opinions and the frequent labeling of critics as "enemies", "anti-Slovak" or "anti-state" were replicated by local autocrats loyal to the central government. Fear of government became widespread, especially in the countryside. Sharp political divisions reached deep into families and upset neighborly relations. Slovakia entered a period of "unconsolidated democracy" characterized by the exercise of power *ad hoc* and *ad hominem* and by the absence of firm rules.[3] And, even if the country had a vocal political opposition, some independent media, relatively autonomous trade unions and universities and a vibrant civil society, not to mention an independent constitutional court and president, the Slovak Republic fell behind its neighbors, not meeting the criteria for integration into the European Union and NATO and considered likely to be excluded from the first wave of enlargement.

---

2 See Marián Leško, Mečiar a mečiarizmus. Politik bez škrupúľ, politika bez zábran (VMV, Bratislava, 1996).

3 Philippe C. Schmitter, "Democratic Dangers and Dilemmas", Journal of Democracy, vol. 5, no. 2 (April 1994), pp. 57-74.

The country became increasingly internationally isolated, described as "a black hole in the heart of Europe" by U.S. Secretary of State Madeleine Albright.[4]

However, the government's authoritarian behavior also had unintended positive outcomes. Citizens began to pay greater attention to the question of democracy. If during the first years of postcommunist transformation people were most concerned with living standards, social insecurity, unemployment, crime and health care, in the second half of the nineties issues of political culture, democracy and the rule of law became increasingly important. People started to put more emphasis on pluralism, compliance with the law, the search for consensus and respect for minority rights. Critical intellectuals debated how the state could be "founded anew" and endowed with democratic content.[5] Of course, attitudes as revealed by opinion polls cannot guarantee political change, especially in situations where feelings of helplessness are widespread.[6] Increased public discontent becomes an impetus for political change only when groups of people take a particular issue on and organize and engage in civic activities geared at change. This was precisely the challenge that civil society in Slovakia as a whole, and NGOs, in particular, faced.

Civil Society in Slovakia after 1989

Associative life has historically flourished in Slovakia under conditions of democracy, although given the fifty year fate of authoritarianism that befell the country (the war time Slovak state, an ally of Hitler, from 1939 to 1945 was followed soon, thereafter, by state socialism from 1948 to 1989), such periods were rare. History, nevertheless, provides several examples, including the "associative fever" that erupted in the aftermath of the creation of Czechoslovakia in 1918 and the time during and after the Velvet Revolution of November 1989, during which there was an outburst of civic activism and one of the key protagonists of change in Slovakia, the movement *Verejnosť proti násiliu* (Public Against Violence), was created.

With the fall of communism, civil society developed rapidly. New legislation facilitated the upsurge in civic activity, particularly the Civil Association Act adopted in March 1990 by the federal parliament. The environmental movement, one of the primary motors of change in Slovakia, became multi-layered. Some former "green dissent" activists continued to operate in existing organizations, others established new

---

4 See Martin Bútora, Grigorij Mesežnikov and Zora Bútorová, "Diagnóza, ktorá nepustí", in: Sľuby a realita. Slovenská ekonomika 1995-1998 (M.E.S.A. 10, Bratislava, 1998).

5 Milan Šútovec, "Kam povedú tie diaľnice?", Domino Fórum (1, Bratislava, 1997).

6 According to an Institute for Public Affairs (IVO) survey carried out in October 1997, 80 percent of Slovaks felt that they did not have any influence over developments in the country. A depressive social atmosphere reigned, with 55 percent of citizens in June 1998 indicating they were afraid to discuss their political views in public. See Zora Bútorová, "Development of Public Opinion: from Discontent to the Support of Political Change" in: Martin Bútora, Grigorij Mesežnikov, Zora Bútorová and Sharon Fisher (eds.), The 1998 Parliamentary Elections and Democratic Rebirth in Slovakia (Institute for Public Affairs, Bratislava, 1999).

ones and yet others entered public life and became politicians, public officials and legislators. New political parties emerged and new interest groups were founded by students, who had been crucial to the success of the Velvet Revolution, and by artists, journalists, entrepreneurs and human rights activists. Previously suppressed groups, such as Christian associations, were free to pursue their activities. Civil society flourished at all levels from the national to local.[7] In October 1991, nongovernmental organizations held their first national conference, a landmark in the history of civil society in Slovakia that began a tradition of democratic governance in the third sector. In 1994, the *Grémium tretieho sektora* or Gremium of the Third Sector was founded: a voluntary advocacy group of 16 elected NGO representatives from various fields of civic activity including humanitarian and charitable activities, youth and education, the environment, human and minority rights and culture. The Gremium was unique in that it incorporated all key areas of civic action, earning it legitimacy and broad support. The Gremium's emergence coincided with the government's intensifying pressure on the third sector, which undoubtedly increased its unity in defense of the common interests of civil society in Slovakia.

Accompanying this development was the establishment of NGOs assisting the third sector with various services including training, information, legal counseling, the development of community foundations and policy analyses. Long-term grant making programs were launched by the Open Society Foundation, the Civil Society Development Foundation financed by the European Union's PHARE Program, the Democracy Network program of the United States Agency for International Development (USAID) and many other international funders. The Donors' Forum emerged as a service entity for NGOs, while the association ChangeNet influenced electronic communications by providing an independent Internet server for civil society. Many NGOs were involved in activities related to democracy, such as campaigning, educating and holding elected officials accountable. The attention of the broader public was attracted by The Gemma Foundation in Southern Slovakia, which organized a trek across the country to distribute literature and talk to citizens about the importance of the European Union and NATO. The People and Water Association in Eastern Slovakia successfully mobilized local inhabitants, mayors, priests and the media to oppose the construction of a new dam in Tichý Potok, with the result that the environment ministry shelved the plan.

By the mid-1990s, Slovakia had witnessed the emergence of almost every form of nongovernmental and nonprofit organization known in advanced democracies, with the exception perhaps of large endowed philanthropic entities. Slovak NGOs were fighting racism and drug addiction, cared for the sick and the disabled, worked for clearer air and water, taught music, art and sports, helped young workers find their first jobs and trained displaced workers for new jobs. Some were small operations

---

7 For an overview of civic associating, see Jozef Majchrák, Boris Strečanský and Martin Bútora (eds.), Keď ľahostajnosť nie je odpoveď (Inštitút pre verejné otázky, Bratislava, 2004).

driven by the energy and vision of a few volunteers. Others had professional staff, websites and extensive international contacts.

Slovakia's NGOs were much more than islands of isolated idealism or "islands of positive deviance", as independent civic initiatives were called by Slovak sociologists before the fall of communism in the late 1980s, hardened as they were by their clashes with the authorities during the *Tretí sektor SOS* (Third Sector SOS) campaign in 1996 to protest restrictive legislation on foundations. Even though the number of registered organizations fell after the enactment of the new law on foundations in June 1996, they had grown into an impressive force and constituted a vibrant and efficient "civil archipelago" of hope and positive action. In February 1998, on the eve of the OK '98 campaign, 14,400 civil society organizations were registered in Slovakia, including some 12,000 civic associations, societies, unions, movements, clubs and international NGOs, 422 foundations and 161 non-investment funds. These were also visible in public life, as evidenced by the approximated 25,000 articles on NGOs published between 1995 and 1997.

Overcoming Fragmentation in the Democratic Opposition

Under the pressure of adverse political developments, signs of increased civil mobilization gradually began to emerge. They came from all sectors of society. A wide array of civic organizations assembled in The Association of Civil Associations in Slovakia to protest the "Law on the Protection of the Republic", which would have posed a significant threat to freedom and democracy, but which was eventually rejected by parliament. The Center for Environmental Public Advocacy successfully concluded its legal assistance to the citizens of the small village of Ďubákovo, where a construction ban had been imposed by the state in 1982. In December 1997, the constitutional court declared the ban unconstitutional, which established an important precedent for local community rights in the face of the powerful water management and energy lobby. Representatives of the Hungarian minority effectively mobilized their voters to reject the government's implementation of so-called "alternative" education in the Slovak language, imposed without consultation with the Hungarian community. Students at Bratislava's Metodova Street high school stopped the politically motivated dismissal of their principal through protest action. Protest actions by actors and other members of the cultural community, who organized *Zachráňme kultúru* (Save Our Culture) forums, opposing government interference in the cultural sphere, were very popular although they were only partly successful. Many citizens, at least privately, agreed with the protests.[8]

In the political sphere, the democratic opposition in Slovakia underwent much-needed transformation and came to the realization that in order to confront the authoritarian tendencies of the incumbent government they would have to overcome their differences, substantive as they might have been. On the one hand, popular support for the opposition as a whole was significantly higher than support for the ruling coalition. On the other hand, the fragmented political opposition could not take advantage of its popularity with the public, as parties did not sufficiently communicate, cooperate and coordinate their efforts. In July 1997, the chairmen of the *Kresťanskodemokratické hnutie* (Christian Democratic Movement, henceforth KDH), *Demokratická únia* (the Democratic Union, henceforth DU), *Demokratická strana* (the Democratic Party, henceforth DS), *Sociálnodemokratická strana Slovenska* (the Social Democratic Party of Slovakia, henceforth SDSS) and *Strana zelených na Slovensku* (the Green Party of Slovakia, henceforth SZS) signed an agreement pledging to run in the 1998 parliamentary elections as a single bloc under the name of *Slovenská demokratická koalícia* or the Slovak Democratic Coalition (henceforth, SDK). The creation of SDK was an opportunity for smaller opposition parties that did not reach the five-percent threshold, as was the case the 1992 and 1994 elections.

The government's thwarting of the May 1997 referendum on direct presidential elections and on Slovakia's entry into NATO shook public opinion and the opposition into action.[9] The debate on direct presidential elections began in December 1996, when opposition representatives argued that it would be difficult for parliament to build the consensus required for electing a new president at the end of President Kováč's term in 1998. Following the governing coalition's refusal to schedule parliamentary debates on the proposal, the opposition petitioned for a referendum. They gathered more than 520,000 signatures, a significant number in a country of

---

8 In 1996, as much as 64 percent of citizens regarded as justified the protests of physicians and health care providers against government policy, 53 percent approved of the protests by theater artists and other representatives of the cultural community, 52 percent supported the protests by employees of privatized companies against privatization decisions and 50 percent agreed with the protests by university teachers and others in the academic community against the government's draft law on universities. According to IVO findings from July 1998, as much as 70 percent of respondents supported the protests of physicians and health care providers against government policy. See Zora Bútorová, "Development of Public Opinion: from Discontent to the Support of Political Change", in: Martin Bútora, Grigorij Mesežnikov, Zora Bútorová and Sharon Fisher (eds.), The 1998 Parliamentary Elections and Democratic Rebirth in Slovakia (Institute for Public Affairs, Bratislava, 1999), op cit.

9 For more details, see Grigorij Mesežnikov, "Domestic Politics", in: Martin Bútora and Thomas W. Skladony (eds.), Slovakia 1996-1997: A Global Report on the State of Society (Institute for Public Affairs, Bratislava, 1998). A detailed overview and analysis of the obstructed referendum can be found in: Grigorij Mesežnikov and Martin Bútora (eds.), Slovenské referendum '97: zrod, priebeh, dôsledky (Inštitút pre verejné otázky, Bratislava, 1997).

5.3 million inhabitants. According to a March 1997 survey, 57 percent of respondents intended to take part in the referendum and 76 percent declared that they were in favor of direct presidential elections, a clear success in shaping public discourse for the opposition.[10]

Subsequently, the parliament passed a resolution instructing the president to call a referendum on Slovakia's membership in NATO (despite the fact that Slovakia was not invited to join the alliance). President Kováč then decided to merge the referenda. This was vigorously opposed by Mečiar's ruling coalition, and the government instructed Interior Minister Gustáv Krajči to reprint the ballot papers without the question on direct presidential elections. In response, the central referendum commission declared the result void and asked for an investigation, in which the interior minister was later accused of committing a legal offense.[11] The opposition called for a boycott, resulting in 9.8 percent turnout. In the aftermath, doubt spread as to whether upcoming parliamentary elections could be free and fair and the democratic opposition and civil society began discussing how to ensure they would be. This was a political turning point in two respects as it created the impetus for the formation of the Slovak Democratic Coalition (SDK) and raised the challenge of how democratically-minded actors could avert the advent of an authoritarian regime in Slovakia.

Launching the OK '98 Campaign

In preparing for the OK '98 campaign, Slovak NGOs could build on the experience of several earlier campaigns. An early and well-known example of independent thought and action was the 1987 *Bratislava nahlas* (Bratislava Aloud) study, collectively produced by environmentalists, researchers and journalists. The report included facts about damage done to the environment and called for dialogue on the issue. The study's systematic criticism took on a political dimension. Several of the key figures behind this report were persecuted and harassed by the secret police, later appearing at the front line of active citizens in November 1989. After 1989, a noteworthy example was the *Tretí sektor SOS* (Third Sector SOS) campaign, which was launched in 1996 by the Gremium of the Third Sector against a discriminatory bill on foundations. The bill was criticized by the NGOs because, if passed, establishing foundations would be hampered by excessive bureaucracy and artificial barriers. Although it did not succeed in averting the bill, the campaign was influential. Many

---

10 See Public Opinion Research Institute, Názory. Informačný bulletin, vol. 8, no. 1 (Statistical Office of the Slovak Republic, Bratislava, 1997).

11 The district prosecutor dropped the criminal indictment and in November 1997, seven months after the referendum, the government backed the interior minister's actions.

organizations came out of the shadows, allying themselves with others[12] and inspiring citizens to engage in civic resistance.[13] Mečiar's 1994 to 1998 term of government was literally "littered" with protest meetings, petitions, open letters and other forms of expression in opposition to government policies. All of them carried an underlying democratic message, whether they were aimed at defending the social rights of citizens or at the direct defense of democracy and self-government in society.

That these protest activities often met with similar reactions from the authorities, before and after 1989, is no coincidence. If during the communist regime such activities were termed "anti-socialist", under Mečiar "anti-Slovak" was used. Pro-government media commonly claimed that the operation of the civic sector was the result of "stimulation from foreign centers" and accused NGOs of "supporting cosmopolitanism" and of endeavoring to "subvert the Republic". Bitter experience of the referendum, the very real threat of "double exclusion" from integration into the EU and NATO and the arrogance of those in power in flaunting the rule of law strengthened the concern of many Slovaks that the government would manipulate the elections in order to remain in power.[14] People felt that the legacy of the Velvet Revolution was threatened. For civic activists, it was time to think and act.

By the summer of 1997, Slovak NGO leaders had begun discussing their strategies for getting more involved in the parliamentary elections, forthcoming in 1998. An important landmark was the annual conference of the third sector that took place in October 1997 in Košice. Held under the title "Working Actively for Democracy", the conference adopted a final declaration supporting NGO activities aimed at increasing citizen awareness for free and fair elections in 1998. It also urged the presence of international observers during the election campaign. Later, in November 1997, the results of the conference were taken up at an informal meeting of representatives of the Foundation for a Civil Society, the German Marshall Fund of the United States, the Charles Stewart Mott Foundation and other donor organizations in Brussels. At a

---

12 Pavol Demeš and David Daniel, "Third Sector SOS Campaign" in: Building Civil Society Worldwide: Strategies for Successful Communication (CIVICUS Publications, Washington, DC, 1997).

13 Jan Surotchak, a civic activist with foreign experience, who served as the head of the Foundation for a Civil Society Program in Slovakia, underlined the factor of accumulated capacity, as follows, "The Third Sector SOS campaign in 1996 (...) built a great deal of capacity in the sector (...) I personally don't believe that OK '98 would have been that successful, if that experience had not been there (...)". Quoted in Oľga Berecká, Natália Kušnieriková and Dušan Ondrušek, "NGO Campaign for Free and Fair Elections. OK '98 – Lessons Learned" (Partners for Democratic Change, Bratislava, 1999).

14 The general lack of confidence of the citizenry in the possibility of free and fair parliamentary elections was demonstrated in an IVO survey conducted in January 1998. Only 41 percent of respondents believed that the elections would be free and fair, while 37 percent believed that they would not be. As many as 22 percent could not predict how the course of the elections would go. See Zora Bútorová, "Development of Public Opinion: from Discontent to the Support of Political Change", in: Martin Bútora, Grigorij Mesežnikov, Zora Bútorová and Sharon Fisher (eds.), The 1998 Parliamentary Elections and Democratic Rebirth in Slovakia (Institute for Public Affairs, Bratislava, 1999).

subsequent meeting in Vienna, on December 15, 1997, civic leaders from Bulgaria and Romania lent their experience from similar campaigns in their countries.

The framework of OK '98 was developed in January 1998 by the SAIA–Service Center for the Third Sector (henceforth, SAIA-SCTS) and it was presented, discussed and, after amendment, adopted at a meeting of founding NGOs on January 10, 1998.[15] A broader discussion within the NGO community and with various donors, including the Slovak Donors' Forum, took place over the following three months. As a result, on March 3, 1998, over 50 civic leaders met in Zvolen and issued the first statement about the campaign. The declaration included strong criticism of the government, expressing "a fundamental dissatisfaction" with the legislation regulating the electoral process and how it was prepared and approved, and presented the fundamental principles of the campaign to the public. Firstly, it declared its sense of responsibility at a decisive moment in Slovakia's history: "Slovakia is currently at a critical stage in its development. Citizens feel that their votes cannot alter developments in society. For this reason, it is enormously important that we take responsibility for our own future in the coming elections". Secondly, it espoused a moral commitment to civic participation: "We view it as our moral responsibility to contribute to ensuring that citizens take part in the political process and to monitor the course of the elections". Thirdly, it expressed determination to resist: "We declare that, in the case that anyone attempts to disrupt the democratic process in Slovakia, we will make use of our constitutional right to resist these attempts, together with representatives of trade unions, churches, local governments and other democratic forces". [16]

On this basis, the OK '98 campaign was developed as an open nonpartisan public initiative, designed to help ensure free and fair elections. It served the threefold aim of improving voter awareness and information about the parliamentary and local elections in 1998, increasing the turnout of citizens at the polls and increasing the influence of citizens on the preparation of the election law, thereby, ensuring citizen oversight of the fairness of the elections.[17] The fundamental function of the campaign "was to clarify among citizens the link between a responsible attitude in asserting one's right to vote and the potential for solving contemporary individual

15 The Civic Campaign OK '98 was initiated by eleven well-known personalities involved in Slovak NGOs representing organizations active in the field of civil society and democracy building. Subsequently they created the campaign's coordination council. They were: Andrej Bartosiewicz (Association for the Support of Local Democracy), Ingrid Baumannová (The Foundation for a Civil Society [NOS]), Daniel Brezina (Gemma '93), Zora Bútorová (Institute for Public Affairs), Pavol Demeš (SAIA-Service Center for the Third Sector), Péter Hunčík (Sándor Márai Foundation), Michal Kravčík (People and Water), Juraj Mesík (Ekopolis-EPCE), Dušan Ondrušek (Partners for Democratic Change Slovakia), Braňo Orgoník (Informal Association of Trenčín) and Šarlota Pufflerová (Foundation Citizen and Democracy, MRG) who became the spokesperson for the campaign.
16 See Pavol Demeš, OK '98 Campaign of Slovak NGOs for Free and Fair Elections: A Case Study (Slovak Academic Information Agency, Bratislava, October 1998).
17 Ibid.

and collective problems".[18] Contrary to the *Tretí sektor SOS* Campaign of 1996 to 1997, which was established to "defend" the third sector, the OK '98 campaign chose a positive and pro-active approach. The acronym OK '98, that stood for *Občianska kampaň '98* (Civic Campaign '98) reflected this and signaled optimism that, if people got involved, everything would work out.[19] This initiative was critical in fighting the defeatist mood that had developed among citizens, as a result of the proposed amendments to the election law announced by the HZDS. According to legal experts, several of the proposed changes ran counter to the constitution and to international election standards, increasing the risk of election manipulation.[20] Yet, despite protests from NGOs, distinguished public figures and representatives of trade unions and churches, the new legislation, effectively creating an unfair advantage for the HZDS in the forthcoming elections, was enacted in May 1998.

Two months before the elections, as much as 51 percent of the population expected Prime Minister Mečiar to become head of the government once again, only 24 percent expected that he would not and 25 percent were unable to predict the outcome of the election. Almost all supporters of the HZDS (94 percent) and the majority of SNS supporters (66 percent) counted on Mečiar's victory. In contrast, the belief of opposition supporters in victory over Mečiar was even slightly weaker than it had been in autumn 1997. On the other hand, political polarization in Slovak society increasingly came to reflect socio-cultural differences. While the supporters of the HZDS and SNS were primarily resident in rural areas, the number of people with higher education, young people, students, entrepreneurs, professionals and inhabitants of big cities supporting the opposition was on the rise. This constituency was sensitive to deficiencies in democracy, more critical of authoritarian politicians, more reluctant to adopt an attitude of passivity and resignation, and, thus, more

---

18 See Oľga Berecká, Natália Kušnieriková and Dušan Ondrušek, NGO Campaign for Free and Fair Elections. OK '98 – Lessons Learned (Partners for Democratic Change, Bratislava, 1999), op cit.

19 According to Pavol Demeš who devised it, "(...) we did not want to have it as the SOS for the third sector we had before, when we were defending ourselves. Here I thought more of involving an element of hope and activity. If we go for it, it will be OK in 1998". The positive tone was also emphasized by the media advisor of the campaign, Hana Hanúsková: "From the very beginning we were decided to do the media campaign positively. We even tried to react positively to all the negative attacks and there were quite many of those". Quoted in Oľga Berecká, Natália Kušnieriková and Dušan Ondrušek, NGO Campaign for Free and Fair Elections. OK '98 – Lessons Learned (Partners for Democratic Change, Bratislava, 1999), op cit.

20 The amendment required that each party in a coalition must receive 5 percent of the vote to qualify for seats. The chief target of this provision was undoubtedly the Slovak Democratic Coalition (SDK). Other problematic provisions included restrictions on the transparency of voter lists, inadequate safeguards against unauthorized voting and restrictions on private media access and coverage. See "Comments on the Proposed Amendments to the Slovak Republic's Election Law", manuscript prepared by the National Democratic Institute for International Affairs, April 30, 1998.

prepared to support the opposition. Evidently, there was a potential in citizens' activity that could be mobilized.[21]

The OK '98 Campaign:
"I think, therefore, I vote. I vote, therefore, I am".

Within the scope of the OK '98 campaign, almost 60 independent information, education and monitoring projects were prepared. The majority of these were of a regional character, but there were also several larger projects with nationwide impact, often oriented at young people.

Dissemination of information

The largest and most visible OK '98 project was "Road for Slovakia", organized by the civic association GEMMA 93. During a 15-day march (August 19 – September 3, 1998), some 350 civic activists covered more than 850 towns and villages across Slovakia, distributing 500,000 brochures to inform voters about the elections. Door-to-door campaigning explained voting procedures, stressed basic principles of parliamentary democracy and emphasized the importance of citizen participation in the elections. Theatre performances featuring popular actors were an integral part of this activity.[22]

Citizenship education in the media

The Permanent Conference of the Civic Institute and the private station *Radio Twist* partnered to reach a broader public with a pre-election educational program. In a series entitled "Slovakia and Democracy – the 1998 Elections", 25 Slovak celebrities were interviewed on the radio. At the end of each interview, the guest emphasized that he or she was going to take part in the elections and called on the public to do the same. No one made partisan statements. The personalities interviewed called for activity and civic responsibility and for people to go out to vote.

"Rock the Vote" and other youth projects

"Rock the Vote" was organized by the Foundation for a Civil Society to encourage young people between 18 and 21 years of age to vote. Under the slogan "Don't Let Others Decide about Your Future", a bus with activists passed through 23 towns

---

21 See Zora Bútorová, "Development of Public Opinion: from Discontent to the Support of Political Change", in: Martin Bútora, Grigorij Mesežnikov, Zora Bútorová and Sharon Fisher (eds.), The 1998 Parliamentary Elections and Democratic Rebirth in Slovakia (Institute for Public Affairs, Bratislava, 1999), op cit.

22 For instance Stano Dančiak, a respected member of the Slovak National Theatre. Actor Matej Landl repeatedly said "it is important to go and vote because elections is something that will decide your future"; see Martin Porubjak, "I Think, Therefore I Am: The Artists in the 1998 Election Campaign", in: Martin Bútora, Grigorij Mesežnikov, Zora Bútorová and Sharon Fisher (eds.), The 1998 Parliamentary Elections and Democratic Rebirth in Slovakia (Institute for Public Affairs, Bratislava, 1999), op cit.

from Eastern Slovakia to the packed Main Square in Bratislava, and staged 13 rock concerts featuring popular rock bands.[23] Young activists explained to their peers why it was important to vote, showing them who would benefit from their indifference and describing the procedures for voting. The concerts, the practical advice about election procedures and the repeated calls for young voters to think independently, met with a very positive response. Other projects successful in targeting young people included the "Youth Campaign for the Elections" organized by the Slovak Youth Council, discussions about voting rights and voter responsibility in 30 high schools in 17 towns organized by the European Association of Student Rights (ELSA) and the Student Solidarity Forum (FOŠTUS) project informing young people about the technical aspects of the elections and about the competing parties. Two documentary films prepared by the Institute for Public Affairs (IVO) and dedicated to attracting first-time voters were repeatedly screened on regional TV channels.

TV spots: "I think, therefore, I vote. I vote, therefore, I am".

Aiming to attract young voters, the civic association Hlava '98 (Head '98) organized a series of TV and radio spots airing the slogan "I think, therefore, I vote. I vote, therefore, I am" in cinemas, on the private station TV Markíza, on TV NAŠA in Eastern Slovakia and twelve private radio stations covering different areas of the country. In a non-traditional and artistically imaginative way, these spots stressed freedom and the importance of voting. In the ads, young people called on their peers to take part in the elections. Young people's role models, like athletes and actors, relayed the message. The ads were chic, genuine, humorous, and they had the charm of personal expression.

Political and electoral education

The Institute for Public Affairs (IVO) published educational and analytical materials aimed at journalists, commentators, public intellectuals, civic and student leaders, politicians and diplomats. Publications addressed fundamental principles of democratic electoral systems, the parliamentary mandate in Slovakia and the electoral programs of political parties.[24] The F. A. Hayek Foundation and other think tanks published similar analyses of party political programs.

Monitoring government performance

Besides analyzing the work of political parties, several programs focused on evaluation of the government's performance in various policy areas. Such projects were carried out both within the OK '98 campaign, as well as independently. Among

---

23 See Marek Kapusta, Rock volieb '98 Campaign – Report on Activities and Results: A Case Study (Foundation for a Civil Society, Bratislava, 1998).
24 Kálman Petőcz, Základy demokratických volebných systémov (Inštitút pre verejné otázky, Bratislava,1997); Milan Galanda and Juraj Hrabko, Poslanecký mandát na Slovensku (Inštitút pre verejné otázky, Bratislava, 1998); Grigorij Mesežnikov (ed.), Voľby 1998. Analýza volebných programov politických strán a hnutí (Inštitút pre verejné otázky, Bratislava, 1998).

them were projects by the Confederation of Trade Unions on social and labor policy, by the Society for a Sustainable Life on environmental questions, by Greenpeace on energy, by the Center for the Support for Environmental Public Advocacy on water management and public transportation, by the Alliance of Organizations of Disabled People in Slovakia and the Board for Advising in Social Work on the social sphere, by the Gremium of the Third Sector on NGO legislation, by the Slovak Helsinki Committee on human rights and by the Student Solidarity Forum on matters affecting young people.

Targeting special groups
Several projects addressed specific groups in society. The Association of Expert Seniors prepared a series of pre-election discussion forums for pensioners. Other organizations prepared programs aimed at women, the Roma minority and disabled persons.

Education for members of election commissions
The Anton Tunega Foundation prepared a project to educate members of election commissions. In cooperation with a Košice-based organization, Public Presentation, the foundation prepared a short instruction video, published 25,000 copies of a high-quality manual for members of the polling station committees and trained 250 members of the committees with no party affiliation.

Targeted public opinion surveys and their dissemination
The impact of OK '98 among citizens was reinforced by six targeted public opinion polls, which contributed to the ongoing public discourse about the approaching elections.[25] As for the public's perception of civic activities, the May 1998 poll conducted by IVO showed that the majority of citizens supported the activity of NGOs in all campaign areas covered by OK '98.

Disputes over the electoral law
Another function fulfilled by OK '98, in the area of pre-election education, was to explain to the public the substance of the new election law, enacted just four months before the elections and widely criticized as non-democratic (see above for a detailed description of the controversy over the election law). The campaign against the highly controversial amendments to the election law was conducted on the basis of expert analysis.

---

25 The findings of extensive and in-depth surveys and analyses were presented at regularly held press conferences, published in a series of articles in the widely read daily SME, as well as in two books aimed both at domestic and foreign audiences; see Zora Bútorová (ed.), Slovensko pred voľbami. Ľudia – názory – súvislosti (Inštitút pre verejné otázky, Bratislava, 1997), and an extended English edition: Zora Bútorová (ed.), Democracy and Discontent in Slovakia: A Public Opinion Profile of a Country in Transition (Institute for Public Affairs, Bratislava, 1998).

Public forums, debates, discussions
Organized by a variety of NGOs, some 45 meetings bringing together citizens and the candidates for election were held, mainly in cities. In general, opposition leaders were more willing to participate and better prepared than the representatives of the incumbent government and its political allies.

Monitoring the media
Although not directly under the auspices of the OK '98 campaign, a number of NGOs were involved in monitoring the media during the months prior to the elections. The most prominent of these was MEMO '98, supported by the Slovak Helsinki Citizens' Assembly and the Association for the Support of Local Democracy. They monitored major electronic and print media, regularly publishing analysis of media coverage of the elections, their balance and objectivity or government bias.[26] A complementary project was conducted by the Slovak Syndicate of Journalists, supported by Article 19 and the European Union's PHARE Program, focusing on a different set of print and electronic media. These efforts helped to illustrate "that there was bias and a lack of objectivity, especially on the state-run Slovak television".[27]

Domestic observers in the elections
The Association for Fair Elections organized an independent project called "Civic Eye '98" (Občianske oko '98) to engage and train domestic election observers. While five weeks before the elections the government succumbed to international pressure, finally allowing the presence of international observers from member countries of the Organization for Security and Cooperation in Europe (OSCE), it refused the involvement of domestic observers. Thus, the central election commission did not officially accredit the activists of the "Civic Eye '98". Nevertheless, 1,746 volunteer observers actively carried out their task outside polling stations. Thanks to the chairpersons of many of the local polling station committees, there were also observers inside some polling stations. The OSCE sent 25 long-term and 206 short-term observers. They visited nearly 1,700 polling stations. Though they evaluated the elections positively, one of their objections was precisely governmental "failure to accredit domestic observers". In fact, the pro-government media, particularly Slovak television and the daily Slovenská Republika, systematically discredited both groups.[28]

26 Rastislav Kužel and Marek Mračka, Project MEMO '98: A Case Study (Helsinki Citizens' Committee and the Association for the Support of Local Democracy, Bratislava, 1998).

27 Andrej Školkay, "The Media and Political Communication in the Election Campaign", in: Martin Bútora, Grigorij Mesežnikov, Zora Bútorová and Sharon Fisher (eds.), The 1998 Parliamentary Elections and Democratic Rebirth in Slovakia (Institute for Public Affairs, Bratislava, 1999), op cit.

28 For a description of the role of foreign observers, see Jeremy Druker, "International Observers and the 1998 Elections", in: Martin Bútora, Grigorij Mesežnikov, Zora Bútorová and Sharon Fisher (eds.), The 1998 Parliamentary Elections and Democratic Rebirth in Slovakia (Institute for Public Affairs, Bratislava, 1999), op cit.

Besides the OK '98 campaign, other activities were run autonomously but served similar election-related goals. These included appearances on private TV and radio by celebrities from public cultural life. Many artists openly supported the Slovak Democratic Coalition (SDK) and opposed the cultural policy of Vladimír Mečiar's government, which they considered arrogant and reminiscent of policy under communism. The Confederation of Trade Unions (KOZ), the largest labor organization in Slovakia, analyzed the voting habits of parliamentarians on key social problems and published the results in leaflet form under the title "Big tips from KOZ". KOZ also studied the electoral platforms of the parties and found that the parties closest to trade union goals were those of the opposition.[29]

Inside OK '98:
Communication with a Broad Range of Partners

The OK '98 campaign was a large-scale effort of numerous NGOs, volunteers and donors. It required mechanisms to formulate and implement a joint strategy and to cooperate effectively with many partners in Slovakia and abroad. Decision making took place on several levels, which reflected the diverse composition of participating actors and the decentralized nature of the campaign.

On the national level, the 11-member coordination council of OK '98 was the key decision maker. Initially, its role was to develop a strategy and to mobilize interest and support for the campaign in the NGO community and among donors. Later, supporting communication among NGOs and their initiatives became more important, as did providing contacts with domestic and foreign institutions and experts and helping to establish partnerships and coalitions. In order to increase the flexibility of the coordination council, a three member executive committee was created.[30] Public and media relations and dialogue with political representatives, trade union leaders, mayors and other groups were an important part of its activities. The secretariat of the campaign was established at the Foundation for a Civil Society in Bratislava. Individual projects were autonomous in decision making and implementation. The independence of the projects led, initially, to some difficulties and frustrations in communication between different partners. The situation improved when common rules were settled. Several regional ad hoc groups or coalitions of NGOs were created, designing strategies according to local needs. Regional coordination meetings were held on a regular basis in Košice, Zvolen and Stupava.

---

29 See Darina Malová, "From Hesitation to a Calculated Strategy: The Confederation of Trade Unions in the 1998 Elections", in: Martin Bútora, Grigorij Mesežnikov, Zora Bútorová and Sharon Fisher (eds.), The 1998 Parliamentary Elections and Democratic Rebirth in Slovakia (Institute for Public Affairs, Bratislava, 1999), op cit.

30 The members of the executive committee were Šarlota Pufflerová from the Foundation Citizen and Democracy (spokesperson), Andrej Bartosiewicz from the Association for Support of Local Democracy and Pavol Demeš from the SAIA-Service Center for the Third Sector.

There were also some problems of coordination with other partners, such as the opposition political parties. This is attributable to the novel nature of the OK '98 campaign and it took the opposition political parties some time to understand the potential of mutually coordinated activities. Communication with the parties of the governing coalition was a different matter, however. Suspicious of free civic initiatives, representatives of these parties often refused to participate in public forums and debates or were opposed to civic monitoring of the elections. Worse, some politicians and journalists openly attacked NGOs and their leaders, accusing them of undermining the independence of Slovakia, of serving Slovakia's enemies and of not respecting the law. These attacks were repeated several times in the state-owned media (especially on public television).

Given the increasingly pro-government bias of state media, it was crucial to work efficiently with private media, like the private *TV Markíza* and *Radio Twist*, as well as with daily newspapers like *SME*. The OK '98 campaign organizers had to be proactive and preempt disinformation conducted by the government. "It was not clear at all to people how our campaign could be nonpartisan and political at the same time. The stereotypes that existed in this society during the years of socialism caused politics to be identified with party leadership (...) our people have never even heard of something like civil politics." [31] For the OK '98 campaign, this meant that its goals and activities had to be explained in a very accessible manner.

A large-scale campaign, such as OK '98, requires considerable resources and funding. An effective system and procedure for the submission of NGO projects was created by the Donors' Forum, an informal association of grantmaking foundations supporting democracy and civic participation.[32] Donors built a flexible funding system, simplified application procedures and provided co-financing for projects. Information about these activities was regularly published in the *NonProfit* magazine and on the Internet. While the campaign benefited from an enormous amount of voluntary work, from in-kind contributions like, for instance, the creative input of artists and professionals specializing in "social campaigns", as well as from smaller contributions made by local business and private donations, the support provided by European and U.S. donors, coming from both the private and public sectors, was of critical importance.[33]

---

31 Hana Hanúsková, media advisor of the campaign, quoted in: Oľga Berecká, Natália Kušnieriková and Dušan Ondrušek, NGO Campaign for Free and Fair Elections. OK '98 – Lessons Learned (Partners for Democratic Change, Bratislava, 1999), op cit.

32 These included the Civil Society Development Foundation, the Open Society Foundation, the Foundation for a Civil Society, the Children of Slovakia Foundation, the Carpathian Foundation, the Charles Stewart Mott Foundation, the German Marshall Fund of the United States, the Jan Hus Educational Foundation, the British Know How Fund, the Fund of Canada, the United States Information Service (USIS) and others.

33 The overall financial volume of the campaign was estimated at approx. 30 million Slovak Crowns or, at that time, US$ 857,000; see Pavol Demeš, OK '98 Campaign of Slovak NGOs for Free and Fair Elections: A Case Study (Slovak Academic Information Agency, Bratislava, 1998).

International contacts, however, went beyond external funding. For years before the 1998 elections, the democratic community in Slovakia had maintained communication with their counterparts in western democracies. There was ample space for western politicians and experts, international institutions and independent organizations to reflect on developments in Slovakia. The political opposition had partners in international organizations and independent media, academia, the cultural community, and NGOs maintained their own relationships. For civil activists in Slovakia, identification with a "global civil society" was not just a slogan. They lived that identification through worldwide partnerships. In January 1998, eleven presidents of Central European states met in the Eastern Slovak town of Levoča. As the theme of the meeting was civil society, the heads of state also held talks with representatives of Slovak NGOs. In May 1998, the European Union and the United States presented awards for democracy and civil society to fifty organizations and individuals from Central and Eastern Europe. In a clear gesture of support for democratic forces, three associations in Slovakia received awards "in recognition of achievements in promoting democratic values and a civil society", including two that were involved in the OK '98 campaign (the People and Water Association and the Gremium of the Third Sector).

A unique tool for coordinating the efforts of all democratic forces before the elections was the Democratic Round Table, an informal platform that included representatives of opposition parties, trade unions, towns and municipalities, youth organizations and the third sector with the aims of ensuring the free and fair conduct of the elections, preventing electoral fraud and securing a smooth transfer of political power after the election. It was launched in June 1998, with seven meetings taking place prior to the elections, and was attended by four democratic opposition partners: SDK (Slovak Democratic Coalition), SMK (Party of the Hungarian Coalition), *Strana demokratickej ľavice* or SDĽ (Party of the Democratic Left), *Strana občianskeho porozumenia* or SOP (Party of Civic Understanding) and four nonpartisan actors: the Confederation of Trade Unions (KOZ), the Gremium of the Third Sector, the Union of Cities and Villages and the Youth Council of Slovakia.

These gatherings represented a new form of political dialogue. The Democratic Round Table epitomized the most important achievement of pre-election efforts in Slovakia: the ability to create democratic alliances. Independent media and the majority of the representatives of important churches, although not represented in the Democratic Round Table, were an informal part of the broader social effort for democratic change. In some cases, this cooperation was based on the implicit relationship of actors adhering to the same democratic values. In the case of the Democratic Round Table, this alliance took the form of a public, visible and effective association of pro-democratic forces. It became increasingly clear that this semi-institutionalized grouping, which associated parties as actors of representative democracy and civic groups that stood for participatory democracy, was ready to defend the democratic character of the elections and, should the opposition succeed, would not allow victory to be snatched from its hands.

A Second Chance for Democracy: Achievements of the OK '98 Campaign

The civic activism developed in the OK '98 campaign played a critical role in informing and educating citizens, monitoring the elections and in mobilizing voters, with 84 percent turning out to vote, among them eight out of ten first-time voters.[34] Post-election surveys indicated that the OK '98 campaign captured the attention of the majority of citizens (70 percent), and the majority of those who had an opinion on the campaign, evaluated it positively.[35]

The extent and spectrum of activities, events, materials and products of the campaign was impressive. Hundreds of reports in national and regional print and electronic media covered these election-related efforts, thousands of volunteers participated and over 2 million posters, leaflets, postcards, stickers, brochures, publications, pens, pencils, hats and t-shirts gave a visual image to the campaign.

People supported the change. The word *change* became one of the buzzwords of the electoral campaign. The result was that the new Slovak government, under Prime Minister Mikuláš Dzurinda, could begin the process of transforming Slovakia, giving the country the opportunity to take its place in the community of democracies. In the new parliament, parties previously in the opposition had a constitutional majority (93 of 150 seats), enough to make changes in a decisive manner after four years of "Mečiarism". Despite the broad variety of their political programs, ideological profiles and different approaches to solving societal problems, they were committed to principles of democracy and supported the integration of Slovakia into the EU and NATO.

One of the remarkable features of the campaign was the previously unseen outburst of creativity it unleashed. New and imaginative techniques and approaches were applied, including interactive communication, TV spots in the style of MTV and so on. The youngest voters liked the elements of irony and ridicule, poking fun at the obtuseness of the authoritarian mentality. In some situations, the campaign took on

---

34 According to a survey carried out by the FOCUS agency in November 1998 in cooperation with the International Republican Institute, 19 percent of first-time voters and 9 percent of all voters stated that it was the NGO campaign that encouraged them to participate in the elections.

35 While 38 percent of respondents gave the campaign a grade of 1 or 2, only 8 percent rated it with a 4 or 5 (1-positive, 5-negative). Only 11 percent of citizens regarded the activities of the OK '98 campaign as being useless although harmless. The significance of the campaign was most appreciated by people with higher education; see Zora Bútorová, "Development of Public Opinion: from Discontent to the Support of Political Change", in: Martin Bútora, Grigorij Mesežnikov, Zora Bútorová and Sharon Fisher (eds.), The 1998 Parliamentary Elections and Democratic Rebirth in Slovakia (Institute for Public Affairs, Bratislava, 1999), op cit.

an almost "carnival character". This mobilized a degree of dynamism, romanticism, passion and excess, important in at least two respects. First, it encouraged people's feeling of communion and togetherness in a kindred collective spirit. Second, it was an attractive and fresh alternative to the grayness of an authoritarian-bureaucratic regime, its institutions, symbols and officials. A feeling of "justified ownership" took hold of the country. For thousands of people, especially young people, the campaign was an important emotional experience. Similar eruptions of creativity have taken place in other countries under similar circumstances (Serbia and Ukraine, for example) but Slovakia was the first case of decisive national elections in which creativity played such an important role. A further and related key to success was the "ethos of victory" presented by the campaign to the outside world, contrasting with the often gloomy mood of the general public. This was important in helping citizens to overcome their fear of political participation and civic activism, fear that is a hallmark of authoritarian societies.

Gaining the trust of the citizens was important to the success of the OK '98 campaign.[36] It succeeded in doing so, filling the gap between the passive position of isolated individuals and the competing political parties. Even though the election was carried out in accordance with the then election law (unfair as it was), it was deemed not to have been manipulated. This can be attributed to the presence of local and international observers and the parallel vote count conducted by the members of the Slovak Democratic Coalition (SDK), mobilized successfully by the campaign.

The large-scale involvement of citizens in political life, images of town squares packed with people, along with occasions of euphoria, brought back memories of November 1989, when the communist regime in Czechoslovakia collapsed. Nevertheless, if compared to the Velvet Revolution, there are striking differences. First, unlike in 1989 when change was only vaguely conceptualized, 1998 saw one clear and crucial demand: Slovaks wanted more democracy. Secondly, the leaders of the 1989 opposition were largely unknown to the public. In September 1998, Slovaks opted for change by voting for politicians who were publicly known from previous high profile political battles. Third, the changes of 1989 were rather unexpected and came about without the long-term active engagement of the majority of citizens. In 1998, Slovaks had to make a conscious effort to bring about political change. When it did happen, it was instigated primarily from within, at the initiative of Slovak society and fed largely by its own resources, ideas and values.

These important differences notwithstanding, the events of November 1989 and September 1998 are linked by their political significance. In both cases, a

---

36 See Zora Bútorová and Martin Bútora, Mimovládne organizácie a dobrovoľníctvo na Slovensku očami verejnej mienky (SPACE – Centrum pre analýzu sociálnej politiky, Bratislava, 1996) and Zuzana Fialová, Neziskový sektor na stránkach slovenskej tlače (SPACE – Centrum pre analýzu sociálnej politiky, Bratislava, 1997).

full turnabout was achieved in the political orientation of the country. The 1998 elections in Slovakia were not merely about a move towards the left or right of the political spectrum. Instead, they represented a choice between two alternatives: the continuation of a non-democratic, semi-authoritarian trend, or the return to the original ideals of 1989, towards democracy and an open society, the rule of law and a market economy. In this sense, the 1998 elections represented a "delayed" or "second" Velvet Revolution and OK '98 was one of its key catalysts.[37]

Long-Term Effects on Democracy in Slovakia

Slovak NGOs did not disappear from the public scene after the elections. Civil society considered it important to avoid the well-known "burn-out" effect following large-scale social mobilization. NGOs wanted to preserve some fundamental mechanisms of integration, communication and cooperation within civil society, to consolidate their credibility in the eyes of the public, to continue to act as watchdogs of democratic governance and to define a new agenda for improving the quality of democracy.

With this in mind, Slovak civic organizations held an extraordinary conference at the end of September 1998 in Stupava, the result of which was a call for the continuation of public oversight, for the extensive decentralization of the state and the strengthening of local self-government and for the acceptance of civic initiatives as equal partners in governance, which would require revised tax legislation to facilitate the sustainability of civil society. In October 1998, a number of civic associations called on the former democratic opposition to adhere to their pre-election agreements and to include the Party of the Hungarian Coalition (SMK) in the new government. In November 1998, dozens of NGOs and hundreds of individuals addressed the government with an open letter entitled "We want real change!", challenging it "not to confuse tolerance with a lack of principle in judging those who are responsible for criminal acts and for the widespread devastation of the country and society", asking them not to "misinterpret the change in society simply as a new division of power and government seats, but to see it rather as a principal change in the manner of managing public affairs".

More broadly, and in accordance with a continued shift "from politics to public policies", several NGOs, NGO coalitions and platforms became actively involved in promoting a variety of public policy issues and some developed over time into powerhouses of structural reform. They prepared analyses, special studies and publications on democratic governance, the rule of law and human rights, economic and social reforms, the environment, foreign policy, corruption, the problems of

---

37 See Martin Bútora and Zora Bútorová, "Slovakia's Democratic Awakening", Journal of Democracy vol. 10, no. 1 (January 1999), pp. 80-95.

the Roma community, gender issues, education and many other challenges facing Slovakia.

Several of the successful reforms Slovakia implemented since 1998, or the initial reform concepts, were conceived or debated in independent think tanks before they gained a practical political foothold. In "making change happen", civil society exerted its influence through the media, put pressure on political actors, defended public interests, appealed to citizens at large and initiated new legislation. Domestic advocacy was supplemented by the development of the role of Slovak civil society in international democracy assistance. Several NGOs active in the OK '98 campaign, used their experience to support democratic efforts elsewhere in Central and Eastern Europe, lending assistance to activists in Croatia, Serbia, and later in Ukraine and Belarus, among others. Slovak NGOs have also become active in development assistance, through technical assistance in the Balkans and humanitarian missions in Africa and Asia.

The continued role of civil society in strengthening democracy inside Slovakia has taken the form of civic campaigns on several further occasions. In 2000, a campaign demanding the thorough reform of public administration and its decentralization (*Za skutočnú reformu verejnej správy*) was launched. The Civic Initiative for a Good Information Act under the slogan of "What Is Not Secret Should Be Made Public" launched in 2000 was supported by over 120 nongovernmental organizations associating over 100,000 members. This alliance and its successful appeal to the public resulted in groundbreaking legislation that grants citizens free access to information and requires civil servants to provide it. In 2001, campaigns were launched to ensure the enactment of a strict law on waste management (*Za dobrý zákon o odpadoch*) and to highlight government responsibility for coping with ethnic intolerance (*Rasizmus je aj Tvoj problem*).

Part of civil society again engaged in specific election-related activities in the run-up to the 2002 parliamentary elections. However, the overall climate in society was very different from that in 1998. While the fear and tension of the Mečiar years had waned, so had the enthusiasm of 1998 and unfulfilled expectations gave rise to skepticism among many who had supported democratic change four years earlier. This depressed social climate gave rise to concerns that radical and national-populist parties would receive strong support, with likely negative effects on further democratic reform and Euroatlantic integration. Compared to 1998, NGO activities in the 2002 elections were more elaborate and sophisticated.[38] Priority was given to information, education and motivation activities to ensure the highest possible turnout. Evaluations of the government's performance compared to its original

---

38 Peter Novotný, Daniel Forgács and Marián Velšic, "Non-Governmental Organizations in the 2002 Elections", in: Grigorij Mesežnikov, Oľga Gyárfášová, Miroslav Kollár and Tom Nicholson, Slovak Elections '02. Results, Consequences, Context (Institute for Public Affairs, Bratislava, 2003).

program, examinations of the fulfillment of pre-election promises and analyses of political party programs helped voters in making election decisions. Many civic groups aimed their projects at specific target groups (youth, Roma, women) or themes (social policy, foreign policy, economic reform, rural development).

Two highly visible activities were the *"Nie je nám to jedno"* (We Are Not Indifferent) and *"Šetri si svoj hlas na september"* (Save Your Voice for September – *hlas* in Slovak means both "voice" and "vote"). The authors of the "We Are Not Indifferent" campaign, *Občianske Oko* (Civic Eye) and *Hlava '98* (Head '98), used an unusual tactic to get people to join the initiative. They asked them to put their fingerprints on the petition sheet supporting election participation, and to write personal statements as to "why I am not indifferent".[39]

The influence of all these activities is most noticeable when one looks at results for first-time voters. While before the summer of 2002, only 50 percent of eligible first-time voters had decided to vote, during the summer (the peak of NGO campaigning) this figure had reached 70 percent. While the contribution of such activity to increasing voter turnout is very difficult to quantify, it is sure that had NGOs not campaigned before the elections, the turnout would have been far lower. The result was unequivocal, with a new government that ensured the continuity of democratic development, bringing Slovakia into NATO and the EU, being elected.

Conclusion: Hallmarks of the OK '98 Campaign

The OK '98 campaign owed its success to several favorable circumstances. Its innovative character proved important. Although OK '98 was not the first of its kind, as comparable efforts had preceded presidential elections in Romania and Bulgaria previously, the organizers could not draw on generally applicable models. But, this could also be said of the opponents of democratic change, who underestimated the effectiveness of civil society driven voter mobilization and who did not put in place measures to obstruct its efforts.

The heritage of the nonviolent struggle of 1989 and the accumulation of experience from previous civic initiatives in Slovakia proved critical. These provided a degree of tested cooperation, mutual trust and personal connections between civic actors and organizations, which was a valuable basis for conducting OK '98. Cooperation among democratic political forces was another important factor: an alliance for democracy emerged that included opposition political parties. They had to learn

39 Altogether, the activists collected 15,000 fingerprints and hundreds of personal statements. The second phase of the campaign culminated in press advertisements, rock concerts, public appeals by respected figures, a series of 19 television spots and a concert tour, which visited 14 cities in Slovakia; see Peter Novotný, Daniel Forgács and Marián Velšic, "Non-Governmental Organizations in the 2002 Elections", in: Grigorij Mesežnikov, Oľga Gyárfášová, Miroslav Kollár and Tom Nicholson, Slovak Elections '02. Results, Consequences, Context (Institute for Public Affairs, Bratislava, 2003), op cit.

from their earlier defeats at the hands of disunity and a lack of cooperation. Moreover, this civic mobilization should be seen as one of the more recent building blocks of democratic modernization in Slovakia. Especially after independence, Slovak society needed to mature politically and overcome its traditional passivity. The country needed to develop responsibility for its own affairs and for proposing constructive alternatives, the habit of public engagement beyond "rebellion". The OK '98 campaign was a reflection of the marriage of intelligent civic defiance and a positive vision for the future.

Slovak NGOs were also successful in breaking into the public domain, previously colonized by authoritarian politicians. Whereas in the past, political communication usually flowed from Prime Minister Mečiar in the direction of the opposition, the pro-democracy camp succeeded in reversing the direction of communication. This was instrumental in mobilizing a broad based change-oriented constituency, another factor of importance. The OK '98 campaign appealed to first-time voters and to an educated, urban, constituency that often showed below-average turnout. These groups were decisive for the result. The appeal to change-oriented voters was persuasive because of the creative input of professionals specializing in "social campaigns", whose participation was characteristic. Artists, media professionals and others from the nongovernmental milieu lent their skill with enthusiasm and belief in change, rather than performing yet another professional assignment.

Critically important was also the reluctance of the authorities to resort to extreme measures and/or to manipulating the elections on this occasion. Exceptions notwithstanding, the incumbent political elite was not ready to brutally violate standard procedures. Its formal adherence to democratic principles, not least to avoid jeopardizing its international legitimacy, created sufficient space to challenge the government through elections. Further, Slovakia enjoyed a favorable international environment. The country's Visegrad neighbors were well on their way to EU and NATO membership, and both organizations and their member states were well disposed to embracing Slovakia under a democratic government. Several of them provided political and financial support. In Slovakia, EU conditionality played a seminal role.

Finally, the Slovak story has become an inspiring example for some other countries, even if this has to date not been sufficiently reflected in the media and academic literature on "electoral revolutions".[40] The experience of OK '98 was used in 1999 in Croatia, systematically studied and applied in Serbia 2000[41] and the intensive communication of former OK '98 activists with civic leaders was useful in Ukraine in 2004.

---

40 Valerie J. Bunce and Sharon L. Wolchik, "Favorable Conditions and Electoral Revolutions", Journal of Democracy, vol. 17, no. 4 (October 2006), pp. 5-18.

41 That Pavol Demeš was presented with the Democracy and Civil Society Award by Serbian NGOs in 2000 is a reflection of this fact.

Slovak activists agreed that the fact that similar campaigns were carried out in other countries previously was encouraging and motivating.[42] In Slovakia, it was not just any "campaign". It helped to achieve "a political earthquake", a real breakthrough that was not pre-determined from the outset. It has shown that a vital civil society can significantly influence political processes in societies that have rulers that engage in authoritarian practices. Today, after campaigns in Croatia, Serbia, Ukraine and Georgia, this sounds more familiar, but this was not as obvious in 1997 to 1998.

Successful campaigns are "domestic products", developed from within the country and are heavily dependent on local circumstances, traditions and culture. Yet, some techniques are transferable, for instance, training civil observers, organizers and moderators of candidate forums, media monitoring and get-out-the-vote activities, especially for young people. The universality of engaging people is also crucial, "encouraging them to become engaged because it is fun, not because it is a duty".[43] Slovak activists have emphasized the need for a dedicated domestic leadership, committed to a common goal, engaged in cooperation and service, being able to develop and maintain good relations with the media, legal experts, politicians, labor unions, mayors, churches and the international community.

The Slovak experience has confirmed that under favorable circumstances, illiberal trends may be reversed through free elections. Since 1998, populist autocrats have learned lessons and seem to have become more effective in preventing freedom-loving citizens from challenging their rule. Overcoming contemporary authoritarian regimes will, therefore, require new thinking and new procedures. In doing so, it might be useful to take a fresh look at the Slovak story of 1998 and afterwards.

Chronology

January 7, 1997

Opposition political parties launch a petition to demand a referendum on direct presidential elections. Supported by civic activists, 520,000 signatures are collected, enough for the petition to be considered valid.

---

42 "It showed us the way, the light appeared at the end of the tunnel and I think that vision was fundamental for OK '98's efforts", confirmed Marek Kapusta. "Because at the beginning only a handful of people believed it would be possible, and that something could really be changed by our activities and exactly that positive example of Romania and Bulgaria (…) the bare fact that it is possible, that it has been done in three countries already, is a fascinating thing, I think"; quoted in: Oľga Berecká, Natália Kušnieriková and Dušan Ondrušek, NGO Campaign for Free and Fair Elections. OK '98 – Lessons Learned (Partners for Democratic Change, Bratislava, 1999), op cit.
43 Jan Surotchak, quoted in: Oľga Berecká, Natália Kušnieriková and Dušan Ondrušek, NGO Campaign for Free and Fair Elections. OK '98 – Lessons Learned (Partners for Democratic Change, Bratislava, 1999), op cit.

February 14, 1997
In an attempt to obstruct the petition, the ruling coalition in the Slovak parliament calls for a referendum on Slovakia's accession to NATO, although the country has not been invited to join.

March 13, 1997
President Michal Kováč decides to combine both issues in one referendum scheduled for May 23, 1997. Civic organizations and prominent personalities encourage citizens to participate, in order for the referendum to reach the required 50 percent turnout.

May 24, 1997
After the government reprints the ballots, removing the question on direct presidential elections, the central referendum commission declares the referendum void and asks for an investigation. On recommendation by the opposition, the vast majority of voters refuse to participate, resulting in 9.8 percent turnout. Following the referendum, civil society begins discussions on how to ensure free and fair elections.

July 8, 1997
The Madrid NATO Summit formally invites Poland, the Czech Republic and Hungary to join the Alliance. Slovakia is not even mentioned among likely future candidates.

July 15, 1997
A European Commission report on ten countries aspiring to EU membership singles out Slovakia as the only country not meeting the Copenhagen political criteria.

Summer 1997
Informal debates among civic leaders result in preparations for a national conference to discuss the role of the NGOs in democratic elections.

October 1, 1997
Mikuláš Dzurinda from the opposition Slovak Democratic Coalition, a newly created coalition of opposition parties, asks the government to invite international election observers. In response, Prime Minister Mečiar claims that "Slovakia can guarantee democratic elections alone".

October 28 – 29, 1997
The Fifth Annual Stupava Conference of the Third Sector, a countrywide gathering of NGOs, is held in Košice. Entitled "Working Actively for Democracy", the conference ends with a declaration in support of NGO activities to improve citizen information and to create conditions for free and fair parliamentary elections in 1998. The conference also calls for the presence of international observers.

November 6 – 9, 1997

Results of the Košice conference are presented to international donor organizations at an informal meeting in Brussels.

December 15, 1997

A meeting in Vienna brings together representatives of Slovak NGOs with international donors. Civic activists from Bulgaria and Romania share their experiences from pre-election activities in their countries.

End December 1997

Principles of a civic campaign are discussed. Pavol Demeš, a leader of the Third Sector SOS campaign in 1996 and spokesman of the Gremium of the Third Sector, proposes a positively oriented campaign promoting the democratization of Slovak society.

January 10, 1998

Representatives of democracy and advocacy NGOs participate in the founding meeting of the campaign at the Institute for Public Affairs (IVO). Agreement is reached on the name of the initiative: Civic Campaign OK '98. Subsequently, members of this group and representatives of the Gremium of the Third Sector and the Donors' Forum compose the coordination council of the campaign.

January 29, 1998

President Kováč visits Washington. The Helsinki Commission of the U.S. Congress expresses concern that "the regularity of the Slovak elections is not fully secured".

January – February 1998

The coordination council develops the campaign strategy and seeks support in the NGO community and among donors. Informal communication begins with representatives of democratic opposition parties.

March 3, 1998

President Kováč's term of office ends and Prime Minister Mečiar acquires interim presidential powers, which he uses to pardon associates and persons implicated in abuses of power and legal violations. Over 50 civic leaders representing 35 nongovernmental organizations attend a meeting in Zvolen. The OK '98 campaign is declared as an open nonpartisan public initiative that is designed to ensure free and fair parliamentary and local elections. The participants announce nationwide civic mobilization and promise to resist any violations of the democratic process in Slovakia.

April 1998

The Slovak Donors' Forum launches a program to support civic initiatives related to the elections. It creates a standardized format and procedure for nonpartisan NGO projects to access financial support provided by European and U.S. donors.

Spring 1998
The coordination council creates a three-member executive committee to support flexible communication with civic initiatives, ensure contact with domestic and foreign institutions and experts and establish partnerships and coalitions. A campaign secretariat is set up at the Foundation for a Civil Society in Bratislava. Several regional *ad hoc* coalitions of NGOs are created to design strategies targeting local needs. Regional coordination meetings are held in Košice, Zvolen and Stupava.

May 20, 1998
Despite international criticism, the governing coalition moves to amend the election law, requiring each party in any coalition to receive five percent of the votes, in the wake of growing support for the democratic opposition platform, the Slovak Democratic Coalition (SDK).

Summer 1998
Nearly 60 independent projects within the OK '98 campaign are launched. Taking place across Slovakia, these include dozens of information events and discussion forums, 13 rock concerts, TV spots and radio programs, several media monitoring projects and trainings for 1,700 election observers, six public opinion polls, regular press conferences and, during a "March through Slovakia", the mass distribution of election-related information to citizens, altogether 500,000 brochures, 570,600 leaflets, 197,500 posters, 253,000 postcards and 375,010 stickers.

June 4, 1998
The Democratic Round Table is launched and attended by four democratic opposition parties and four nonpartisan actors. Seven meetings of the round table will be held in the run-up to the elections.

August 18, 1998
Under international pressure, the Slovak foreign ministry officially invites an OSCE monitoring mission to observe the parliamentary elections. The government refuses any involvement of domestic observers and one of its officials labels Slovak NGOs engaged in election monitoring as *provocateurs*.

September 25 – 26, 1998
Parliamentary elections are held. The democratic opposition wins 93 of 150 seats, with turnout estimated at 84.2 percent.

September 27, 1998
An OSCE report gives a positive evaluation of the elections and praises the high turnout. It criticizes the election law, biased coverage by state television and "the failure to accredit domestic observers".

October 30, 1998

The new Slovak government, consisting of the four parties of the democratic opposition and headed by Mikuláš Dzurinda, is appointed. The new government promises to overcome the democratic deficits in the country, renew the reform process and pursue swift Euroatlantic integration.

"Road for Slovakia" volunteers, summer 1998, in t-shirts sporting the slogan. "Think? Vote? YES, Civic Campaign OK '98".

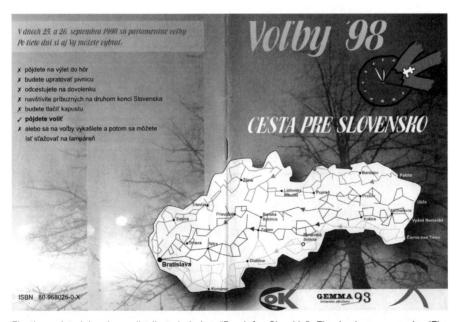

Election related brochure distributed during "Road for Slovakia". The back cover reads: "The parliamentary elections will take place on 25-26 September 1998. On these days you have the choice to go to the mountains, clean out the basement, go away on holiday, visit relatives on the other side of Slovakia, make sauerkraut, vote, forget about the elections and complain to the heavens".

Marek Kapusta, coordinator of the "Rock the Vote" campaign, Košice, summer 1998.

OK '98 volunteers involved in a theatre performance.

OK '98 volunteers with the Slovak national flag handing out information brochures in the countryside.

15 days before the elections: The dollar driven OK '98 campaign bus with activists.

14 days before the elections: "Mushroom season in Slovakia". A field full of poisonous mushrooms (international organisations) surrounding Slovakia's "Free Democratic Elections".

3 days before the elections: "Don't get excited! I'm a 'civic' observer ...".

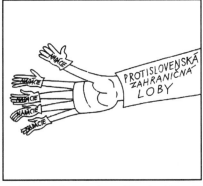

2nd day of the elections: "The 'anti-Slovak' foreign (foundation) lobby".

9 days after the elections: "A well deserved rest after a job well done!". Spokesperson of the Gremium of the Third Sector, Pavol Demeš, relaxing with a "Soros" cigar.

Anti–OK '98 cartoons published in Slovenská Republika, a pro-government newspaper, September 1998.

GLAS 99: CIVIL SOCIETY PREPARING THE GROUND FOR A POST-TUĐMAN CROATIA

Sharon Fisher and Biljana Bijelić

When Croatia's January 2000 parliamentary elections brought about the overwhelming defeat of the Croatian Democratic Union (HDZ), observers initially expressed new hope for the country, seeing the election results as a sign of re-invigorated democratization. Following Slovakia, Croatia was the second country in Central and Eastern Europe to experience the defeat of a semi-authoritarian regime through a "peaceful civic revolution" or electoral breakthrough, later serving as an inspiration for political changes in Serbia and elsewhere in the region. While the election results were partly a consequence of HDZ's own mistakes, they were also the result of two additional factors: the growing unity of Croatia's political opposition and the strengthening role of civil society organizations in changing public discourse. On both accounts, foreign actors were key: in line with the approach that brought peaceful regime change to Slovakia in 1998, the international community encouraged cooperation among the six main opposition parties and provided funding and training for civil society organizations, culminating in the launch of a get-out-the-vote campaign prior to the elections.

This chapter focuses on the pre-election campaign run by Croatian nongovernmental organizations. It deals primarily with the Civic Coalition for Free and Fair Elections, commonly known as GLAS 99, which means both "voice" and "vote" in the Croatian language. GLAS 99 was modeled on Slovakia's OK '98 campaign and its organization was greatly helped by the international support it received. Although it is impossible to quantify its role precisely, the pre-election campaign of Croatian civil society organizations helped to guarantee a high turnout in the elections, at the same time as ensuring that the population's frustration was not channeled into radical parties. Achieving a high turnout was especially important because undecided voters, particularly youth and inhabitants of urban areas, were widely expected to back the opposition rather than the ruling parties, if they could only be motivated to vote. The positive impact of the Croatian NGO sector's pre-election get-out-the-vote campaign was demonstrated not only by the 75 percent election turnout, which was high considering that the elections were held on January 3, immediately after New Year's Day, but also by the fact that the opposition parties won an overwhelming majority

This chapter is based on research conducted by Sharon Fisher for the book Political Change in Postcommunist Slovakia and Croatia: From Nationalist to Europeanist (Palgrave Macmillan, New York, 2006).

in the parliament. Although GLAS 99 was successful as a once-off pre-election campaign, assisting in bringing about political change, the longer-term effects of its activities are not as readily apparent. One undeniable benefit was that the campaign abolished the culture of fear that prevented voices of political dissent from speaking out against the political and social injustices of Croatia's authoritarian regime.

The first section of this chapter offers a brief overview of Croatia's politics and society during the 1990s, looking at political factors as well as the development of civil society, including both NGOs and the media. The second section examines the emergence of the GLAS 99 campaign, investigating its initiators and the lessons that they learned from Slovakia's example. The third section looks at the campaign's approach and activities, while also providing detail on the structures and resources underlying them. Finally, the fourth section deals with the lessons that can be learned from the campaign, as well as its aftermath and the outlook for the future.

Politics, Society and Civic Initiatives in Croatia during the 1990s

In relation to other countries in Central and Eastern Europe, Croatia was in many ways in an advantageous position during the communist period because of the openness of the Yugoslav regime and because its citizens were allowed to travel and work abroad. Nonetheless, Croatian civil society was slow to develop. Although the Republic could boast the 1971 Croatian Spring protest movement, its character was generally considered more nationalist than liberalizing, with its main triggers being concerns such as the transfer of Croatia's economic wealth to poorer republics within Yugoslavia and the recognition of Croatian and Serbian as separate languages.[2] While initially finding favor in the eyes of Yugoslav leader Josip Broz Tito, the movement was crushed in December 1971 out of concern that it was getting out of hand, with comparisons to the situation in Croatia's Nazi-allied *Ustaša* state during World War II abounding. During the rest of the 1970s and most of the 1980s, civil society activity in Croatia was largely stifled and the political opposition remained weak. Any subsequent manifestations of nationalism or calls for liberalization were perceived in Belgrade as a step back toward the World War II *Ustaša* state. Some Croatians accounted for the lack of widespread dissidence by the fact that the regime was never repressive enough to warrant it. Nonetheless, social movements flourished in neighboring Slovenia in the 1980s, particularly among young people, environmentalists, pacifists, feminists and homosexuals, forcing

---

2 See Barbara Jelavich, History of the Balkans: Twentieth Century (Cambridge University Press, Cambridge, 1983), pp. 396-397.

the ruling communist party to soften its stance.[3] That contributed to a shift of the centers of political dialogue from Belgrade and Zagreb to Belgrade and Ljubljana.

Signs of activity in Croatian civil society did start to emerge during the last years of the communist period, particularly in the area of women's issues and environmental protection. For example, the group Women and Society was formed in 1979, and although it was primarily an academic circle, it became the cradle for many future civic initiatives among women. Moreover, with the problem of domestic violence emerging as an important issue, Women and Society helped to establish an emergency hotline for women in 1989, the first of its kind in Central and Eastern Europe. By the late 1980s, a lively opposition movement had emerged, reflected partly in the launch of two liberal weekly magazines: Start and Danas.[4]

After 1990, when Croatia's first multi-party elections brought about the end of communism and the formation of a one-party government led by the HDZ, the focus on the national question again took precedence over questions of democratization and economic liberalization. President Franjo Tuđman led Croatia through a war of independence that served to heighten nationalism and increase allegiance to the new state and the ruling HDZ. During much of the 1990s, the political opposition gave the impression of helplessness in the face of government policies. In certain respects this was understandable, given HDZ's domination of the Croatian political scene. The party won an absolute majority in seven national elections during the 1990s. Those victories were partly the result of manipulation of the electoral system, but also a reflection of the tense political atmosphere created by HDZ, which tended to label independent elements in society as "enemies" of the nation.

Still, much of the blame for the opposition's weak position lay with the parties themselves, as they lacked unity and were reluctant to launch serious protests against the HDZ regime or even to move into the traditional role of the primary critic of government.[5] One of the central questions for Croatia's opposition during the 1990s was whether and to which extent to cooperate with HDZ, and a number of opposition representatives suggested that a period of cohabitation with HDZ would be appropriate for the transition to democratic rule. Meanwhile, the church, rather than the political opposition, was the first to call attention to HDZ's unfair approach to economic policy. In his Christmas message in 1997, Archbishop Josip Bozanić pointed to the country's difficult social situation and criticized the fact that a few government officials were quickly growing rich at the expense of the average citizen, while the great majority of the population was becoming poorer.[6] Only later did the

---

3 See Tomaž Mastnak, "Civil Society in Slovenia: From Opposition to Power", in: Paul G. Lewis (ed.), Democracy and Civil Society in Eastern Europe (Macmillan, London, 1992), pp. 134-151.

4 "Danas" means "today" in Croatian language.

5 See Zoran Daskalovic, "Tuđman Triumphs Over Divided Opposition", War Report, no. 51 (May 1997), pp. 3-5, and Jelena Lovrić, "Who Will Lead the Mass Protests?", AIM, September 20, 1996.

6 RFE/RL Newsline, December 12, 1997.

main opposition party, the postcommunist Social Democratic Party (SDP), begin to present itself as a real social alternative to HDZ.

After the liberation of the Krajina region from Serbian control in 1995, the Croatian public started to distance itself from nationalism, as ordinary people no longer perceived any real threat to the country's existence. While opposition to HDZ was weak during the early 1990s, in the second half of the decade competing elites gradually learned from their earlier mistakes and started to cooperate and intensify their efforts at bringing about political change. That was true not only of the political opposition, but also of civil society organizations, including civic groups, trade unions and the media. The media were especially important in turning people away from the ruling parties, as journalists tended to be far more daring than politicians in questioning national myths. While Croatia's three "state-wide" television channels, as well as most daily newspapers, remained under strong government control throughout the 1990s, a few voices in the media were consistently anti-nationalist, including the weekly *Feral Tribune*, the daily *Novi list* (New Paper), as well as *ARKzin*, a monthly journal published by the Anti–War Campaign (ARK). Of equal importance were the sensationalist tabloid weeklies *Globus* (Globe) and *Nacional* (National), which continually dug up dirt on scandals related to the HDZ and generally reached a wider audience than publications such as the *Feral Tribune*.

In addition to the media, trade unions played a crucial role in developing an alternative public discourse, particularly on economic issues. While Croatian workers were reluctant to demonstrate against the government before 1996 because of the need to present a unified front during a time of war, trade unions staged frequent protests during the second half of the 1990s, beginning with a one-day strike at Croatian Post and Telecommunications in February 1996. Subsequently, metal workers, pensioners, teachers, research workers and railway employees launched demonstrations, mainly to protest their weak economic and social positions. As the economic situation deteriorated further in the late 1990s, and as the lavish lifestyles of those with connections to HDZ became increasingly apparent, the strength of the trade union movement grew.

As in the case of other elements of Croatian society, the country's NGO sector was slow to emerge as a critic of government, partly because of the war, but also because of obstacles put in place by the ruling elite. The NGO community was not popular with the HDZ, an attitude that was hardly surprising given the party's general reluctance to relinquish control to groups that were beyond its influence. Together with its allies in the media, HDZ worked to promote a negative image of NGOs. One key criticism was that NGOs were controlled by the foreign "enemy" and aimed at subverting the Republic. For example, in 1996, Tuđman accused western foundations and embassies of supporting the Croatian opposition and vowed to crack down on "foundations, organizations and individuals" funded by foreign sources for "often illegal and subversive intentions." He continued by referring to such organizations as "tools in the hands of foreign powers" aimed at "undermining the government".[7] In 1998, pro-HDZ journalist Milan Ivkošić wrote that "80 percent of the activists from women's and similar marginal organizations are Serbs, and the rest are more or less Croats with political or family backgrounds in the Yugoslav secret service, the Yugoslav police, or Yugoslav army officers". He added that women in those NGOs "present in their personal lives a model that directly opposes that of the ideal and desirable Croatian family", meaning that they are "married without children", "old but unmarried" or "lesbians". Ivkošić concluded that these groups would be "quite insignificant" without the support they received from abroad.[8] One organization that was subjected to special criticism was George Soros' Open Society Institute.

In addition to verbal attacks, HDZ tried to stifle the third sector through legislation. Although an estimated 20,000 civic associations were registered in Croatia in the mid-1990s, new legislation contributed to reducing that number.[9] The parliament approved a law on associations in July 1997, giving the state the authority to control the work of NGOs, impose hefty fines and to ban groups on suspicion of acting illegally. Existing organizations were required to reregister by January 1998. However, only a small percentage was actually in a position to do.[10] The group Attack, for example, had problems registering as the new law prohibited organizations from using foreign names.[11]

Although verbal and legislative attacks created a difficult working environment for NGO activists, a number of enthusiasts in Croatia continued their efforts, and a whole new set of NGOs conducting activities relating to the war and its effects emerged. One of the most important centers of activism was the Anti-War Campaign (ARK), which was founded in 1991. A number of other politically conscious organizations grew out of ARK, forming a network of NGOs in Zagreb and the countryside that was aimed at building peace, bringing about reconciliation, strengthening human rights and protecting the rights of women. Many peace activists worked in the Western Slavonian town of Pakrac,[12] creating a project called Pakrac's Volunteers that distributed humanitarian aid, provided legal assistance, worked with victims of war trauma and held educational workshops for youth and women. Such groups did not discriminate based on nationality, so they gained significant funding and recognition from the international donor community. Women's groups continued to

---

7 AP, December 12, 1996.

8 Večernji list, June 14, 1998.

9 Milivoj Đilas, "NGOs in Croatia", AIM, September 22, 1999.

10 Feral Tribune, January 19, 1998.

11 Milivoj Đilas, "NGOs in Croatia", AIM, September 22, 1999, op cit.

12 Prior to the war, Pakrac's population was 46 percent Serb and 36 percent Croat, with the rest consisting of a smattering of twenty national minorities; see Laura Silber and Allan Little, The Death of Yugoslavia (Penguin and BBC, London, 1995), pp. 134-135, 146.

flourish through the 1990s, forming a central element of Croatian civil society in the postcommunist period by addressing such problems as female war victims, political participation and abortion rights. Somewhat surprisingly, the environmental groups that were a key center of dissent during the last years of the communist regime dwindled.

The Croatian Helsinki Committee for Human Rights (HHO) was established in 1993, helping to raise awareness of the importance of human rights as a key public issue. That was especially true after the 1995 police and military operations that drove the majority of ethnic Serbs out of Croatia, at which time the HHO became one of the main defenders of the rights of Croatian Serbs. Ivan Zvonimir Čičak, who served as the organization's chairman from the time of its establishment until his replacement in October 1998, ranked among the most controversial personalities in Croatia. That was especially true due to the nature of HHO statements, which brought domestic and international attention to a number of problems in Croatia, including the atmosphere of intolerance against ethnic Serb returnees, the use of "hate speech" in the media and the rise in political violence.

Written complaints and press conferences were among the common methods used by many NGOs, but some groups focused on other means of protest to stimulate public debate. Although NGO-sponsored events often failed to attract significant crowds, the Citizens' Committee for Human Rights was known for its annual demonstrations aimed at returning Zagreb's Square of Croatian Heroes (*Trg hrvatskih velikana*) to its communist era name, the Square of the Victims of Fascism (*Trg žrtava fašizma*). The demonstrations traditionally included several well-known actresses and other public figures and the 1999 protest became the subject of special attention when a group of *Ustaša* sympathizers turned up and police chose to use violence against the anti-fascists. Women's groups also sponsored important forms of protest, including, for example, the 1995 petition for legal and safe abortion that attracted 20,000 signatures and the demonstration in front of the parliament in March 1995, during which activists questioned deputies on women's issues.

Despite those positive steps forward, unity in the NGO sector was often lacking. There was a split between some groups within the ARK network and those socially oriented humanitarian NGOs that did not have their roots in the peace movement. The work of many among the latter NGOs was seen as being primarily aimed at helping ethnic Croats, having a fundamentally different view on basic questions such as the war and nationalism. Efforts at cooperation were launched by groups such as the umbrella group, the Center for the Development of Nonprofit Organizations (CERANEO), founded in 1995 in an attempt to strengthen the sector through the organization of workshops and annual forums and the publication of a newsletter. In 1996, more than 100 Croatian NGOs came together in an effort to amend the government's draft Law on Associations, even if unsuccessful. Nonetheless, unlike the situation in Slovakia, where a similar campaign against a law on foundations brought the NGO sector together, unity was short lived in Croatia.

It should be noted that the entire spectrum of values existed within Croatia's NGO sector and many organizations had close ties to the government. One example is the Humanitarian Foundation for the Children of Croatia, of which President Tuđman's wife, Ankica, served as director in the 1990s. The organization benefited from special privileges, including the right to place collection boxes in public places and to distribute its flyers on Croatia Airlines flights. Another NGO with HDZ ties was the Foundation of the Croatian State Vow, whose director, Ivić Pašalić, was one of President Tuđman's closest advisors. The foundation offered student scholarships and published a journal entitled *Državnost* (Statehood). In some articles this journal attempted to build a personality cult around Tuđman.[13] One of the most controversial aspects of Croatian civil society during the Tuđman era were the numerous groups of veterans and other victims from Croatia's war of independence in the early 1990s, commonly known as the "Homeland War". These veterans groups received significant funding from the state budget and had a privileged position in society.[14]

Despite HDZ's confrontational stance toward civil society organizations, in October 1998 the cabinet set up an Office for Associations, which provided funds to certain NGOs (including women's groups), to which receiving government support was previously unimaginable. That same month, the Croatian government co-sponsored a three-day NGO fair in Zagreb, together with the United Nations High Commissioner for Refugees (UNHCR), intended as a gathering of organizations focused on humanitarian questions and the protection of human rights. In the end, the fair presented an awkward mix, attended by a wide range of NGOs, ranging from feminists and pro-life groups to ethnic Serb organizations and groups defending the interests of veterans of the recent "Homeland War".[15]

It is unclear why HDZ took a more favorable approach to the NGO sector in the late 1990s, although its shifting stance may have been part of an attempt to appease the international community, which was putting increasing emphasis on the development of NGOs in the region. In May 1998, the European Union and the United States awarded the Prize for Democracy and Civil Society to 50 organizations and individuals from 29 countries of Central and Eastern Europe, including three from Croatia: the women's human rights group Be active, Be emancipated (B.a.B.e.), which was part of the ARK network, the Forum 21 media pressure group and the Serbian Democratic Forum's Legal Advice Centers. One HDZ publication from 1999

13 Tomislav Čadež, "Zaklada hrvatskog državnog zavjeta: kako se kultivira kult ličnosti", Globus, November 27, 1998, pp. 32-35.
14 See Sharon Fisher, "Contentious Politics in Croatia: The War Veterans' Movement", in: Petr Kopecký and Cas Mudde (eds.), Uncivil Society? Contentious Politics in Postcommunist Europe (Routledge, London, 2003), pp. 74-92.
15 See, for example, Goran Borković, "Smotra nevladinih udruga postala sajam taštine i incidenata", Vjesnik, November 5, 1998.

recognized an individual country's level of NGO development as a "basic indicator" of its democracy, adding that "the role of Croatian nongovernmental organizations in the development of Croatian democratic society has been large".[16] As demonstrated during the pre-election period, however, HDZ's newly found affection for NGOs would not last long.

Emerging Unity among Croatian Democrats: The GLAS 99 Campaign

In certain respects, HDZ set the stage for its own defeat in the 2000 elections. This was reflected in the party's controversial policies on the economy and its alienating public discourse. In light of growing opposition during the second half of the 1990s, HDZ was faced with the choice between altering its discourse in an attempt to expand its shrinking constituency and risking defeat in the forthcoming elections. Although there were various attempts by HDZ to move in the direction of the political center after 1995, the shift never actually occurred. Instead of moderating its discourse, the party further radicalized its rhetoric with the aim of frightening the population about potential threats to the nation. For example, HDZ warned the electorate of the catastrophes that an opposition victory would entail, including the restoration of Yugoslavia.[17] While HDZ had been successful in "feeling the pulse" of the population in the early 1990s, the party appeared to have lost touch with ordinary voters, who had become increasingly concerned with economic problems and limitations on democracy, by the end of the decade. Opinion polls taken in late 1998 show that the vast majority of citizens did not believe Tuđman's discourse and was not fearful for the nation's future, even if the opposition did come to power.[18] Although Tuđman had managed to pull together support for HDZ before previous elections, his death in December 1999 threw the party into chaos.

Even with support for HDZ falling, it sometimes appeared that the political opposition lacked the necessary unity to win the elections and form a new government. However, with encouragement from the international community, some Croatians looked to Slovakia as a model of coalition building.[19] It was the issue of electoral legislation that finally brought together Croatia's six main opposition parties, and the Opposition Six held its first meetings in September 1998 to work out a joint draft election law.[20] The unity of the Opposition Six was signaled most notably by the signing, on 30 November 1999, of the "Declaration on the Fundamental Direction of

16 Izborni pojmovnik HDZ-a, HDZ, Zagreb, 1999, p. 250.

17 See Ivo Žanić, "Tuđmanov 'sovjetski' diskurs", Jutarnji list, December 9, 1998, and Zoran Daskalović, "Tuđman Triumphs Over Divided Opposition", War Report no. 51, May 1997, pp. 3-5.

18 See Globus, October 16, 1998, pp. 24-26 and December 18, 1998, pp. 16-17.

19 See interview with Deputy Chairman of the Croatian Social-Liberal Party (HSLS), Vilim Herman in: Novi list, January 19, 1999.

20 Vjesnik, September 2, 1998; Večernji list, September 22 and 23, 1998.

Post-Election Activity", in which the parties vowed to create a common government, promised not to form a coalition with the HDZ and agreed on various policy issues. Due to the fact that the electoral law was changed to a purely proportional system, the six parties established two coalitions: the Coalition of Two and the Coalition of Four. While the Coalition of Two included the Social Democratic Party (SDP) and the Croatian Social Liberal Party (HSLS), the Coalition of Four grouped together the conservative Croatian Peasants' Party (HSS) with three small liberal parties, including the Croatian People's Party (HNS), the Liberal Party (LS) and the Istrian Democratic Assembly (IDS).

In Croatian society, despite growing dissatisfaction among the population, the extent of public protest was disappointingly low during the late 1990s, with passivity and distrust prevailing. The property of "civic competence"[21] was slow to take hold, meaning that the public mood was often characterized by a feeling of helplessness concerning its ability to affect government policies, thereby reinforcing the political culture of alienation that was inherited from the communist regime.[22] This was also reflected in decreasing interest in elections. Although voter turnout reached a respectable 71 percent in the upper house elections in April 1997, only 55 percent of eligible voters took part in the presidential elections in June of that year, despite the opposition's arguments that a large turnout was needed to force Tuđman into a second-round runoff. Tuđman, therefore, prevailed in the first round.

Shortly before the 2000 elections to the lower house of parliament, public opinion polls revealed that the main issues of concern included high unemployment, a low standard of living and pensions, rather than concerns about democracy.[23] The task of NGOs was to ensure that people had not completely lost hope and to encourage them to come out and vote in the elections. Especially important were the estimated 200,000 first-time voters, representing more than five percent of the total electorate.

Many Croatian NGO representatives were doubtful about whether they would be capable of running a get-out-the-vote campaign like the one in Slovakia in 1998. One problem was the lack of unity in the NGO community, disjointed as a result of personality conflicts, personal ambitions and deeper ideological debates that plagued the sector throughout the 1990s. One group that was often criticized by the rest of the NGO community for its lack of cooperation was HHO, which had by far the most media coverage of any civic organization. The lack of a state-wide private

---

21 See Gabriel A. Almond and Sidney Verba, The Civic Culture: Political Attitudes and Democracy in Five Nations (Princeton University Press, Princeton, 1963), pp. 180-183.
22 Pavle Novosel, "Croatian Political Culture in Times of Great Expectations", in: Fritz Plasser and Andreas Pribersky (eds.), Political Culture in East Central Europe (Avebury, Aldershot, 1996), pp. 109-110.
23 International Republican Institute, Istraživanje javnog mnijenja, November 1999, p. 8.

television station on which to broadcast the campaign caused concern.[24] Unlike in Slovakia, Croatia's NGO community did not have the widespread respect of the population. International donors had focused their efforts mainly on advocacy groups that were promoting issues such as human and minority rights. In an economically impoverished country, with a history of authoritarian political culture, NGO activists whose salaries were paid by foreign agencies were perceived as careerists at best or foreign spies at worst, rather than as professionals engaged in enhancing public political consciousness.

Despite those challenges, the NGO community started discussions in February 1999 on the possibility of launching a Slovak-style campaign. A preliminary meeting held that month was attended by representatives of HHO, OSI, ARK, Attack, the environmental organization *Zelena akcija* (Green Action), several women's NGOs and the U.S. Agency for International Development (USAID). Croatian NGOs learned from their Slovak counterparts through a number of seminars and exchanges sponsored by the international community, marking the first of many cases in which Slovak NGO activists shared their experiences in an effort to help forge democracy abroad. For example, at a Bratislava conference held in February 1999 that included NGO representatives from Croatia, Serbia, Ukraine, Belarus and Russia, Slovak activists shared their expertise, highlighting programs such as "Rock the Vote", *Občianske oko* (Civic Eye) (civic election observation) and MEMO '98 (media monitoring).

In March 1999, a group of intellectuals and NGO activists announced that organizations and individuals engaged in developing democracy and civil society would participate in the electoral campaign. The following day activists from women's groups said they would form a coalition for monitoring and influencing the elections. The NGO sector finally came together in April and May 1999, with 35 groups uniting to create the Civic Coalition for Free and Fair Elections or GLAS 99. One month before the elections, the number of organizations involved had reached 145 and was still growing.[25] GLAS 99's main task was to run a get-out-the-vote campaign prior to the elections in an effort to ensure broader public participation in the democratic process and to help steer people away from apathy and extremism.

Another group that was active throughout the pre-election period was *Gradjani organizovano nadgledaju glasanje* or GONG (Citizens Organized to Monitor Elections), which was established in early 1997 with the aim of conducting domestic election observation and increasing the interest of voters in the electoral process. GONG received significant financial support from USAID's Office of Transition Initiatives (OTI) as well as training from the U.S.-based National Democratic Institute (NDI). By the time of the 2000 elections, GONG was widely respected as a professional and nonpartisan organization, partly since it had already scored a key victory in

---

24 Novi list, February 15, 1999; personal interview with Marija Raos of CERANEO, October 19, 1998.

25 Personal interview with GLAS 99 Director, Tin Gazivoda, December 10, 1999.

October 1998, when the constitutional court recognized the right of NGOs to send domestic observers to elections, after police had prohibited GONG observers from entering polling stations during by-elections in Dubrovnik earlier that month.[26] As in the case of Slovakia, the presence of independent observers was especially important in Croatia's 2000 elections, since many citizens feared that HDZ would try to manipulate the results.

The HDZ was clearly afraid of the application of the "Slovak model" to Croatia. In his speech to HDZ's tenth party congress in June 1999, Tuđman stressed that "despite the fact that Croatia has friendly partner relations with some European countries and the United States", it is faced with "intense efforts by so-called nongovernmental organizations that desire some other Croatia". He warned that such groups were trying "in any way possible" to use the elections to bring about political change.[27] Shortly before Croatia's parliamentary elections, former Slovak Prime Minister Vladimír Mečiar was interviewed by the pro-HDZ daily *Večernji list* about the "Slovak model" and the international community's role in his party's 1998 electoral defeat.[28] That interview triggered a smear campaign against several U.S. organizations in the pro-HDZ media. One article even referred to Mečiar as "living proof" of how America decided who would win the Slovak elections.[29]

GLAS 99: Activities, Structures and Resources

Although GLAS 99 had a central office in Zagreb coordinating campaign activities, the structure of the organization was meant to be as democratic as possible, with each NGO having one vote in the general assembly. Tin Gazivoda, formerly a student in the United States and the United Kingdom and an employee of HHO, became director of the main office. He was joined by Sonja Vuković (marketing coordinator), Darko Jurišić (program coordinator) and Koraljka Dilić (public relations representative).

The first pre-election activities of the NGO community related to the electoral law itself. In October 1999, GLAS 99 publicly presented its action program and demanded the right to participate in the parliamentary discussion of the election law, acting in concert with HHO and the Movement for Democracy and Social Justice in calling for amendments to the government's draft. At the time the draft was put forward, GLAS 99 ran a campaign inviting voters to call top politicians and present their opinions about the elections and the election law. GLAS 99 also distributed brochures on "how the new election law would cheat voters". The campaign helped to improve the image of the NGO sector among the population. A November 1999 poll showed that

---

26 See Novi list, October 17, 1998.
27 Croatia Watch, no. 6, July 30, 1999.
28 Večernji list, November 17, 1999.
29 Dunja Ujević, "Slovački izbori u Hrvatskoj", Večernji list, November 18, 1999. See also "Američki obavještajci sjede u IRI-ju i USAID-u koji financiraju šestoricu, a odgovaraju Montgomeryju!", Vjesnik, December 1, 1999.

25 percent of respondents said they were "very interested" in the NGOs' thoughts about the elections and 35 percent said they were "somewhat interested".[30] Other GLAS 99 pre-election activities included educating citizens about voter rights, monitoring the campaigns of political parties, and, most importantly, motivating citizens to vote.

GLAS 99 officially launched its get-out-the-vote campaign in September 1999. The campaign was run through posters and billboards, radio jingles, TV spots, as well as brochures, flyers and rock concerts for young people. Some of the GLAS 99 materials focused solely on voter education, informing citizens who has the right to vote and why elections are important. It is noteworthy that GLAS 99 began its pre-election campaign well before that of the political opposition. Even after the official campaign period for parties began, its ads were often more visible and persuasive than those of the opposition parties. The main requirement of all organizations involved in GLAS 99 was that they should be nonpartisan. The rest was up to them. Still, being nonpartisan did not mean being apolitical, and some of the groups' ads and materials strongly criticized the government.

The main slogan of the overall GLAS 99 campaign was *Zaokruži i dobivaš* ("Circle and Win"), and the "o" in *zaokruži* was drawn to symbolize the circling of a party on an election ballot. This slogan was intended to play on the prize competitions that had been launched by a number of newspapers. The group's main billboard referred to the elections as "the most popular prize competition", which was "coming soon to Croatia". The billboard added that there would be "more than 3,000,000 winners", corresponding to the number of voters in Croatia. One magazine advertisement using the "Circle and Win" slogan called on Croatians to vote and told them that the elections were "the essential prize competition". One of GLAS 99's most eye-catching magazine and newspaper ads showed a scene inside Zagreb airport, featuring the signs for international arrivals and departures, together with the slogan "I want to live in a normal country". In its final call to voters, GLAS 99 published a full-page advertisement reading: "Let's get out to the elections. Our fate and that of our children and our homeland is again in our hands. Let's vote seriously and responsibly".

Among the main TV spots of GLAS 99 was a fast moving, MTV-style presentation, showing well-known musicians and singers. The song *"Novo vrijeme"* (A new age), was featured. According to one observer, the song demonstrates a rare combination of utopian and ironic nostalgia.[31] Although there was no direct reference to GLAS 99, the ad showed people making a circle on the screen, thus showing the group's main symbol. Following attacks on GLAS 99 by HDZ representatives, state-controlled *Croatian TV* prohibited the airing of two GLAS 99 ads, including the *"Novo vrijeme"*

30 International Republican Institute, Istraživanje javnog mnijenja, November 1999, p. 14.

31 Paul Stubbs, "New Times? Towards a Political Economy of 'Civil Society' in Contemporary Croatia", Narodna Umjetnost, vol. 38, no. 1, 2001, pp. 89-103.

clip, claiming that they gave "indirect political messages". At the request of *Croatian TV*, the central electoral commission reviewed the advertisements and announced in mid-December that GLAS 99 had no right to any pre-election campaigning. Although the constitutional court ruled later that month that the ads could be aired,[32] the decision was made just a few days before the elections, ensuring that *Croatian TV* won its bid to stop GLAS 99 from airing its message.

GLAS 99 was made up of four separate groups: one focusing on youth, another on women, a third on environmental organizations and a fourth on pensioners. The youth campaign was led by the Union of Nongovernmental Organizations (UNO 99), marking the first time that such a network was established in Croatia. The campaign for women was run by the Women's Ad Hoc Coalition, which grouped together 27 women's organizations that had a history of cooperation, as they had already run campaigns prior to the 1995 and 1997 elections. The campaign aimed at retired persons was run by the Union of Pensioners, while *Zelena akcija* oversaw the environmental campaign. In addition to the four targeted campaigns, there was also a coordination committee with representatives of four regions (Osijek, Rijeka, Zagreb and Split).

The campaigns by environmental NGOs and pensioners were less visible, and hence the following considerations will focus largely on the youth and women campaigns. The youth campaign was considered particularly important, as attracting first-time voters would be key to producing a stronger victory for the political opposition. While HDZ had significant backing from youth in the elections that initially brought it to power,[33] it had largely lost the support of young voters, despite the party's control over the education system. An opinion poll conducted shortly before the 2000 elections showed that just 12 percent of first-time voters supported HDZ, compared with 29 percent of pensioners.[34] One development that angered young voters in the months prior to the elections was police intrusions into cafés and nightclubs. In that regard, one journalist accused the police of attacking "the last oasis of urban culture."[35]

The youth campaign's main slogan was *"Izađi i bori se"* (Get out and fight), with a "z" added between *"i"* and *"bori"* to form the word "elections" (*izbori*). One of the youth campaign's main ads featured a turtle with its head and legs in its shell at the top of the page and with the same turtle at the bottom of the page, apparently walking with a purpose. Another of the campaign's ads showed three young people in black and white (but with brightly colored hair) standing facing a wall, with "Raid or Democracy" as the main slogan. A playful youth campaign pamphlet showed on its cover a man breaking a stack of concrete slabs with his head, together with the slogan "Think

32 Foreign Press Bureau, Daily Bulletin, Zagreb, December 22 and 29, 1999.

33 See Dejan Jović, Kakvu Hrvatsku žele, Danas, April 3, 1990, p. 7.

34 Globus, November 12 and 19, 1998.

35 Ivan Vidić, Urbana kultura na udaru represije, Globus, November 12, 1999, pp. 82-84.

with your head!". Inside the brochure was a series in which readers were asked to spot the differences between two photographs. One page featured a photo of three sexily dressed blonde women, juxtaposed with another of middle-aged female demonstrators in central Zagreb holding signs with slogans such as "Why did you lie to us?". Another showed pictures of a rock musician versus Croatian folk dancers, alluding to HDZ's preference for traditional forms of culture. Through various texts, the pamphlet tried to appeal to young voters by dealing with issues that concerned them and using familiar language. A second pamphlet encouraged voters to focus on the future of Croatia, with the words "Happy New 2000!" on the cover. Inside, it included quotations from a number of politicians and journalists connected with HDZ, demonstrating their unfavorable views on elections, opposition, democracy and youth. One picture showed the evolution of man, with the most recent stage being referred to as "Homo Croaticus". That stage was said to have begun around the year 1995 (the year of Croatia's last parliamentary elections), in which the people "chose between a better life and false promises", but selected the latter. A third pamphlet designed for the youth campaign explained to voters the meaning of democracy. The Student Information Center also joined in the youth campaign, producing flyers that encouraged students to "take things into your hands" and vote.

Referring to the female part of the Croatian electorate, the women's campaign was marked by the slogan "51 %". The Woman's Coalition election platform listed the following demands: employment with regular pay; shared responsibility for the home and participation in decision making; an end to violence against women; legal, safe and free abortion and contraception; and education for tolerance and human rights in schools. One ad showed the face of a smiling and pensive woman, with "partner and not subject" as the main slogan. One poster featured a woman's face with the slogan "Let's change positions and vote for partners", while another consisted of small pictures of various female NGO activists, together with the slogan "Women! Let's show our strength!". The Coalition also produced a pre-election quiz for women, getting them focused on key issues. On the occasion of the International Day against Violence against Women, November 25, 1999, the Coalition distributed materials to citizens relating to the theme of elections. Shortly before the vote, the women's human rights group B.a.B.e. published its analysis of the treatment of women and women's issues in the media and it distributed posters showing quotes about women. One quotation from a Japanese woman read: "If it is true that men are better than women because they are stronger, why aren't sumo wrestlers sitting in the government?". In addition to B.a.B.e., the Women's Information Center and the Split-based women's organization *Stop Nade* created their own materials for women on elections. While the former produced a booklet on women and elections, the latter prepared a brochure on elections and democracy and another on women's issues that included the slogan "A better world for women is better for all humankind".

According to Gazivoda, the main problems faced by the GLAS 99 campaign included both a lack of coordination among participants and a lack of coordination among donors.[36] The two biggest contributors to the group's finance were USAID's OTI and the OSI, and the two organizations were often on different wavelengths about what GLAS was expected to do. While U.S. groups such as NDI, the International Republic Institute (IRI) and the Information Research and Exchange Board (IREX) provided training and expertise, most of the key private foundations that helped fund the campaign were based in the United States (the National Endowment for Democracy, Freedom House and the Charles Stewart Mott Foundation). From Western Europe, the European Commission provided some funding, as did organizations such as the British Know-How Fund and the Westminster Foundation for Democracy. Meanwhile, the Swedish group *Kvinna Till Kvinna* supported women's NGOs. Various western embassies also contributed financial support, particularly the U.S. and British Embassies. However, that assistance was largely uncoordinated.[37]

In certain respects, HDZ's arguments about an international conspiracy were not entirely unfounded, as some western funders did not hide their aim of altering the country's political situation through assistance to civic activity. USAID was careful to avoid being too forthright about its goals in Slovakia. By the time of the Croatian elections, however, OTI representatives had decided to take on a more active role in the pre-election campaign, going as far as instructing local activists on what to include in their literature.[38] OTI contributed US$ 3.7 million to Croatia in 1999 alone, most of which was focused on pre-election activities, and even provided a professional media team to help work out the details of the campaign. Moreover, USAID provided a further US$ 1.3 million that year through its Democracy Network program, while the U.S. Embassy's Democracy Commission distributed some US$ 200,000 in small grants.[39]

It is noteworthy that cooperation and contact with the political opposition was limited, despite the fact that the NGOs were helping their election bid. As the elections approached, the opposition parties gradually became more interested in meeting NGOs. However, when it came to making on important political decisions, they did not involve NGOs.[40] Representatives of all political parties were invited to discuss the role of NGOs in the elections during an NGO gathering sponsored by CERANEO a month before the elections. However, no one from HDZ or from three of the six main opposition parties attended.

---

36 Speech by Gazivoda at 3rd Annual NGO Forum sponsored by CERANEO, December 3, 1999 in Zagreb.
37 Personal interview with Gazivoda, December 10, 1999.
38 Personal interviews with Croatian NGO activists, December 1999.
39 Support for East European Democracy (SEED) Report, Financial Year 1999, March 2000, p. 55.
40 Personal interview with Gazivoda, December 10, 1999.

Lessons and Prospects

The GLAS 99 campaign launched by NGOs in Croatia had a number of positive results. By organizing a get-out-the vote campaign, NGOs helped to ensure that the majority of Croatian voters participated in the electoral process, as demonstrated by the 75 percent turnout. Moreover, despite HDZ's continued efforts to warn the population about the danger of an opposition victory, voters overwhelmingly supported the opposition parties, giving the Coalition of Two and the Coalition of Four more than three-fifths of the parliamentary seats and, thereby, setting the stage for a more democratically oriented political administration in Croatia under the leadership of Prime Minister Ivica Račan. In the presidential elections that were held one month later, the NGO community organized the GLAS 2000 campaign, helping to elect Stipe Mesić, who had quit HDZ in 1994 and was one of the few vocal critics of Tuđman's nationalist policies in the political opposition. A secondary, but nonetheless positive, result of the GLAS 99 campaign was that it assisted in creating an atmosphere of civic activism that until then had been largely absent.

Such successes should not be ignored, especially given the skepticism of many Croatian NGO activists that the situation in Slovakia could not be repeated, given the very different circumstances in Croatia. Nevertheless, the longer-term effects of the GLAS 99 campaign are less obvious and its impact on strengthening Croatian civil society appears to have been limited. One of the key problems was the NGO sector's public image. Even after the change of government, civic groups were not viewed favorably by many Croatians, partly due to the HDZ's rhetoric about international influence on the NGO community.

A further lesson learned relates to domestic politicians. While NGOs and trade unions helped Račan in January 2000, the ruling parties quickly forgot how and with whose assistance they were elected. During Račan's term, few efforts were made to make use of the NGO sector's expertise. According to one analysis, no concrete changes took place during the new government's first year in office, despite rhetorical backing for NGOs. The only positive shift related to the public image of NGOs, which were no longer widely perceived as "anti-Croatian".[41] The situation began to improve in 2001 to 2002, with the approval of new legislation on NGOs and the establishment of formal cooperation between NGOs and the government. Nevertheless, research shows that few ministries saw NGOs as reliable partners and few NGOs had formed real partnerships with government institutions, partly due to the weakness of public advocacy.[42] The European Commission's first annual Stabilization and Association Report on Croatia, published in April 2002, criticized the absence of NGOs from

---

41 USAID, The 2000 NGO Sustainability Index for Central and Eastern Europe and Eurasia (USAID, Washington, DC, 2001), p. 60.

42 Igor Vidačak, "The Non-Governmental Sector and the Government: A Dialogue for Europe", in: Katarina Ott (ed.), Croatian Accession to the European Union: Economic and Legal Challenges (Institute of Public Finance and Friedrich Ebert Stiftung, Zagreb, 2003), pp. 260-79.

policymaking and the legislative process and recommended increased cooperation. Even so, by 2004, Croatian NGOs were achieving only limited success in advocacy activities, as the new government of Ivo Sanader backtracked with regard to cooperation.[43]

Several problems related to the strategies of donors. For example, the inflow of large amounts of international funding for the pre-election campaign created an artificial unity that turned out to be short lived, as joint activities fizzled out shortly after the GLAS 2000 campaign for the presidential elections. In the country's next parliamentary elections, held in November 2003, the NGO sector did not organize a get-out-the-vote campaign and HDZ returned to power, although in a new, more internationally acceptable form under the leadership of Prime Minister Sanader. One USAID official said that the donor community only took its cue from Croatia and that international organizations did not provide assistance for another get-out-the-vote campaign because, unlike in the Slovak case in 2002, the country's NGOs did not ask for help.[44]

Moreover, the fact that the international funding for civic campaigns was only short-term in nature and did not continue much beyond elections created enormous cynicism on the part of NGOs. Croatia had a position in the spotlight for about 10 months before the changes in Serbia took place, causing the international community to promptly shift its attention. OTI closed its Croatia program in March 2000, leaving support for civil society to other donors, such as the Charles Stewart Mott Foundation, the British Know-How Fund and the USAID Mission. At the same time, the total amount of funds coming from U.S. donors for Croatia's NGO sector shrank considerably, with USAID's Democracy Network providing just US$ 750,000 in 2000 and the U.S. Embassy's Democracy Commission again giving approximately US$ 200,000 worth of small grants.[45]

Nevertheless, USAID does seem to have evaluated its role as one of the main donors supporting Croatian civil society. The organization is now concerned about its role in helping to create a third sector that is self-sustaining. In the aftermath of the "Homeland War," there was a strong focus among foreign donors on promoting human rights and advocacy, and their financing strategies reflected that. Some, however, have argued that this was an unnatural development that has distorted the third sector.[46] In the second phase of USAID's Democracy Network program for Croatia, launched in late 2001, the organization deliberately shifted its approach, focusing mainly on non-controversial social service NGOs, partly with the intention

43 USAID, The 2004 NGO Sustainability Index for Central and Eastern Europe and Eurasia (USAID, Washington, DC, 2005), p. 103.
44 Personal interview with USAID official, Washington, DC, November 2004.
45 Support for East European Democracy (SEED) Report, Financial Year 2000, March 2001, p. 62, op cit.
46 Personal interview with former Academy for Educational Development (AED) country director for Croatia, Michael Kott, Washington, DC, November 19, 2004.

of helping to improve the sector's image and sustainability. While previously, most funding went to NGOs that were concentrated in Zagreb and the three regional centers, donor efforts have helped spur the opening of new organizations in smaller municipalities. By 2003, the total number of Croatian NGOs had increased to approximately 23,800.[47]

The problems that have plagued the Croatian NGO community during the recent past will be difficult to overcome. USAID put Croatia's 2004 NGO sustainability rating at 3.5 points, demonstrating that the country's sector is still in the mid-transition phase. That is a considerable improvement over the country's 1999 rating of 5.0, mainly due to a sharp drop in the scores for legal environment and financial viability (both of which were previously at 6.0 points). Still, much work needs to be done to bring the overall score down to the levels seen in Croatia's regional peers that joined the European Union in 2004, with all countries except for Slovenia having sustainability scores of 2.1 to 2.7 points.

The latest evaluation by USAID considers financial viability to be the main problem for NGOs in Croatia, particularly given the reduction in foreign assistance. That is especially true since USAID funding for Croatia was phased out in 2006. Prospects for more domestic funding have improved somewhat, thanks to the Račan government's establishment in late 2003 of the National Foundation for Civil Society Development, which is supported by lottery revenues and state funds with the aim of making the NGO sector more sustainable, while also promoting networking and volunteerism. Still, the Foundation was tainted by controversy in January 2005, when it was revealed that funds were allocated to those NGOs whose organizational coordinators were represented on its management board.[48]

Public perceptions of the NGO community remain one of the key challenges for Croatia's third sector, as they continue to vary from indifference to generally negative attitudes. One public opinion poll commissioned in 2002 by the Women's Human Rights Group B.a.B.e. showed that more than half of the population was not aware of public activities by NGOs, while a relative majority found their work unsuccessful.[49]

Croatia's NGO sector in the 21st century has continued to face the same hardships and opportunities as other elements of society, presenting many contradictions. Despite healthy GDP growth, scarce domestic financial resources have contributed to rising foreign debt. Despite rhetoric of multinational tolerance and greater openness toward the states of the former Yugoslavia, individual instances of ethnic violence have continued in Croatia. Despite elaborate legislative and institutional

---

47 USAID, The 2003 NGO Sustainability Index for Central and Eastern Europe and Eurasia (USAID, Washington, DC, June 2004), p. 55.

48 For more information on that scandal, see http://www.zamirzine.net under "Stalne rubrike: Nevladine udruge".

49 "Percepcija NVO u Hrvatskoj", available at http://www.babe.hr/istrazivanja/percepcijaNVO_ BaBe.pdf.

protection for a woman's right to live free of violence, cases of domestic violence have increased and have become more serious recently.

In such a social and political context, Croatian civil society faces at least two important dilemmas of "political normalization". First, it remains unclear whether NGOs can become partners to the ruling elite without losing their critical stance as independent observers. Second, it is unclear how civic organizations can widen the scope of their activism to issues that were not explored during the 1990s (such as the right to asylum, gay and lesbian rights and animal rights) without being constantly reminded that Croatian civil society has more important issues to deal with.

Political changes after the 2000 elections brought about reforms that included better legal protection for social and ethnic groups whose human rights were violated in the previous era, while also transforming the country's political rhetoric along the lines of European Union requirements. However, formal political changes can only achieve limited effects if they are not followed by a transformation of civic culture. While the GLAS 99 campaign was successful in abolishing the culture of fear that had characterized the 1990s, more work needs to be done. A shift from the political rhetoric of tolerance toward a civic culture of tolerance requires that civil society organizations are equipped with professionalism, perseverance and civic courage, in addition to sufficient financial means, as they face new political and social tensions and challenges.

Chronology

January 1, 1999
In his New Year interview with *Croatian TV*, President Franjo Tuđman states that as far as social policy is concerned it would be hard to find a state as socially conscious as Croatia. At the same time, Freedom House classifies Croatia as "partly free" in terms of media freedom, with a lower level of democracy than in 1997.

January 26, 1999
Tuđman speaks with opposition leaders Dražen Budiša (Croatian Social Liberal Party) and Ivica Račan (Social Democratic Party) about the reconstruction of the government and offers Budiša participation in the cabinet.

February 12, 1999
NGO representatives hold a preliminary meeting in which they decide to launch a joint campaign prior to the elections scheduled for the beginning of the following year.

March 7, 1999
Public intellectuals and NGO activists Gojko Bežovan, Ivan Zvonimir Čičak, Damir Grubiša, Darko Jurišić and Čedo Prodanović state that organizations and individuals engaged in developing democracy and civil society will participate in the electoral campaign. On the next day, activists from women's groups announce they are forming a coalition for monitoring and influencing the elections.

March 19, 1999
A new electoral law is drafted, dividing Croatia into 10 electoral units, with a proportional electoral system. That is considered beneficial for large parties and for regional parties, but not advantageous for smaller parties and coalitions. The draft remains open to amendments.

May 10, 1999
Violence breaks out in Zagreb's Square of Croatian Heroes during the annual civic protest aimed at returning the square to its old name, the Square of the Victims of Fascism. Right-wing *Ustaše* sympathizers throw teargas at anti-fascist protesters. The police do not react, choosing to view the event as a conflict between "anti-fascists" and "anti-communists".

July 2, 1999
President Tuđman's legal advisor, Mirko Ramušćak, publicly calls on Croatian citizens to boycott newspapers "that serve [George] Soros and his sick idea to subjugate nations and states to his evil empire".

July 8, 1999
GONG starts preparing for the election monitoring campaign.

August 6, 1999

Opposition leaders Ivica Račan and Dražen Budiša announce the formation of a coalition in which the Social Democratic Party (SDP) will be represented by two thirds of the candidates and the Croatian Social Liberal Party (HSLS) by one third.

August 1999

The United Nations Security Council threatens Croatia with economic sanctions for its lack of cooperation with the International War Crimes Tribunal for Former Yugoslavia. The Organization for Security and Cooperation in Europe (OSCE) criticizes state-run *Croatian TV* because the airtime devoted to the ruling Croatian Democratic Community (HDZ) is disproportionately larger than that for the opposition parties.

September 2, 1999

A coalition of NGOs known as GLAS 99 officially starts a get-out-the-vote campaign.

October 7, 1999

Women's rights activists publicly campaign for greater participation of women in politics as part of GLAS 99.

October 21, 1999

GLAS 99 publicly presents its program of action and demands the right to participate in parliamentary discussions on the electoral law.

October 26, 1999

The International Helsinki Federation for Human Rights declares its support for GLAS 99.

November 11, 1999

President Tuđman falls fatally ill.

November 24, 1999

The OSCE starts monitoring the pre-election campaign in Croatia and preparing its international election observation mission.

December 12, 1999

The defense minister announces that the army will respect the electoral results. President Tuđman dies.

December 22, 1999

The state electoral commission rules that GLAS 99 has "no right to any pre-election campaigning". The decision is made in response to GLAS 99's television ads.

December 29, 1999

Days before the elections, the constitutional court rules that GLAS 99 advertising can be aired.

January 3, 2000

Parliamentary elections bring an overwhelming victory to two opposition coalitions, which win more than 60 percent of the seats in parliament. Voter turnout reaches 75 percent.

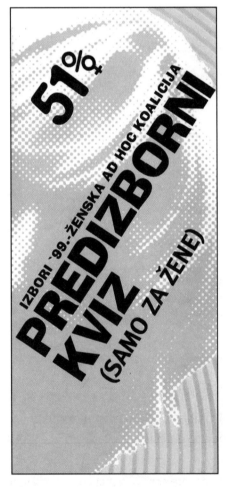

51%. Elections 99 – Women's ad hoc coalition. Pre-election quiz (for women only).

Take the matter into your own hands! 8:00-12:00 – lectures. 12:00-13:00 – canteen. 13:00-17:00 – library. 17:00 – vote

Come out! GLAS 99 – Vote / Have your say!

Think with your head! Get out! Vote and win!

B.a.B.e volunteers campaigning in downtown Zagreb.

Spot the difference!

Spot the difference!

The protest poster reads: "Why did you lie to us?".

IZLAZ 2000:
AN EXIT TO DEMOCRACY IN SERBIA

Jelica Minić and Miljenko Dereta

IZLAZ 2000 (Exit 2000) is the umbrella name given to the campaign for free and fair presidential elections in 2000 of a group of Serbian NGOs. A common campaign image and slogan invited citizens to participate in the elections and to take the opportunity to exit from the political and social crisis, economic deprivation and international isolation, in which Serbia increasingly found itself as a result of the 13-year long neo-authoritarian rule of Slobodan Milošević.[1]

The main purposes of the campaign were to encourage high voter turnout, to monitor the election process and to ensure that the ballot was at all stages free, fair and reflected the will of the citizens. The joint approach of more than 150 NGOs, involving an estimated 25-30,000 volunteers, was intended to increase the effectiveness and influence of civil society. The campaign was part of a broad, coordinated, strategy on the part of all democratic forces in Serbia including free media, opposition political parties, independent unions and nongovernmental organizations. All these groups were united by their wish for democratic change, their otherwise differing interests notwithstanding.

The contribution of civil society to pro-democracy activities prior to the 2000 federal and presidential elections in Serbia has been noted as exemplary, both domestically and internationally. Civic campaigns and activities were carried out in an extremely tense political and social atmosphere, as the Milošević regime did not hesitate to use repression and arrests, to disrupt activities or confiscate materials or to direct threats at persons and organizations involved. Among ordinary citizens, fear of reprisals was widespread.

Nevertheless, on election day (September 24, 2000) over 71 percent of voters turned out, with over 50 percent casting their ballot in favor of Vojislav Koštunica, the democratic challenger to Slobodan Milošević, whose long and non-democratic reign was ended through an impressive demonstration of the will of Serbian citizens for democratic change. The parliamentary elections on December 23, 2000, in which the Democratic Opposition of Serbia won a landslide victory, confirmed this sea change in Serbian politics. Civil society made a considerable contribution to the re-establishment of democracy in Serbia and it can be rightfully proud of the role it played then and since.

---

1 "Izlaz" (Serbian for "exit") has a double meaning: to exit a place or a problem situation and to show up somewhere (at elections, going out socially in the evening, appearing in public, etc.).

Today, in hindsight, it is difficult to say which of the many civic efforts around the September 2000 elections made the most important contribution, whether the large and mediatized projects at the national level such as those of the Center for Free Elections and Democracy (henceforth, CeSID), the youth movement OTPOR[2], G17+, Civic Initiatives or the European Movement in Serbia, or the smaller ones that involved many marginalized groups without significant resources or media coverage. More importantly, all these activities demonstrated the strength and influence of the nongovernmental sector, its creativity and ability to mobilize citizens and its power to resist even the most non-democratic regime. This experience continues to be an inspiration to all those in Serbia, and elsewhere, that are committed to democracy and human rights and to political, social and economic reform.

Representative of all of these civic efforts, this case study presents the civic campaign IZLAZ 2000, provides an overview of the general context in which this campaign was developed and implemented, describes its main protagonists and activities and assesses its main results.

Milošević's Serbia:
Society and Politics before the 2000 Elections

The pre-election activities that made up the IZLAZ 2000 campaign were an integral part of the wider struggle by democratic forces in Serbia for political change in favor of democracy. These included opposition political parties, independent trade unions, universities, youth organizations, numerous professional associations, as well as the independent media. The context in which these forces developed their activities was the regime of Slobodan Milošević under which all pro-democracy actors faced significant challenges to their existence and survival. However, that civic campaigns eventually succeeded in contributing to bringing Milošević's rule to an end, can be attributed to the nature and structure of civil society in the country, at the time and historically.

Political context

In 2000, the Federal Republic of Yugoslavia (FRY) was a federal state consisting of Serbia and Montenegro, the two states remaining in the federation a decade after the progressive dismemberment and dissolution of the Socialist Federal Republic of Yugoslavia. After the international recognition of Slovenia, Croatia, Bosnia & Herzegovina and Macedonia, a series of wars broke out (1991). The Dayton Agreement, signed in December 1995, brought with it three years of peace to the territory of the former Yugoslavia. The outbreak of the Kosovo conflict led to NATO air strikes against Yugoslavia in March 1999.

---

2 Detailed information about OTPOR is available with the Center for Applied Non-Violent Action and Strategies in Belgrade, Serbia; see http://www.canvasopedia.org/

In the two years prior to the federal elections in 2000, the situation for the democratically oriented nongovernmental sector in Serbia was characterized by increased government pressure and, therefore, highly precarious. Repression began with the elimination of university independence and a crackdown on the independent media, on both the national and local levels. The subsequent NATO intervention and the bombing of Belgrade in response to the regime's actions in Kosovo only increased the repressiveness of the Milošević regime. State controlled media issued nationalistic and xenophobic propaganda and systematically bashed the democratic opposition and all the other democratically-minded activists. The ultimate goal of this type of propaganda was to discredit democratic forces in the eyes of the public by labeling them as collaborators and traitors, thereby, disqualifying them from political and public life. Such propaganda also spread fear among citizens that the regime would retaliate against anyone who was associated with democratically-minded groups.

The regime intensified its repressive actions further at the beginning of 2000, when it became obvious that pro-democracy groups had made significant progress in developing their cooperation and in creating a strategy for joint action. The regime launched a concerted attack on the remnants of the free and independent media, with numerous local media being banned or taken over by regime sympathizers. A systematic crackdown on the OTPOR youth resistance movement took place, during which almost 2,000 activists were arrested. Many were beaten-up by police.

During spring 2000, nongovernmental organizations came under systematic attack, being labeled terrorists, NATO mercenaries and traitors. Activities were misrepresented in the media. Regular legal-financial inspections of civic associations were used by the authorities as a pretense to increase scrutiny of their activities. Equipment and public relations materials were confiscated and activists and employees of nongovernmental organizations were summoned for questioning by the police, all in an attempt to create a psychology of fear and to impede activities. Without a doubt, this polarization of public life and the psychological war unleashed by the regime on pro-democracy forces contributed to shaping the resolve of the opposition and nongovernmental sector.

At the same time, the NATO bombing of Belgrade significantly increased the level of social and political consciousness of pro-democracy activists and groups. They quickly realized that effecting lasting change in Serbia could only be achieved if they joined forces and built cross-sectoral cooperation to oust the ruling Socialist Party of Serbia (SPS), which for more than a decade had been an increasingly destructive force in Serbia's political and social development.

As early as September 1999, a process to unite the parties of the democratic opposition was initiated in the form of a round table, resulting in the creation of the Democratic Opposition of Serbia (DOS) and, subsequently, in its victory in the federal elections in 2000. 18 parties constituted DOS, including the Democratic Party of Zoran Đinđić, the Democratic Party of Serbia of Vojislav Koštunica, the Civic Alliance of Serbia of Goran Svilanović, the Demo-Christian Party of Serbia of Vladan Batić, New Serbia under Velimir Velja Ilić, the League of Vojvodina's Social Democrats of Nenad Čanak, the Social Democratic Union of Žarko Korać, the Alliance of Hungarians from Vojvodina of Jožef Kasa, the Reformist Democratic Party of Vojvodina of Miodrag Mile Isakov, the Vojvodina Coalition of Dragan Veselinov, the Social Democracy of Vuk Obradović, the Movement for Democratic Serbia of Momčilo Perišić, the Sandžak Democratic Party of Rasim Ljajić, the League for Šumadija of Branislav Kovačević and the Association of Independent Unions of Serbia of Dragan Milovanović. NGO partners involved in the dialogue included the Center for Democracy, CeSID, the Yugoslav Committee of Lawyers for Human Rights, Civic Initiatives, the Center for the Development of the Non-Profit Sector, the youth movement OTPOR and others. The unity demonstrated by the democratic opposition also led to a shift in public opinion, as ordinary citizens gained trust and confidence in the democratic opposition and warmed to the idea that political change could be achieved through elections.

During the months preceding the September 2000 elections, it became increasingly obvious that the ballot had come to be understood as a referendum on the regime and on political change in the country. The regime resorted to populist demagogy in communicating with citizens. The government made promises to distribute hard currency savings, which were blocked in individual bank accounts and off limits to account holders, offered to issue bonds and announced measures against corruption in the social and health care systems. The regime proclaimed that the elections would be a referendum on the future of Kosovo and claimed that the reconstruction and development activities that had been conducted by the government to date proved that Serbia did not need international aid. The opposition, for its part, spoke about change, about re-establishing the country's relations with the international community, returning to the rule of law, reforming the legal and educational systems and the media and about re-instating democracy.[3]

Social context

The years of government by Milošević and his SPS had brought about considerable discontent among ordinary citizens. SPS presided over the discrediting of the legal system, the flaunting of the rule of law, a continuous and unstoppable deterioration in the standard of living, a breakdown of social values, the ruin of the social welfare and health care systems, rampant corruption in all state institutions and the continuous rise of personal, legal and financial insecurity among ordinary people. As early as

---

3 Exemplary of the democratic opposition's views were the "White Book", published by the G17+ think tank in 2000, covering the consequences of the previous ten years of Milošević's regime for Serbia, and the European Movement in Serbia's publication entitled "Preparing Serbia for European Integration".

September 1999, analysts of public opinion reported that 80 percent of citizens were in favor of change and that the principal reason for their dissatisfaction was economic in nature. An indication of this is that at the time, 35 percent of citizens were estimated as poor and another 35 percent lived on the poverty line. There were 1.25 million pensioners in Serbia and approximately 50 percent of working age citizens were unemployed or only formally employed.[4]

On the other hand, public opinion analyses conducted until summer 2000 also indicated that the citizens were largely apathetic and that many doubted that peaceful change through elections was possible. By the end of July 2000, when the date of the elections was made public, opinion research indicated that 42.2 percent of citizens believed in the possibility of change through elections.[5] At the same time, longer-term survey results and previous elections indicated that a very low turnout was a distinct possibility. The largest group abstaining from voting was to be found in the 55 plus age group, consisting mainly of women, without university education, living in suburban or in rural areas.[6] Furthermore, analyses indicated that large numbers of young people would also stay away from the ballot boxes, despite the fact that they had reached the age of majority and had the opportunity to vote for the first time. According to the analysts, one out of six young voters was in favor of the incumbent political parties, while among the remaining five, three were likely not to vote in the forthcoming elections.[7]

General civic dissatisfaction, on the one hand, and indications in public opinion that many voters would abstain from casting their ballot, on the other, all implied that in order for democratic forces to win the elections, it was necessary to motivate as many voters as possible to take part in the elections, which would serve as a channel for that civil dissatisfaction to be redefined as votes against the regime and in favor of democratic change.

The Situation in the Nongovernmental Sector

It is estimated that in 2000, there were 1,500 new and independent NGOs, whose work focused on the problems resulting from the social crisis in the country and on promoting social activism and change, on putting new social issues on the agenda and on mobilizing new target groups. Until 1995, civil society developed fast, with the number of organizations promoting anti-war, humanitarian, feminist and human

---

4 Žarko Paunović et al (eds.), Exit 2000 – Nongovernmental Organizations for Democratic and Fair Elections (Center for Democracy Foundation, Center for Development of the Non-Profit Sector, Civil Initiatives, Belgrade, 2001).

5 Results of the CPS-CPA Center for Policy Studies, a think tank.

6 Analysis by G17+, a think tank.

7 Žarko Paunović et al (eds.), Exit 2000 – Nongovernmental Organizations for Democratic and Fair Elections (Center for Democracy Foundation, Center for Development of the Non-Profit Sector, Civil Initiatives, Belgrade, 2001), p. 7, op cit.

rights causes consistently growing. Alternative educational, research and cultural organizations and associations also grew in popularity. Promotion of the principle of the rule of law was the common denominator among all independent NGOs. The NGO sector contributed to the development of alternative value systems, the articulation of the pluralism of interests among different social groups in the country and to the development of critical public opinion.

After the civic protests that took place in winter 1996 to 1997 as a result of Milošević's refusal to accept the results of the 1996 local elections, the NGO sector proved to be an important promotor of democratic values and began to grow. Coalition building between the civic and governmental sectors, in the form of support to the newly elected local authorities, strengthened it further. After the war in Kosovo and the NATO intervention in March to June 1999, new types of organizations and networks began to appear all over the Federal Republic of Yugoslavia, including advocacy groups, civic parliaments, civic resistance movements, trade unions and new professional associations of journalists, university professors and judges. The following organizations are exemplary of the development of Serbian civil society in the late 1990s and evolved into important drivers of the civic activities around the elections in 2000.

The Center for Free Elections and Democracy (CeSID) was established in Belgrade in 1997 with the aim of improving public understanding of elections and democratic processes. Through training activities, pre-election campaigning and monitoring, CeSID played a key role in strengthening democratic processes. It developed a countrywide network consisting of 21,000 volunteer election monitors, 165 municipal teams, 16 local and 5 regional offices and a pool of experts and researchers. Further, a number of prominent public personalities were involved in its advisory board.

Civic Initiatives was founded in May 1996 to strengthen citizen participation, education and training for democracy, as well as the development of NGO networking and common lobbying activities. Civic Initiatives focused its activities on NGOs outside the capital Belgrade, reaching smaller cities and rural locations throughout Serbia (and Montenegro) and connecting local groups to the capital. This was crucial during the IZLAZ 2000 campaign.

The European Movement in Serbia was founded with the mission of raising awareness of and promoting European integration for Serbia, regional cooperation and local development. The movement developed a strong network structure in 20 towns in Serbia. Through its Forum for International Relations it put foreign policy issues on the public agenda.

OTPOR (Resistance) emerged as a pro-democracy youth movement at Belgrade University in October 1998. After the NATO intervention in 1999, OTPOR started a political campaign against President Slobodan Milošević. It continued directly addressing the president during the presidential campaign in 2000, when it launched its campaign called *"Gotov je"* (He's finished) and came to be widely credited for its role in ousting Milošević. Since then, OTPOR has inspired and trained youth groups in numerous countries, including Georgia, Ukraine and Belarus.

G17+ was established as an experts' network in 1998. It started as a group of 17 distinguished economists and sociologists from Serbia and Montenegro, who criticized the political economy of war of Milošević's regime and its disastrous outcome for the country, including sanctions and international isolation. Through the production of numerous pamphlets, publications and the organization of public events, this group encouraged the development of a pro-reform bloc in Serbia.

Civil society also played an important para-diplomatic role during the intense political and economic isolation of Serbia. Some groups of important actors on the domestic scene became involved in regional and European processes of cooperation such as the Szeged Process "for free towns and municipalities in Serbia", the Timişoara Initiative for Free Media, the Graz Process including networks working in the fields of alternative and non-formal education, the Royaumont Process including nongovernmental organizations from the wider region, special forms of humanitarian work (for example, "energy for democracy", "asphalt for democracy" and "schools for democracy"[8]) and networking between independent institutes and research centers.

The number of registered nongovernmental organizations continuously increased in the years prior to the 2000 elections. In addition, the capacity and competence of nongovernmental organizations increased with their exposure to knowledge about methods and techniques of public organizing. During 1999 and 2000, experiences from the civil society sector activity during pre-election campaigns in Slovakia (OK '98) and in Croatia (GLAS 99) were presented at several NGO conferences, workshops and meetings held in Belgrade and elsewhere in Serbia, in Bratislava, Szeged and Timişoara, and were, thus, made available to civil society.

During the same year, NGOs made efforts to intensify their contacts with citizens, especially at the local level. This new approach consisted of organizing forum discussions, talking with members of local communities and organizing small-scale activities at the local level to solve problems considered current and important within those communities. The NGO leaders took part in public debates and electronic media programs at the local level and a huge number of brochures, booklets and promotional materials were distributed. In addition, many local events were organized challenging official politics and offering a new vision of the Yugoslav – European future, peace in the region and cooperation with neighboring countries.

8 These concrete projects were mostly designed by G17+ and supported by a number of European governments and the European Commission. These projects provided support to the towns and municipalities where the opposition parties had power and helped to build a constituency for change.

The socio-political reality clearly pointed to the need for the inclusion of the NGO sector in the pre-election process. NGOs understood their role primarily in terms of civic education, especially as concerns elections and the electoral process. In addition, they recognized that they could be instrumental in motivating citizens to come out and vote in the elections. They were clear about the goal of this mobilization, though. Their aim was to harness the high level of civil dissatisfaction and to transform it into votes for change. Their activities stressed the promotion of social change within a European perspective, more broadly.

It became increasingly clear as the elections approached that citizens had to understand that it was they who would win against Milošević and that all citizens should have the chance to clearly say what kind of future they wanted for themselves and for their children. Having recognized this, the civil society sector's primary goal became that of restoring citizen trust in the importance of their votes, of convincing them that every vote counts and of re-establishing their faith in the ability of the people to win democratic change.

The IZLAZ 2000 Campaign

IZLAZ 2000 was a political, but nonpartisan, campaign. Discussion about nongovernmental activities and get-out-the-vote campaigns began when Serbian activists learned about the success of the Civic Campaign OK '98 in Slovakia. At the beginning of 2000, and having in mind the upcoming federal and local elections, the nongovernmental sector started looking into the possibility of organizing similar campaigns. Some organizations prepared preliminary programs of activities, initiated agreements and cooperation with similar organizations, started cooperative networking and carried out some preliminary activities. Eventually, a threefold campaign goal was defined.

To enable citizens to better understand the electoral process

In the past, Milošević's regime had repeatedly tampered with election processes and results. After the regime's refusal to recognize the results of local elections in winter 1996 to 1997, citizens protested for three months. That was a first victory for the democratic opposition. Yet for a more decisive democratic change through elections, public knowledge about elections was insufficient.

To increase the number of citizens voting in the elections

The only way to win the elections was to get citizens out to vote, as the ruling parties benefited from the ability to mobilize their usual voting constituencies, who were highly disciplined in going to the ballot boxes. It was crucial to convince undecided and disappointed voters, a large group whose votes could (and in the end, did) ensure electoral victory for the democratic opposition, to come out to vote.

To increase the number of citizens actively participating in the electoral process

A decisive factor was to mobilize a large number of citizens as volunteers to get them involved in checking electoral lists, monitoring the elections, participating in electoral boards and ensuring a free and fair electoral process.

The IZLAZ 2000 campaign was implemented in two phases. In the first phase, the campaign was prepared, and in the second, it was launched and run. The starting point of the preparation in conceptual terms was a conference entitled "A View into the Future", organized by Civic Initiatives in September 1999, at which a workshop about the Slovak experience with OK '98 was held. A month later, representatives of the opposition parties, independent media and independent trade unions met with NGOs and decided to work together in a wide opposition bloc for the first time.

In February 2000, a group of 30 NGOs started talks on the campaign strategy, inspired by presentations of the GLAS 99 campaign by Croatian NGOs in Belgrade and several other cities. The following month a campaign preparation board was set up, including representatives of the Association of Independent Media, CeSID, the Center for Policy Alternatives, the Center for the Development of the Non-Profit Sector, the Center for Democracy Foundation, Civic Initiatives, G17+, OTPOR, the Partnership for Change, Timok Club Intake and the Women's Network.[9] In June 2000, several further members joined the board, including the European Movement in Serbia, Women's Political Action, AZIN and the Group for the Promotion of Women's Political Rights. An information and support center and a secretariat for the campaign were also established.

After July 27, 2000, when it was finally announced that the election would take place in September of that year, coordination meetings of the campaign were organized on a weekly basis, and in the immediate run-up to the elections, they even took place twice a week. Close cooperation with local networks was established and it was recommended to set up local coordination bodies for the campaign. Coordination also involved the setting up of a joint fund for activities and rapid interventions.

Developing effective channels of communication on the campaign was a further important task. In the late spring of 2000, a bulletin called "Nongovernmental organizations and the 'Get-out-the-Vote' campaign" was issued in order to provide the public with basic information about the campaign. Later, regular information was distributed daily by the Center for the Development of the Non-Profit Sector and published through a special edition of *IZLAZ News*. Web presentations and press releases of IZLAZ 2000 were carried by *Free Serbia* and ANEM.

---

9 Žarko Paunović et al (eds.), Exit 2000 – Nongovernmental Organizations for Democratic and Fair Elections (Center for Democracy Foundation, Center for Development of the Non-Profit Sector, Civic Initiatives, Belgrade, 2001), p. 10, op cit.

In August 2000, IZLAZ 2000 was launched and activities intensified at the beginning of September. By mid-September, most activities reached their peak to ensure maximum impact of the campaign in time for the elections. More than 150 NGOs took part in the get-out-the-vote campaign by carrying out over 60 different projects under the common logo of IZLAZ 2000. Local NGOs, which did not have their own campaign projects, joined other NGOs and helped them recruit volunteers and distribute pre-election materials to citizens. The IZLAZ 2000 campaign had a countrywide reach, with hardly a single municipality among the 164 in Serbia not seeing at least one event inviting citizens to vote. The cooperation between the participating NGOs was exemplary, with local, regional and national campaigns being united and coordinated.

Besides nationwide activities targeted at citizens in general, like those organized by OTPOR, G17+ or Civic Initiatives, other projects addressed specific target groups. Youth campaigns were organized by 37 NGOs, supported by the B92 radio station and ANEM, under the common name *"Vreme je"* (It's time), by the European Movement in Serbia and the Students' Union of Serbia. These campaigns included concerts and performances, the distribution of leaflets, posters, stickers, pencils, balloons and other promotional materials, as well as radio and TV jingles.

Projects specifically targeting women were carried out in 50 towns across the Federal Republic of Yugoslavia and in many villages. The aim was to motivate as many women as possible to participate and use their right to vote in the elections. The variety of activities included volunteer training sessions for women, public debates with voters, the distribution of printed materials, media promotion activities (videos and radio jingles), billboards, badges and stickers. These campaigns were conducted by the Group for the Promotion of Women's Political Rights and Women's Movement – Women's Network, along with some local NGOs.

Actions to reach rural communities were carried out by the Center for Anti-War Action, Village Step 98, the Alternative Citizens' Parliament and others. Further projects included one for the Roma population, carried out by the Roma Information Center and the YUROM Center, and one for workers and retired persons, carried out by the Partnership for Democratic Change. CeSID, along with the Yugoslav Lawyers Committee for Human Rights and the Belgrade Center for Human Rights, organized a campaign to ensure election monitoring.

The course of the IZLAZ 2000 campaign was also conditioned by external factors. Financial assistance to the campaigns at all levels, from national to local, was regularly obstructed and received with significant delay. In addition, the national and many local media were state controlled and, thus, not open to covering the campaign.

The Role of International Cooperation

Several social and political initiatives, or campaigns, have been instrumental in recent years in bringing about democratic change through elections in Central and Eastern Europe. Prior to Serbia in 2000, the notable cases were those of Slovakia and Croatia. International cooperation and the exchange of good practice of pre- and post-election civic activism were a critical element of success in Serbia.

During the preparation of the get-out-the-vote campaign, a number of meetings and trainings with colleagues from the NGO sectors in Croatia and Slovakia were organized both outside and inside Serbia. The "Bratislava Process" was launched at an international conference held in Bratislava, Slovakia, in July 1999, entitled "The Future of the Federal Republic of Yugoslavia in Light of Post-War Developments", organized by the East-West Institute and the Ministry of Foreign Affairs of the Slovak Republic. Part of the Bratislava Process, a task force was created to enable dialogue and joint action among members of different pro-democracy forces in Serbia and organizations from the international community. Representatives of opposition parties, NGOs, unions, student organizations and the independent media, were brought together through this process.

The task force, as an international initiative, contributed decisively to the victory of democratic forces in Serbia. It was an important innovation in international relations. The form of cooperation, contents and main players, all contributed to the initiative's experimental and innovative nature. This unilateral initiative on the part of a small European country (Slovakia), gave crucial support to political change in another small European country (the Federal Republic of Yugoslavia), with which it had neither common borders nor special historical ties, other than through the small Slovak minority living in the Vojvodina region. The representatives of the Slovak authorities and NGOs successfully mobilized international multilateral organizations, international institutions and foundations, including the Council of Europe, the Organization for Security and Cooperation in Europe (OSCE), the European Parliament, the East West Institute, the Fund for an Open Society, the Rockefeller Foundation, the German Marshall Fund of the United States and the Stability Pact for South East Europe, among others, to support political change and the consolidation of reform in the Federal Republic of Yugoslavia.

The main task was to consolidate and structure the unity of the various forces in favor of change, through open dialogue between opposition parties and representatives of local authorities, NGOs, independent media, trade unions and business, with the support of Slovak and international partners, who facilitated the process of building consensus and a common platform on the desired political change.

An important aspect of this international dimension of the campaign's preparation was the Donors' Forum, which started its activities at the beginning of July 2000. It was composed of the Canadian International Development Agency, the Fund for an

Open Society, the Know How Fund of Great Britain, the Dutch and Swiss Embassies in Belgrade and the German interest section in Belgrade. Subsequently the German Marshall Fund of the United States joined this initiative and provided support for the election-related activities of 50 NGOs. The Donors' Forum ensured a process, by which the submission of project proposals, their review and the decision making on funding was accelerated and coordinated. The objectives were to provide financing to as many NGO projects as possible, to prevent duplication of financing and to ensure a well balanced territorial distribution of approved projects. The donor organizations provided significant resources, which the NGO pre-election campaigns were able to engage.

However, that was not the only assistance the donor organizations provided, even though funding was critical. Efforts were made to establish cooperation between NGOs and other relevant partners within the country and internationally. The experiences, suggestions and advice received from the Slovak and Croatian colleagues proved useful. Representatives of donor organizations helped NGOs to acquire the necessary know-how by organizing trainings for civic activists, providing relevant training materials and publications. At the same time, and although cooperation was very close, donors did not impose their approaches or ideas on Serbian NGOs.

Outcomes and Lessons

Although the exact extent may be hard to determine, it is beyond doubt that the described civil society engagement made a considerable contribution to democratic change in Serbia. At the presidential elections on September 24, 2000, over 71 percent of citizens cast their vote and gave a clear victory to democratic candidate Vojislav Koštunica (50.24 percent) over the incumbent Slobodan Milošević (37.15 percent).[10] In the elections to the federal parliament of Yugoslavia on the same day, the Democratic Opposition of Serbia received a majority in both houses, with 11 deputies in the House of the Republics and 55 in the House of the Citizens.[11] This clear desire of Serbian citizens for democratic change was confirmed in the parliamentary elections on December 23, 2000, when the Democratic Opposition of Serbia won an overwhelming 64.7 percent of the votes.

This democratic breakthrough was clearly the result of the joint effort of all pro-democratic and change-oriented forces in the country. The high level of consensus, the common platform and the coordination of the effort for change brought new quality to the political life of the country and provided a good starting point for the new governments of Serbia and the Federal Republic of Yugoslavia. In spite of all the difficulties and the increasing level of repression in the run-up to the elections,

---

10 Official Gazette of the FRY, no.55, vol. IX, October 10, 2000, p.1.
11 Official Gazette of the FRY, no. 56, vol. IX, October 13, 2000, p.1.

the key to success was the consolidated and united front presented against the Milošević regime.

This unified stance was the result of long-term development. The success of the public protests against the refusal of the government to recognize the results of the local elections in December 1996 and the ensuing cooperation between civil society and the newly elected local authorities prepared the ground for the change that took place in 2000. By then, there existed mutual understanding and confidence between those working at the local level, especially through the Association of Independent Towns and Municipalities, which was established at the beginning of 1997. Independent local media in many towns in the Federal Republic of Yugoslavia were a very important factor of change and helped to develop the common platform on which the opposition could gain the confidence of the wider public.

The IZLAZ 2000 campaign, despite a very limited time frame, was highly effective because of the enormous social energy that had accumulated and could be tapped into. In addition, and for the first time in the ten-year history of public civic protest in Serbia, the campaign received logistical, financial and moral support from the international community. Given the long standing isolation of the country, democratic opposition and civil society were significantly galvanized by the sense of solidarity and moral support provided by the international community, not least because it was also matched with significant resources in support of the civic campaign.

The central momentum for change, however, came from citizens. According to an analysis of public opinion in Serbia carried out by the Center for Policy Studies (CPA/CPS) in October 2000, "the citizens consider their decision to finally get rid of the old regime, which had catastrophic effects for the state, a crucial factor which led to the turn of events and to electoral victory and democratic changes".[12] Despite a lack of knowledge regarding the activities of the civil sector expressed by the majority of citizens, a large number of citizens believed that the NGO contribution to the victory of the Democratic Opposition of Serbia (DOS) was significant (29 percent), or of medium significance (23 percent), which clearly illustrates that the campaign to motivate citizens to take part in the elections and to be involved in monitoring the electoral process was successful.

The contribution of the IZLAZ 2000 campaign and other civic efforts to the electoral victory was mainly reflected in the high turnout of citizens with higher education, especially high school and university students and professionals. However, it should be pointed out that blue-collar workers also indicated their belief that the civic pre-election campaign was instrumental in the victory of democratic forces. The NGO campaign was, of course, also evaluated positively by the followers of DOS. In sum,

---

12 Žarko Paunović et al (eds.), Exit 2000 – Nongovernmental Organizations for Democratic and Fair Elections (Center for Democracy Foundation, Center for Development of the Non-Profit Sector, Civil Initiatives, Belgrade, 2001), p. 26, op cit.

it appears that the NGO campaign had a positive effect on almost all social groups, other than senior citizens and those with little or no education. The CPA expert research team compared the above results with those of research carried out in September 1999, and concluded that "the organizations of civil society have played an extremely significant role in exercising their authority over political issues".[13] According to another expert, Vukasin Pavlović, "NGOs here took over a role of social opposition".[14]

Beyond the very political change in 2000, some effects of the NGO campaign were also felt in the longer run. From the perspective of civil society, the conditions under which NGOs work have changed significantly since the democratic breakthrough. While the elections in 2000 represented a milestone in the development of democracy and civil society, the further development of democratic institutions and the implementation of democratic principles and values in Serbia have remained a priority for the sector ever since. In spring 2005, two studies on civil society in Serbia were published and revealed public perceptions of the sector and of the conditions, in which it works.[15] Both showed the great importance the public assigns to the nongovernmental sector in the political, social and even economic stabilization of Serbia, in the promotion of reform and in the improvement of the country's position in the international community.

Although there has been a lot of criticism, and even some attacks on the NGO sector in Serbia, and a new and improved legal framework for the activities of the civic sector has not yet been put in place, the confidence of citizens in their role as actors of change has grown significantly and has even surpassed their confidence in political parties. The main functions of NGOs in Serbia include education, the resolution of social problems, the promotion and protection of human and minority rights, support to the reform of state institutions and to the improvement of public policy, local community development and environmental protection. In addition, NGOs are active in promoting entrepreneurship, regional and international cooperation and European integration.

NGOs have become an important partner to the different branches of power (parliament, government, the judiciary) and at different levels of government (local, regional, national). They have played an important role in passing resolutions on European integration in Serbia, Montenegro and their State Union in 2005, as well as putting and keeping the issue of the 1995 Srebrenica genocide on the agenda of the Serbian assembly. A great number of international activities including research,

13 Quoted in Žarko Paunović et al (eds.), Exit 2000 – Nongovernmental Organizations for Democratic and Fair Elections (Center for Democracy Foundation, Center for Development of the Non-Profit Sector, Civil Initiatives, Belgrade, 2001), p. 26, op cit.

14 Ibid.

15 Center for Free Elections and Democracy, Political Divisions in Serbia in the Context of Civil Society (CeSID, Belgrade, 2005); Civic Initiatives, The NGO Sector in Serbia (Civic Initiatives, Belgrade, 2005).

analyses, international conferences, seminars and publications in different fields would not be possible without the expertise of the NGO sector and other forms of support it provides.

Civil society and its organizations, thus, continue to play their role in shaping Serbia and its democratic future. In so doing, they can still draw inspiration and motivation from the central role they played in ending Milošević's authoritarian rule and putting the country on track towards democracy.

Chronology

September 3 – 5, 1999
Civic Initiatives organizes the NGO conference "A View into the Future" to discuss a common platform and activities for democratic change in Serbia, as well as relevant experiences of Slovakia, Romania and other countries.

October 26 – 27, 1999
The conference "How to Achieve Changes" is organized by the Foundation for Peace and Crisis Management and the United Trade Unions *Nezavisnost* (Independence). Opposition parties, independent media, trade unions and civil society groups agree that concerted action of a broad-based opposition movement is a pre-requisite for democratic change.

February 18, 2000
Representatives of some 30 NGOs and opposition political parties adopt a joint declaration.

February 21, 2000
With a meeting organized by Civic Initiatives, Serbian civil society starts discussions of a campaign strategy. NGOs from Croatia present the GLAS 99 campaign in Belgrade and other towns across Serbia.

April 13, 2000
The campaign preparation board meets to collect information on activities and campaigns planned by civil society in the run-up to the September 2000 presidential, parliamentary and local elections.

June 2000
Two conferences are organized by civil society groups to exchange ideas and plan activities related to the pre-election campaign. Some 400 representatives of civil society and political parties from across Serbia and abroad attend these meetings.

June 21 – 23, 2000
Serbian NGOs and international donors meet in Szeged, Hungary. The Donors' Forum is established to bring together funding bodies present in Serbia and to liaise with further foreign donors.

July 6, 2000
Constitutional amendments are adopted to introduce direct presidential elections. Analysts predict that these changes will secure Milošević another four years in power.

July 27, 2000

After weeks of speculation over the date of the election, Milošević announces September 24, 2000, as election day. Besides the presidential poll, a new federal legislature for Serbia & Montenegro, a new parliament for the autonomous province of Vojvodina and local councils in Serbia are to be elected.

August 17, 2000

The IZLAZ 2000 campaign starts with a youth project in Kraljevo under the slogan *"Vreme je"* (It's Time).

September 1, 2000

The political opposition forms an 18-party alliance known as the Democratic Opposition of Serbia (DOS). Vojislav Koštunica, a 56 year-old constitutional lawyer, is elected joint presidential candidate of the opposition. In the immediate run-up to the election, opinion polls consistently give Koštunica a lead over Milošević.

September 24, 2000

Elections are held in Serbia & Montenegro. International observers are banned from monitoring the elections. Calls by the government of Montenegro for the election to be boycotted are widely heeded.

September 25, 2000

The Democratic Opposition of Serbia (DOS) claims victory, stating that it has won 55 percent of the votes. Vojislav Koštunica declares himself the "peoples' president".

September 26, 2000

The election commission of the Federal Republic of Yugoslavia calls for a second ballot, as neither candidate received a majority of the votes. According to the commission, Koštunica won 48 percent of the vote compared to 40 percent for Milošević.

September 27, 2000

Hundreds of thousands of opposition supporters take to the streets of Belgrade and other cities to demand Milošević's resignation.

October 2, 2000

A general strike begins in Serbia. Schools close, roads are blocked and coal mines stop working. Milošević stresses his intention to run in a second round of voting.

October 3, 2000

A press conference is organized by the Center for Free Elections and Democracy (CeSID) and the Center for Liberal Democratic Studies (CLDS) to present in detail the irregularities observed during the elections.

October 4, 2000

Koštunica goes to the Kolubara coal mine and is welcomed by thousands of supporters as the general strike spreads across Serbia. The constitutional court annuls the election results, but proposes that Milošević serve until new elections in 2001, a deal subsequently rejected by the opposition.

October 5, 2000

The opposition sets a deadline of 3pm local time for Milošević to cede power and calls for a mass rally in the center of Belgrade to back this demand. Thousands of farmers, miners and other opposition supporters from across Serbia converge on Belgrade. After the 3pm deadline passes without a response from Milošević, protesters take over parliament and state television. At 6.30pm, Vojislav Koštunica addresses half a million supporters from the balcony of Belgrade City Hall, declares Serbia to be free and himself proud to have been elected "president of the Federal Republic of Yugoslavia".

October 6, 2000

The constitutional court confirms Koštunica as winner of the presidential elections. Milošević congratulates the new president.

October 7, 2000

The parliament of the Federal Republic of Yugoslavia holds its constituent session. Vojislav Koštunica takes the presidential oath.

December 23, 2000

The Democratic Opposition of Serbia (DOS) wins a landslide in parliamentary elections in Serbia. Its 64.7 percent compare to 13.2 percent for Milošević's Socialist Party of Serbia (SPS) and 8.6 percent for the Serbian Radical Party.

OTPOR! graffiti and volunteers putting up campaign posters.

Campaign poster: "Time to clean up! Serbia for Europe. Only change will bring us back to Europe".

Campaign poster: "If not elections, then what?".

ГОТОВ ЈЕ!

OTPOR sticker: "He's finished!".

ОТПОР!
БУЂЕЊЕ

OTPOR poster: "Resist! Wake up!".

Protestor in front of the Parliament, Belgrade, October 5, 2000.

IZLAZ 2000 poster: "There is a way out! Get out! Choose! Choose change! Exit 2000".

IZLAZ 2000 poster: "There are more of us. Get out and choose change! Exit 2000".

ENOUGH! KMARA AND THE ROSE REVOLUTION IN GEORGIA

Giorgi Kandelaki and Giorgi Meladze

Unlike in western democracies, popular and well-organized student movements in the former Soviet Union, and particularly in the Caucasus, have been less than significant from a political perspective. No longer: with its appearance in April 2003, the Georgian youth movement KMARA (Enough) quickly seized a central spot in the political life of this weakened postcommunist country. KMARA is widely acknowledged to have played an instrumental role in bringing about the Rose Revolution that ended President Eduard Shevardnadze's three-decade-long reign.

The Rose Revolution, effectively the first bloodless change of power in the Caucasus region's history, brought with it renewed hope that democracy could triumph in Georgia and the region, something many believed was intrinsically foreign to this part of the world. Observers, among them Georgia's new president, Mikheil Saakashvili, have referred to the Rose Revolution as among the inspirations for a "new wave of democratization" and as having led to increased attention and support for democracy activists in the former Soviet Union. The Georgian experience convinced western policymakers that regime change to democracy is indeed possible in the former Soviet Union and will not lead to much-feared civil war, as long as certain conditions are present.

Despite the attention the Rose Revolution received both inside and outside the country, the actual extent and impact of western assistance available for the struggle was remarkably limited. Why, of all post-Soviet countries, was Georgia the one where such a democratic breakthrough was possible for the first time? What factors and actors made the revolution possible? How important and substantial was western assistance? The following analysis endeavors to explore these questions.

Shevardnadze's "Liberal Autocracy"

Many writers and scholars have attempted to classify the kind of regime that existed in Georgia and that could also be found in other countries of the former Soviet Union. According to democracy theorists Juan J. Linz and Alfred Stepan, the regime would most probably fit into the broader category of "post-totalitarianism".[1]

---

1 Juan Linz and Alfred Stepan, Problems of Democratic Transition and Consolidation: Southern Europe, South America and Postcommunist Europe (The Johns Hopkins University Press, Baltimore and London, 1996), pp. 42-51.

Georgian political scientist, Ghia Nodia, defines Shevardnadze's regime as a "liberal autocracy" or even a "liberal oligarchy".[2] However, the defining characteristic of the regime was that a number of fundamental freedoms, such as freedom of expression and freedom of association, were more or less allowed, despite the regime's overall authoritarian tendencies.

When Eduard Shevardnadze was elected president of Georgia in 1995, the country was beset by ethnic and civil strife, with local warlords controlling individual regions. Seeking allies in outmaneuvering these warlords and aspiring to being considered a democrat abroad, Shevardnadze allowed for the emergence of alternative centers of power, including political opposition, independent media and civil society. Until 1999, this earned Shevardnadze an unjustified reputation as a success story of post-Soviet democratization among many western observers and governments.[3] The 1995 Constitution was labeled as a significant step forward in the democratic development in Georgia. The government recognized the need for holding regular elections and the opposition was even able to score some successes in local ballots. Nevertheless, "real power" was to remain concentrated inside a restricted network of political elites. Shevardnadze believed that it would always be possible for him to win elections and that, if the necessity arose, they could be rigged. And, while there would be international criticism, it would soon fizzle out.

Importantly, allowing such freedoms as were permitted was not exclusively altruistic on the part of the government. Both the government and elements within the ruling elites saw such freedoms as a tool to outmanoeuvre political enemies. The relatively liberal climate and legislative framework, however, led to the development of a civil society that did not accept the rules and practices of the ruling oligarchy.[4] Shortly after being elected president in 1995, Shevardnadze surrounded himself with a group of western-educated reformers, referred to as the "Zhvania-Saakashvili team", with the intention of developing Georgia's relations with western governments and international financial institutions, an important source of loans and grants, given the ailing economic situation of the country. The administration also hoped that the reformers would be useful for domestic public relations purposes.

With the reformers "contained" and with little influence on real policymaking, while the old, corrupt, party nomenclatura remained in key decision making positions,

2 According to Nodia, "the assumption of the rulers was that they had to conform to certain basic norms of liberal democracy. To be clear, all this did not mean that the opposition should be allowed to actually displace the ruling elite from power through elections. The political system had to be "civilized", "progressive" and "reformist", but political power should be held within relatively small network of elites". See Ghia Nodia, "Breaking the Mold of Powerlessness: The Meaning of Georgia's Latest Revolution", in: Zurab Karumidze and James V. Wertsch (eds.), Revolution of Roses in the Republic of Georgia (Nova Publishers, New York, 2004), pp. 96-97.
3 Laurence Broers, "After the 'Revolution': Civil Society and the Challenges of Consolidating Democracy in Georgia", paper presented at the University of London, December 2004, p. 1.
4 Ghia Nodia, The Development of Civil Society in Georgia: Achievements and Challenges (Citizens' Advocate! Program, Tbilisi, 2005), in Georgian.

President Shevardnadze thought the country could be run the old way. However, once the reforms initiated by the new team began to conflict with the interests of the nomenclatura and Shevardnadze's close (corrupt) allies, Georgia witnessed a turnaround. The reforms were all but abandoned.

In the meantime, however, the Georgian parliament had adopted more than 2,000 laws regulating aspects of private and public life. Perhaps most important of all was the General Administrative Code, making virtually all information in state bodies public. The code became a crucial weapon in the hands of civil society and investigative journalists for exposing the wrongdoings of officials and mobilizing the public to engage in political debate. However, the Shevardnadze administration believed that for as long as it could claim credit for the introduction of greater political freedoms (in contrast to the situation in many other post-Soviet states), challenges coming from civic sector could be simply contained and the scope of action of rebellious NGOs would be limited to writing complaints to international organizations.

The system was steadily being eroded, however, and over time Shevardnadze's assumptions would be proven wrong. Vested interests and informal political deals became well-embedded in the political and economic life of Georgia. The state soon had difficulties to discharge its key responsibilities, so reduced was tax revenue as a result of rampant corruption.[5] It became increasingly difficult to satisfy the manifold interests of the variety of groups surrounding the president.[6] Georgian politics at that time did, indeed, bear the hallmarks of what some scholars describe as the "blackmail state".[7] The government's inability and lack of will to confront the problem of corruption led to the suspension of International Monetary Fund programs already running and planned.

It was impossible for the president to maintain even a semblance of his image as a reformer. When in 2001, the authorities attempted to shut down *Rustavi 2*, an outspoken private TV channel, the reformers surrounding the president abandoned the administration and went into opposition. By this time the decision had been made. President Shevardnadze dropped the pretence of being a reformist leader once and for all. While, admittedly, Shevardnadze can justly claim credit for the fact that civil society in Georgia developed significantly during his term in office, he, nevertheless, considered it his major mistake. In several interviews after the Rose Revolution, he stated that he regretted not having made sure that the mechanisms necessary for "managing democracy" were put in place in Georgia.

---

5 Lawrence Broers, "After the 'Revolution': Civil Society and the Challenges of Consolidating Democracy in Georgia", paper presented at the University of London, December 2004, p. 2, op cit.

6 Ibid.

7 Keith A. Darden, "Blackmail as a Tool of State Domination: Ukraine and Kuchma", East European Constitutional Review, vol. 10, no. 2/3 (Spring/Summer 2003).

From the perspective of political culture, Georgia was a typical post-Soviet society. Popular attitudes towards any kind of participation, particularly political participation, were significantly conditioned by experiences of the Soviet era and, therefore, nihilistic and distrustful. In the public mindset, all elections were unfair and, therefore, a change of government through elections was not considered a viable prospect.[8] Such attitudes were particularly widespread among young people. Political parties and politicians were considered with great suspicion. In people's perceptions, joining a political party or its election campaign was considered an act of personal material self-interest and an attempt to enrich oneself. Truth be told, many people did get involved in politics for the wrong reasons and some did, indeed, succeed in lining their pockets.

In this context, political parties were clearly an insufficient condition and a weak instrument for mobilizing a public so reduced by political apathy. An additional obstacle was that the youth wings of the political parties were relatively weak. Further, civic campaigns carried out in Georgia before 2003 were limited in reach to small circles and urban areas and were not easily understandable for the common Georgian layperson. The one positive effect of this was that people living in outlying regions of Georgia were less exposed to previous campaigns and generally had a higher motivation and enthusiasm, making their mass mobilization easier.

Three actors are believed to have played a crucial role in making the Rose Revolution possible: the youth movement KMARA and civil society more broadly, the opposition parties, especially Mikheil Saakashvili's National Movement, and *Rustavi 2*, the most prominent independent media actor at that time. Each of these groups played a distinctive role in making successful democratic and nonviolent change possible in Georgia. The identities and roles of these groups during the revolution will be elaborated upon in the following sections.

The Emergence of Civil Society in Georgia

The emergence of civil society in Georgia began in the post-Stalinist era of Soviet history. Embryonic elements of civil society developed in universities and different unions that existed under the control of the state. In the context of Krushchev's attempt to develop the "human face" of the Soviet state, these associations were permitted to voice some, although admittedly very little, criticism. These groups were pivotal in the events of 1978, when Georgians defended the official status of the Georgian language, as well as in the turbulent events of 1989, that later led to the collapse of the Soviet Union. In the late 1980s, environmental issues were articulated as part of the national question and became a strong motivation for civil

8 Summary of 32 focus groups conducted by BCG Research, August 12-19, 2003.

society to organize.[9] Simultaneously, political parties concerned with similar issues began to emerge, producing issue overlap.

The landscape changed considerably after 1995, when Eduard Shevardnadze's ruling Citizens' Union of Georgia offered NGOs the possibility to participate in its "reformist" political agenda. This led to another wave of development in the civil sector. Many NGOs emerged around the ruling party and its political competitors, all of which were seeking legitimacy in the eyes of the public. As a result, there was a real boom in the establishment of NGOs, with their number rocketing to 3,000, of which approximately 500 became recipients of two or more grants from western donors. Despite these impressive numbers, membership of NGOs was not widespread and many organizations consisted of little more than their founding member or members, looking more like generals without armies than civil society organizations. Finally, NGO activity was largely concentrated in the capital, Tbilisi, and did not manage to develop countrywide outreach. Understandably, NGO impact on political decision making was rather weak, dependent on political, rather than genuine grass roots, support.

The government's decision to allow limited liberal freedoms was a political calculation and did not demonstrate commitment to an open society. Nevertheless, it led to the development of a civil society that did not accept at face value the rules and practices of the ruling oligarchy.[10] However, Shevardnadze and his aides continuously thought that while he could claim credit for greater political freedoms, challenges coming from the opposition or the civic sector could be easily contained. Rebellious NGOs were seen as weak, lacking leverage and intrinsic agency. Civil society was not taken seriously and Shevardnadze lived to regret his own complacency.

The Emergence of KMARA: "These Young People"

Shortly after his resignation, Eduard Shevardnadze was quoted as saying "I did not think I should pay serious attention to these young people running around waving flags and painting graffiti on the streets. I was wrong". Few could have anticipated that "these young people" would come to occupy such a central spot in Shevardnadze's memoirs.

The origins of KMARA can be traced back to 2000, when a group of reform-minded students established student self-government at Georgia's largest institution of higher education, Tbilisi State University. This group's primary concern was the situation in higher education. It campaigned for radical reform of the education

9 Levan Tarkhnishvili, The Democratic Transition of Georgia (Warsaw, 1997).
10 Ghia Nodia, The Development of Civil Society in Georgia: Achievements and Challenges (Citizens' Advocate! Program, Tbilisi, 2005), in Georgian, op cit.

sector, which since Shevardnadze's return to Georgia had witnessed an ongoing and dramatic decline in quality and an increase in bribery.[11]

This group's activities were successful, widely publicized and included a campaign that involved legal action against the university administration and revelations of corruption in education to the media. With time, however, it became increasingly evident that no reform would be possible in higher education without a change of government.[12] During the student protests following Shevardnadze's attempt to shut down *Rustavi 2* in October 2001, a second group of student activists formed, calling themselves the Student Movement for Georgia. The two groups joined to form KMARA in early 2003, in an attempt to broaden the scope of civil society activity to mobilize the masses.

Several other NGOs, namely the Liberty Institute, the Georgian Young Lawyers Association (GYLA) and the Association for Law and Public Education (ALPE) shaped the creation of KMARA. They were instrumental in facilitating the creation of both material and networking opportunities for KMARA. The Liberty Institute was responsible for coordination with the political opposition, training young activists, regional outreach and public relations. They also networked with international NGOs, the concrete result of which was a trip to Belgrade to meet OTPOR activists and subsequent visits of OTPOR and OK '98 campaign activists to Tbilisi in early 2003 to inform their Georgian counterparts about how civic campaigns emerged in Serbia and Slovakia, respectively. GYLA ensured legal representation and services for KMARA activists and ALPE was active in developing training activities and public awareness-raising on topics such as fair elections, police brutality and corruption.

After 2001, civil society was patently aware that further elections were going to be rigged and that mass mobilization would be necessary to defend democracy and fair elections. Mobilization efforts had proved their worth in other countries where authoritarian regimes were ousted by mass protests. Finally, it was clear that the traditional actors of Georgian politics would not be able to achieve the much-needed democratic breakthrough alone. These realizations prompted the creation of KMARA.

KMARA's campaign differed from those of the political parties in that it had countrywide outreach, making significant efforts to include traditionally isolated communities, ethnic-religious minorities and the rural population. In addition, nonviolent resistance was the form of protest chosen. Both the political opposition and the general public were in favor of nonviolence, boosting the popularity of the campaign and providing a strong counter-argument to the often-cited bogey: mass

---

11 Tinatin Zurabishvili and Tamara Zurabishvili, "Serving Bilateral Interests? Corruption in the System of Higher Education in Georgia", in: Evangelina Papoutsaki and Tinatin Zurabishvili (eds.), Caucasus Higher Education in Transition (Civic Education Project, Tbilisi, 2005), pp. 41-55.

12 In one notorious case, the person named as the most corrupt member of faculty as a result of a survey conducted by the group was publicly promoted and praised the day after.

mobilization inevitably leads to bloodshed. Also of significance is that KMARA made it clear that it was not running for political office and positioned itself as a civic force, thus, creating the conditions for cooperation with opposition parties.

Initially, the long-term planning of KMARA and the broader opposition coalition targeted the presidential elections scheduled for 2005. However, a number of factors, including mass fraud, the high level of mobilization among the population and the nonviolent discipline of the protest movement made it possible to achieve the sought-after democratic breakthrough as early as November 2003, when parliamentary elections were held in Georgia.

The Political Opposition

Having joined Shevardnadze's administration in 1995, the reform-minded "Zhvania-Saakashvili team" found themselves "contained", without significant influence on the executive branch. President Shevardnadze believed the country could still be run the old way and reform was quickly abandoned in the wake of attempts by the reform team to confront the corruption of the regime.

The crisis point was reached with the government's attempt to shut down *Rustavi 2* TV in October 2001. Reformers faced the difficult decision of whether to continue to attempt to change the situation from inside the government or to strike out on their own and start an independent political struggle: the familiar choice between change from within or from outside the system. Mikheil Saakashvili, then Minister of Justice, resigned and formed the National Movement Party. After an attempt to rescue the old Citizens Union of Georgia, Zurab Zhvania followed suit and formed the United Democrats Party. He advocated a more moderate strategy and more gradual change than did Saakashvili.

Saakashvili's main strategy could be summarized as the radicalization of the political situation and the widening of the political space. He realized that even with fair elections, something no one believed would be possible, several rounds would be needed for the National Movement and other opposition parties to build their electoral and organizational strength. He was aware that it would be difficult to retain a disciplined and networked political force throughout this long period and that it was necessary to show concrete results to his supporters in the form of a breakthrough.[13] At the same time, it was clear that in the existing political space, and with the people already involved in the political process, a breakthrough was impossible, demonstrating the need for new and more motivated elements to get involved in the struggle. The 2001 rallies demonstrated that mobilizing urban-educated groups alone was insufficient for such a breakthrough to succeed. The enlisting of supporters beyond those groups had to be ensured. Groups that

---

13 Personal interview with Levan Ramishvili, Tbilisi, June 25, 2005.

emerged as targets of further mobilization efforts included members of the lower middle classes, provincial populations and middle-aged persons.

One of the National Movement's most important achievements was its success in effectively reaching out to the populations in the (rural) provinces. In contemporary Georgian history, the last occasion when the provinces played a significant political role was when they supported Zviad Gamsakhurdia in the lead-up to the civil war in 1991. In fact, any opportunity to take part in post-Gamsakhurdia Georgian politics had been effectively destroyed for that group and Saakashvili made numerous efforts to re-open politics for this highly frustrated segment of the public. As Saakashvili radicalized the political space and opened it up for more alienated groups to participate, he also bolstered his reputation as a brave anti-regime oppositionist. He suggested that the reason for his split with Shevardnadze was that his strong anti-corruption position was unacceptable within the government.

These political realities worked together in Saakashvili's favor, as particularly illustrated during the National Movement's rallies in Kvemo Kartli and Adjara, held in the immediate run-up to the elections in November 2003. No visible opposition activity had taken place in either of these provinces. Kvemo Kartli, a province to the south of the capital, Tbilisi, is inhabited by more than 400,000 ethnic Azeris, most of whom do not speak Georgian and chose to stay out of national politics. Traditionally, the central government easily succeeded in securing votes in this region, boosting the numbers of the pro-administration "electorate". Adjara, ruled by pro-Russian dictator Aslan Abashidze always served as a political base for the Revival Union Party. As expected, demonstrations in both of the provinces provoked a violent reaction from the government.[14] The courage of the National Movement to step into so-called "politically protected areas" largely influenced its swift advance in the approval ratings and eventual victory in the elections, even though the rallies were disrupted and violence was used. Hundreds were beaten in Adjara and the National Movement's office in Batumi was burned down. The rallies were also important for prompting people in these regions, who had been too overcome with fear and apathy to participate in politics, to get involved.

These rallies showed the opposition's, and especially the National Movement's, success at broadening political participation by energetically and courageously confronting the Shevardnadze regime. As a result, more Georgians took an active role in voting, and then in defending their democratic freedom to vote in free and fair elections, as the fraud became apparent.

---

14 Within the framework of the cooperation, KMARA made available more than one hundred activists for the demonstration in Batumi.

Election Dynamics

The mass protests that eventually led to President Shevardnadze's resignation continued for exactly 20 days: from November 3 to November 23, 2003. Following the November 2, 2003, parliamentary elections, official results positioned Shevardnadze's For a New Georgia bloc in the lead with 21 percent, followed by Saakashvili's National Movement, the Labor Party, the United Democrats, the Revival Union and the New Rights Party, respectively. These results sharply contradicted exit polls conducted by *Rustavi 2* and parallel vote tabulations carried out by the election watchdog, the International Society for Fair Elections and Democracy.[15] This prompted, on November 3, a small number of demonstrators to gather in Freedom Square in central Tbilisi, growing in numbers every evening. As long as the numbers of protesters remained relatively small the government chose to ignore their demands. Even after the National Movement and United Democrats announced they were merging forces, the government took no action.

In the run-up to the elections, opposition and civic groups, including KMARA, could not anticipate a scenario that would result in Shevardnadze stepping down, given that the presidency was not even at stake in the parliamentary elections. From the beginning they tried to be realistic, hoping for enough support during the parliamentary elections so that the momentum could influence the presidential elections in 2005, at which point Shevardnadze's last term would expire. But, a number of factors accelerated Shevardnadze's demise, including the blatant electoral fraud in the results from the Adjara province, the total unwillingness of the government to even consider a compromise and the discipline, nonviolence and organizational capacity of opposition groups.

Unfolding the Campaign

Following an initial planning phase in early 2003, which included the representatives of two Serbian organizations (the youth movement OTPOR and the Center for Free Elections and Democracy [CeSID]), the name KMARA began to appear in public through mass graffiti actions. KMARA's first public action was held on April 14, 2003 when more than 500 young people marched from Tbilisi State University to the state chancellery. The student protestors carried flags from the Soviet period bearing the faces of Shevardnadze and leaders of his newly formed For a New Georgia bloc, stressing its implication in Georgia's Soviet past. The protesters condemned the government's alleged intention of rigging the forthcoming November 2 parliamentary elections. The day was purposefully selected to coincide with the anniversary of the student demonstrations that took place in 1978, when Communist Party Secretary Eduard Shevardnadze of the then Georgian Soviet Socialist Republic sided with the

---

15 Available in Georgian at http://www.esp.ge.

protesting youngsters against the planned abolition of the official status of Georgian as the state language.

From this point onwards, Eduard Shevardnadze's government pursued three strategies to contain KMARA and other democratic opposition groups: attempting to discredit the movement, simply ignoring it and exerting limited repression, particularly in the regions. At a press conference held on April 21, 2003, Irina Sarishvili-Chanturia, leader of the National Democratic Party and spokesperson for Shevardnadze's For a New Georgia bloc announced that "Russian special forces are planning a large-scale (...) operation under the code name 'Enough'".[16] The government further accused KMARA of being the National Movement's youth branch and of paying each activist US$ 500 per month to stay involved.[17]

Outraged by KMARA graffiti in front of the Palace of Youth where the congress of the Socialist Party was to be held, party chairman and new Shevardnadze ally Vakhtang Rcheulishvili went as far as accusing KMARA of being part of an Armenian conspiracy. At his monthly press briefing, Eduard Shevadnadze told journalists that on his way to work he stopped his limousine to check whether anyone was reading the KMARA graffiti, stating that "(...) nobody was reading them". In addition to the violence that took place in Adjara, other repressive measures were taken throughout the country. Wary of a strong backlash, the police preferred to beat or intimidate activists, rather than arrest them (although, Adjara was an exception in this respect).

KMARA engaged in the kind of activism that cultivated a certain "mythology", portraying it as much more powerful than it actually was. This bluff-strategy began with the trivially simple, but strikingly powerful, graffiti campaign. Inspired by the OTPOR experience, a group of twenty KMARA founding members painted tens of thousands of KMARA graffiti on the streets of Tbilisi. Within two days of Irina Sarishvili's statement to the press, the graffiti was top of the national news, with journalists emphasizing that the biggest KMARA sign had been daubed in front of the Tbilisi office of the National Democratic Party. Next morning, the authorities mobilized the fire service to remove the graffiti, but soon stopped, realizing the irony of the situation. During the following weeks, the ongoing appearance of KMARA graffiti in nine of Georgia's main cities made headlines nationwide.

Other activities carried out by KMARA varied from assertive nonviolent "actions" to university round table debates with the aim of involving students and recruiting new activists for the campaign. Popular personalities were invited to speak at the roundtables. This attracted attention to events and raised the level of participation

---

16 Giorgi Lomsadze, "Amid Controversy, Georgian Student Protest Movement Grows", Eurasianet, http://eurasianet.org/departments/rights/articles/eav061003.shtml, accessed June 4, 2005.

17 Interior Minister Koba Narchemashvili first made this claim. Georgian special services, skilled in spreading rumors from KGB times, spent some energy on disseminating this rumor as well. As a result, even one of the authors' mothers was almost convinced by her colleagues that he was paid for getting involved in the campaign.

following campaign activities. KMARA also ensured the training of 800 activists focusing on basic skills for participation in civic campaigns with the support and expertise of the Liberty Institute and the Association for Legal and Public Education. Activists and new recruits attending were from different parts of the country and the training also aimed to develop skills for establishing KMARA cells back home.

With most of its activities pursuing the aim of mass mobilization for the elections, KMARA's get-out-the-vote campaign was of central importance. The campaign was carried out with the support of the Open Society Foundation in Georgia and aimed at raising public awareness about the elections and at encouraging active participation in voting. Various activities were carried out within the framework of the program such as TV advertising, concerts, sport competitions and the distribution of posters and t-shirts. This voter education campaign was also strongly supported by the International Society for Fair Elections and Democracy.

Closely linked to the campaign, KMARA's monitoring team disclosed approximately 4,000 instances of election fraud during the parliamentary elections in 2003. Independent monitoring revealed that almost 30 percent of voters were excluded from voter lists and denied their right to vote. Public opinion surveys were crucial to revealing the fraud. Widely publicized by the independent media, these surveys helped inform citizens about the outcomes of the elections and gave them a chance to compare the official results with independent figures.

From the beginning of the campaign, a comprehensive inventory of human resources was undertaken. This inventory was based on reports provided by participating NGOs, the donor community, as well as other individuals. Building on that, it was important to develop networking with a variety of target groups including youth, senior citizens, students, orthodox parishioners, religious and ethnic minorities, local NGOs, local political activists and the local media. KMARA's public outreach effort was guided by baseline surveys regularly conducted in the various regions of Georgia. The surveys sought to identify the mood of voters and differences in attitudes between the various regions. The formulation of the main messages and slogans of the campaign were heavily influenced by the findings of these surveys. Public outreach activities were planned and implemented in three stages: branding, mobilization of volunteers and focusing on elections.

The "Secret" of KMARA's Success

KMARA's success can be attributed to several key organizational characteristics. First and foremost, the movement had a horizontal structure. KMARA did not have any single leader or a significant hierarchy. By default, all activists were considered equal. The horizontal structure served two crucial purposes. If activists were arrested, the functioning of the organization could continue. While repression in Georgia never escalated into mass arrests, this structure proved to be highly effective in Adjara where Abashidze's authorities took a more draconian approach. In this region, the tactic of many unrelated cells being active was crucial for the campaign's survival. This structure also inhibited government and other agents from infiltrating and discrediting the movement. In reality, of course, the movement did have leaders. Some activists had more weight than others. Nevertheless, the absence of a formal hierarchy made it easy for educated and motivated activists to make important contributions and to develop ownership for the campaign.

Keeping all activists busy was crucial to ensuring this sense of ownership and the highest possible motivation to participate among all activists. Headquarters was located in the capital and offices were established in nine other regions. The Tbilisi office coordinated planning, implementation, monitoring and evaluation of national campaigns. All activists worked in four fields: public relations, fieldwork, training and finance. Each group consisted of sub-groups. The public relations group included sub-groups working on media relations, speakers, written materials and media monitoring; the field work group addressed issues of regional networking, Tbilisi headquarters' administrative issues and internal communication; the training group was responsible for training trainers and activists; and the finance group carried out financial planning and oversaw spending.

KMARA's most valuable resource was the time contributed to the campaign by volunteer activists. Starting with a core group of just twenty, the number of volunteers reached 3,000 during the campaign's peak. Most of KMARA's activities received funding through the Election Support Program of the Open Society Foundation in Georgia. The funds were not directly provided to the campaign as such, but the materials developed for election-related activities (TV ads, flyers, education materials, etc) were successfully used by the movement for wider purposes. The total amount of expenditure on KMARA activities amounted to approximately US$ 175,000.

KMARA could initially rely on a very limited number of activists which made cooperation with opposition parties in the initial stages of the campaign important and intense. Facilitated by NGOs and contacts in the National Movement and United Democrats, the two parties' youth branches clandestinely made hundreds of activists available for the first KMARA rallies, particularly that of April 14, 2003, adding credibility to the movement and further underpinning its "mythological" power in public.

Other approaches to increasing KMARA's perceived power were the organization of actions simultaneously in different locations and mobility among activists. The first nationwide action was held on May 12, 2003, involving the mass distribution of leaflets outlining the provisions of the Georgian constitution on torture and illegal detention and the picketing of police stations known for misconduct. KMARA activists rallying in Tbilisi, Gori, Kutaisi, Zugdidi, Poti, Telavi, Akhaltsikhe, Ozurgeti, Samtredia and Rustavi were joined by representatives of various human rights

NGOs.[18] KMARA's proactive agenda and assertive behavior helped it to quickly evolve into a legitimate and formidable presence in Georgian politics achieving recognition of its brand at a very early stage.

A further essential feature of KMARA was that it declared that it did not aspire to power and consistently retained a clear distance from opposition parties. This attracted many young people, hitherto, not engaged. Activists made it very clear that their motivation for being involved was exclusively to ensure a change of regime and that they did not aspire to acquire political positions and the personal benefits that were associated with them. By and large, activists did not view their participation in the movement as a step in their careers, which allowed KMARA to avoid some of the typical conflicts experienced in hierarchical organizations in Georgia. Further, involvement in the movement was purely voluntary. Not a single activist was paid. While, after the revolution, a number of activists did accept appointments to positions in the new government, this should be viewed as proof of the effectiveness of KMARA to enable talented young people to develop and succeed, rather than as proof of any profit-making motive on their part.

KMARA's success was also ensured by its clever and continued use of humor in its various activities. In a politically apathetic society such as Georgia, accidental participation in or even viewing of KMARA's funny and positive actions aimed at making fun of the regime, produced sparks of participation among ordinary citizens, some of whom did not even intend to vote. [19] At one such activity, KMARA activists put large-scale banners on display in streets where passers-by could have their picture taken flushing Shevardnadze and his government down a toilet. At another event, they staged a mock funeral, replete with flowers, in an effort to disrupt the presentation of the economic program of For a New Georgia in the garden of the state chancellery. Seven KMARA members were arrested and charged with hooliganism for this attempt to inject some humor into political protest.

The Media

There is wide agreement that another major factor in the success of KMARA, and later the Rose Revolution, was the independent media. In this relation, the independent TV station *Rustavi 2* has been described as "extremely important".[20] Nevertheless, several observers have exaggerated the role of the media in the Georgian revolution. For example, and despite the fact that the printed press in Georgia is very diverse, ranging from liberal broadsheets to tabloids full of conspiracy theories, their very

18 Similar actions were held in Tbilisi on May 4, 5 and 13, July 22 and September 24, in Borjomi on July 6, in Rustavi on October 3 and in Poti on October 17, all in 2003.

19 KMARA's "positive" actions included rock concerts, book collections for schools under the slogan "Enough of the lack of education!" and the collection of rubbish.

20 Interview with Mikheil Saakashvili, in: Zurab Karumidze and James V. Wertsch (eds.), Revolution of Roses in the Republic of Georgia (Nova Publishers, New York, 2004), p. 25.

low circulation prevented them from influencing public opinion substantially in the run-up to and during the Rose Revolution.

Nevertheless, the media was instrumental and in order to examine its role in the events of November 2003, it is necessary to take a step back into recent Georgian history. After the armed coup that ousted Georgia's first nationalist president, Zviad Gamsakhurdia, Eduard Shevardnadze was invited back to Georgia and into government. In the beginning, Shevardnadze's power was nominal, with members of the military council and heads of paramilitary groups, such as Tengis Kitovani and Jaba Ioseliani, sharing in decision making.

Wishing to curb the power of his opponents, Shevardnadze fostered the emergence of a free press, in order to create space for a more experienced political player, such as himself, to claim political advantage.[21] When in 1995, he succeeded in arresting both of these notorious figures and began to crack down on paramilitary groups, Shevardnadze turned to a team of young reformers who could "talk the same language" as the West to help him consolidate his position. The so-called "Zhvania-Sakaashvili team" also needed political allies. They, in turn, supported the emergence of independent media, of which *Rustavi 2* was the strongest and best known. The fact that at that time, no single actor in Georgian politics had a complete monopoly on power, made the development of independent media all the more possible. At the same time, *Rustavi 2* was a purely commercial channel and its leadership engaged in a complex of political games with a variety of political actors prior to the 1999 parliamentary elections.[22]

When Shevardnadze's regime began to waver and reform was abandoned in 2001, the government tried to shut down *Rustavi 2*. This triggered mass protests among students. The entire government was sacked and *Rustavi 2* survived. Nevertheless, Shevardnaze's regime consistently tried to bring the TV channel into line using other means, including attempting to buy it out. After the commercial *Imedi TV* emerged as a strong competitor in 2001, the issue became one of survival, compelling the *Rustavi 2* leadership to develop closer ties with the opposition. *Rustavi 2* also provided a forum for NGOs to voice criticism of the government, enabling them to pursue their own agendas.[23] This signaled a certain radicalization of the political mood in Georgia.

In the context of the revolutionary process itself, *Rustavi 2* co-sponsored an exit poll that, coupled with parallel vote tabulation, proved significant for challenging the

---

21 Personal interview with Levan Ramishvili, Tbilisi, June 25, 2005, op cit.

22 Ibid.

23 James V. Wertsch, "Forces Behind the Rose Revolution", in: Zurab Karumidze and James V. Wertsch (eds.), Revolution of Roses in the Republic of Georgia (Nova Publishers, New York, 2004), p. 136, op cit.

official, and fraudulent, results of the 2003 elections.[24] The poll was released and televised immediately after the closure of polling stations, at 8pm on November 2, 2003, and succeeded in reaching a wide public. This guaranteed public discontent would the official election results considerably differ from the exit poll. Being well aware of the "threat", the government launched a campaign to discredit the exit poll, inviting a foreign pollster to carry out an "alternative" exit poll that, as expected, converged with the official results. The public popularity of *Rustavi 2* compensated for this and undermined the rival exit poll.

Explaining the Nonviolence of the Rose Revolution

A multiplicity of factors contributed to the fact that violence, much feared by both Georgians and western governments, was avoided in November 2003. The majority of Georgian revolutionaries were not committed pacifists, despite the fact that both KMARA and National Movement activists underwent intensive training in nonviolent protest techniques. When the parliament and other government buildings were occupied, the police had the legitimate right to use force, but chose not to. The protestors were perfectly aware that the risk of bloodshed was real, but many also believed that if bloodshed was inevitable, then so be it.[25]

Importantly, the shadow of the violence of the civil war of the early 1990s still loomed large over ordinary Georgians, and even over the government to a certain extent. The semi-liberal nature of Shevardnadze's power made the emergence and strengthening of democratic institutions and democratically-minded actors possible. When Zviad Gamsakhurdia was ousted, such elements were largely absent and their systemic functions were carried out by paramilitary formations and criminal groups. From the mid 1990s, government officials, including many in the police and the armed forces, had to get used to emerging critical pressure from democratic forces, even if limited. Their position became increasingly difficult after 1999, when their legitimacy began to be regularly called into question.[26] Shevardnadze was also not considered as having significant blood on his hands. Although power and position could be lost, it was not expected to result in cataclysmic violence.

During the protests that unfolded in the aftermath of the elections in November 2003, it became increasingly clear that President Shevardnadze's reactions were limited and inadequate. Numerous factions around him were vying for position,

---

24 The undertaking was also funded by the British Council, the Open Society Foundation Georgia and the Eurasia Foundation and carried out by a U.S. polling organization called the Global Strategy Group.

25 Ghia Nodia, "Breaking the Mold of Powerlessness: The Meaning of Georgia's Latest Revolution", in: Zurab Karumidze and James V. Wertsch (eds.), Revolution of Roses in the Republic of Georgia (Nova Publishers, New York, 2004), p. 100, op cit.

26 Chris Miller, Understanding Strategic Nonviolent Struggle: Case Analysis of the Georgian "Rose Revolution", BA Thesis, 2004, p. 39.

contributing to the enlargement of the negotiation space for the opposition.[27] The fragmentation of pro-Shevardnadze groupings was enhanced by the fact that he did not have a clearly identified successor. When an army does not have a consolidated and efficient chain of command, it has difficulties winning battles.

As for the police and the military, the mere fact that their leadership agreed to negotiations indicated they well realized that with virtually the entire country involved in the protest movement, with the "critical mass" already in place, any attempt to use force would sooner or later result in their own downfall. The number of protestors is not only important to legitimize the revolution in the eyes of the public, but it is also key to overwhelming the police and armed forces at key moments in the revolution, such as when government buildings are occupied. Nevertheless, on November 22, 2003, the risk of violence was strongly felt. While opposition leaders knew that some units would not interfere, no news had been received from a number of special-forces units loyal to the president.

Of course, an important dimension of the whole process was the explicit nonviolent rhetoric and discipline maintained by KMARA. This approach is exemplified by the occasions KMARA activists distributed flowers to troops deployed around the city and when sandwiches were distributed to troops with the same care as given to fellow demonstrators.[28] At no point did any group related to KMARA promote or resort to violent actions in the name of the aims of the movement. The impact of this discipline was most apparent during the occupation of the parliament, during which only one window was broken, as the doors were too narrow for the number of demonstrators to get through. Despite the outbreak of a couple of fist fights between citizens and some members of parliament, assigned peacekeepers quickly subdued such incidents. Groups of volunteers stayed in the parliament and the chancellery buildings to ensure that looting and stealing did not take place.[29]

The Role of International Actors

Western governments, particularly the United States, have been both vilified and lauded for supporting the Rose Revolution. Observers' reactions have ranged from enthusiasm about the future of democracy in Georgia and the region to far-reaching conspiracy theories that frequently included crediting the U.S. Ambassador in Tbilisi, Richard Miles, with being the *eminence grise* of the revolution. The fact that Miles was also U.S. Ambassador in Belgrade during the revolution to overthrow Milošević only encouraged such thinking.

27 A good example of this can be found in the interview with Tedo Japaridze, in: Zurab Karumidze and James V. Wertsch (eds.), Revolution of Roses in the Republic of Georgia, (Nova Publishers, New York, 2004), pp. 53-60, op cit.

28 Chris Miller, Understanding Strategic Nonviolent Struggle: Case Analysis of the Georgian 'Rose Revolution', BA Thesis, 2004, p. 48, op cit.

29 The chancellery was voluntarily handed over by its head.

Western assistance to the Rose Revolution can be divided into two categories: assistance to lay the foundations for the elections by spreading democratic values and educating the public and immediate political support in the run-up to and during the revolution. Various western funding schemes for NGOs were important for civic education and informing the public about human rights. But, since the funding was foreign, the agenda was designed in western capitals and frequently focused on the entire region, neglecting problems specific to Georgia. In other words, most, if not all, of the western and US supported programs in Georgia existed in many other post-Soviet countries and, therefore, they cannot be credited with the democratic breakthrough.

Some observers have failed to understand that during the revolution, the participation of western actors was not always helpful. At times, it was even detrimental. For example, Georgian civil society members had to work hard to convince some Council of Europe officials that parties, such as the Revival and Industrialist Parties, could not be considered opposition parties. Not only was U.S. Ambassador Miles not the "mastermind" of the revolution, but, on occasion, his involvement proved problematic. In particular, he strongly discouraged decisive action by the opposition in favor of protracted negotiations and considered Mikheil Saakashvili dangerously radical. The OSCE was similarly reluctant in its critical preliminary report on the parliamentary elections of November 2, 2003.

Conclusion

KMARA's campaign was essential for raising public awareness on election-related issues and overcoming widespread political apathy, particularly among Georgian young people, in the run-up to the 2003 elections. The press conferences, weekly events, demonstrations, charity events and actions such as that entitled "Clean Up Your Street – Clean Up Your Country" all contributed to the popularization of the aims of the KMARA movement and made it a household name within a very short period of time.

The movement's countrywide network made it possible to organize "chain campaigns". An action initiated in the capital was simultaneously supported by events in the regions, thus, creating the impression that KMARA was very powerful. Fear in government circles of the movement's popularity provoked counter measures, contributing to the further popularization of the movement. Overall, KMARA succeeded in informing citizens about their rights and the importance of the elections, considerably increasing turnout and complicating the business of electoral fraud. KMARA's effective capability to project nonviolent power allowed for the mobilization of large numbers of people eager to defend their vote when electoral fraud was disclosed.

After the Rose Revolution, KMARA activists, like all other Georgians, realized that their success had inspired many, to both the East and West of Georgia. They keenly shared their experience and enthusiasm with pro-democracy activists in Kazakhstan, Ukraine and Belarus. Several options were debated as to the further development of the movement, including whether it should become a political party, turn into a civil rights NGO or simply dissolve.

A variety of factors made the Rose Revolution possible: the incumbent regime's systemic weakness, its history of liberal policies, the National Movement Party's success in radicalizing politics and broadening political participation, civic education efforts by civil society organizations during the years immediately prior to the Rose Revolution, free media and the actions of the radical, nonpartisan and nonviolent KMARA.

In Georgia, expectations of disapproval of rigged elections were reduced after the West showed a very reserved attitude to the presidential elections in neighboring Azerbaijan in October 2003. Nonetheless, the successful Rose Revolution convinced many western policymakers that nonviolent regime change was indeed possible in the former Soviet Union and would not inevitably lead to much feared civil war. Thus prepared, the West was ready to engage much more proactively in Ukraine and its Orange Revolution only a year later.

In providing this successful example of democratization, Georgian civil society also contributed to the international debate on democracy assistance in Central and Eastern Europe and elsewhere. It demonstrated which forms of support are critical for making it possible for civil society to contribute to electoral change. These include the necessity to fund and train election observers capable of carrying out parallel vote tabulation and exit polling, ideally with support from similar organizations from other CIS countries. Politically active youth groups, such as KMARA, must be included, as should the broadest possible range of NGOs, advocacy groups, local initiatives and other civic structures.

At the same time, in countries with more repressive and authoritarian regimes like Belarus, where it is highly problematic and even dangerous to carry out comprehensive monitoring, there is a risk that the regime will control election monitoring projects and even successfully approach foreign actors to fund them. The importance of spending on civic education should not be underestimated, but this is a more long-term endeavor on which considerable money needs to be spent over time. Finally, international actors such as the European Union and the United States should abandon the illusion that rigged elections might "not be so bad" or "an improvement over the last elections" in post-Soviet countries.

Today, Russia is a resurgent revisionist power that views the advance of democracy in its immediate neighborhood as a threat to be avoided. In this respect, Russia has launched offensives in the context of its bilateral relations with big democracies, as well as within multilateral organizations such as the Organization for Security and Cooperation in Europe (OSCE). Major stakeholders in the OSCE should not surrender to Russian pressure and lower the organization's standards on election monitoring. Not resisting Russian pressure to increase its share in monitoring missions risks a major loss of credibility. This can also put democratic activists and forces in danger.

Finally, pressure on remaining non-democratic regimes in the post-Soviet space should include sets of measures primarily focusing on the internal situation in the country. For example, pressure should be exerted on authorities to stop arresting people for distributing campaign materials and to release political prisoners. For that matter, western and European Union ambassadors could make good use of their diplomatic status and demonstrate alongside pro-democracy forces to make everyone understand that freedom is a right, not a luxury.

Chronology

April 14, 2003
KMARA holds its first public action. Some 500 students march from Tbilisi State University to the state chancellery to protest against the pro-government bloc called For A New Georgia.

April 21, 2003
The leader of the National Democratic Party, which is part of Shevardnadze's For A New Georgia bloc, Irina Sarishvili-Chanturia, accuses Russian intelligence of providing support to KMARA with the aim of destabilizing Georgia.

April 22, 2003
KMARA graffiti appear all over Tbilisi and subsequently in towns across Georgia.

May 12, 2003
KMARA holds its first nationwide action to condemn police brutality and corruption, with demonstrations taking place in Tbilisi and ten locations across Georgia. Further demonstrations are held over the following days.

June 2, 2003
President Shevardnadze threatens to expel organizations encouraging political instability. Presidential aides later confirm that these accusations were directed at the Open Society Georgia Foundation.

June 3, 2003
KMARA and five opposition parties stage a 5,000-strong protest in front of the parliament to demand the replacement of the central election commission, whose chairman and nine members subsequently resign.

July 13, 2003
Some 1,000 KMARA activists, human rights NGO representatives and members of the three main opposition parties gather in front of the internal affairs ministry to present a mock diploma "for adherence to President Shevardnadze and violation of the law".

September 20, 2003
Over 1,000 people gather in Mziuri Park in Tbilisi for a free concert organized by KMARA. Donations of Georgian books are requested from visitors.

October 2, 2003
50 KMARA activists collect food, clothes and toys for a local orphanage in Telavi. One activist is arrested but the charges are not made public.

October 10, 2003
KMARA activists gather in front of the state chancellery in Tbilisi and stage a mock funeral for Shevardnadze's For A New Georgia bloc. Seven activists are arrested.

October 20, 2003

KMARA activists invite passers-by in Tbilisi to be photographed with the "Bloc Toilet" campaign materials. KMARA and the opposition party National Movement organize a rally in Zestafoni demanding the resignation of President Shevardnadze.

October 23, 2003

The KMARA office in Tbilisi is vandalized by unidentified assailants.

November 2, 2003

Parliamentary elections are held in Georgia.

November 6, 2003

The deadline for the central election commission to announce the official results of the November 2 elections expires. Hundreds of people gather in Tbilisi demanding the resignation of President Shevardnadze. Thousands of riot police are stationed across the city.

November 7, 2003

Thousands gather in Tbilisi and Zugdidi demanding President Shevardnadze's resignation and claiming the parliamentary elections were rigged.

November 8, 2003

Large crowds remain in Tbilisi as army personnel in riot gear block the state chancellery. Hundreds of additional troops and riot police are ordered into Tbilisi from Eastern Georgia.

November 9, 2003

As mass protests continue in front of the parliament, talks are held between Shevardnadze and the three main opposition leaders, but quickly collapse. The central election commission suspends further vote counting and demands that the courts rule on the validity of the election.

November 11, 2003

President Shevardnadze meets with U.S. Ambassador Richard Miles to discuss the political crisis as demonstrators continue to protest outside the parliament.

November 12, 2003

The leader of the National Movement, Mikheil Saakashvili, calls for demonstrators to go on hunger strike until Shevardnadze resigns.

November 13, 2003

With approximately 10,000 protesters gathered in Tbilisi, government officials propose the conscription of all KMARA activists into the Georgian army. Meanwhile, Mikheil Saakashvili calls on citizens to withhold all tax payments. The central election commission calls for repeat elections in nine districts.

November 14, 2003

Thousands of demonstrators surround President Shevardnadze's office, but are blocked by police forces. Mikheil Saakashvili announces his supporters will collect 1 million signatures demanding Shevardnadze's resignation, as several opposition figures call for "full civil disobedience" beginning with November 17. The central election commission files a defamation suit against *Rustavi 2* TV and KMARA for an advertisement claiming the parliamentary elections were rigged.

November 17, 2003

The Governor of Telavi, Medea Mezrishvili, resigns as demanded by a National Movement demonstration on November 16. Elections are reheld in some of the districts identified by the central election commission.

November 18, 2003

Several thousand people gather for pro-Shevardnadze demonstrations in Tbilisi.

November 19, 2003

After criticism from President Shevardnadze, the chairman of the state radio and TV corporation, Zaza Shendelia, calls a press conference to announce his resignation.

November 20, 2003

The central election commission announces the final results of the parliamentary elections: For a New Georgia 21.32 percent; Revival Union 18.84 percent; National Movement 18.08 percent; Labor Party 12.4 percent; Burjanadze-Democrats 8.79 percent; and New Rights Party 7.35 percent.

November 22, 2003

Over 20,000 protesters gather in Tbilisi demanding President Shevardnadze's resignation and new parliamentary and presidential elections. Mikheil Saakashvili leads the demonstrators to the state chancellery and issues an ultimatum to Shevardnadze: resign within one hour and apologize to the Georgian people. Saakashvili then leads demonstrators to parliament and proceeds to storm the building without resistance from interior ministry troops assigned to provide security. Protesters carry roses as they occupy the building.

November 23, 2003

Russian Foreign Minister, Igor Ivanov, meets with President Shevardnadze and opposition leaders Nino Burjanadze, Mikheil Saakashvili and Zurab Zhvania. President Shevardnadze resigns late that evening in return for immunity from prosecution. Speaker of the Parliament Nino Burjanadze assumes responsibilities as interim president.

November 24, 2003

The results of the November 2 parliamentary elections are annulled by the Supreme Court.

KMARA poster: Shevardnadze and his allies with Marx, Engels, Lenin. The slogan reads: "You are a disease! Leave us!".

KMARA photo actions in Tbilisi: Have your picture taken with leaders of the pro-Shevardnadze "For a New Georgia" bloc on their way to prison or being flushed down a toilet.

Caricature masks of President Shevardnadze and leaders of the "For a New Georgia" bloc.

KMARA activists block one of Tbilisi's main streets in protest at the violent suppression of a demonstration in Borjomi in July 2003.

KMARA activists defending the parliament during post-election protests.

November 22, 2003. Demonstrators facing security forces raise their hands to show their protest is nonviolent.

December 22, 2003. Thousands of protestors gather at Freedom Square, Tbilisi.

IT'S TIME! PORA AND THE ORANGE REVOLUTION IN UKRAINE

Vladyslav Kaskiv, Iryna Chupryna, Yevhen Zolotariov

The election of the president of Ukraine in 2004 was a serious test for the maturity of Ukrainian civil society. The Orange Revolution broke out in the aftermath of obvious election fraud. Lasting seventeen days, it brought millions of Ukrainian citizens onto the streets in peaceful demonstration and protest. One in five Ukrainians participated in the Orange Revolution, making it the largest protest movement in Europe since the end of the Cold War. While not a single drop of blood was shed, the Orange Revolution led to a change of regime, established the rule of a legitimately elected president and fundamentally altered the image of Ukraine internationally. This democratic breakthrough demonstrated a high level of civic awareness among Ukrainian citizens and marked the birth of a new political era for the country.

One of the key driving forces behind the Orange Revolution was PORA, a civic campaign whose aim was to ensure the democratic election of the president in 2004. PORA was the first to erect tents on the streets of Kyiv and organized the famous tent city, blockaded administrative buildings and made a crucial contribution to the organization of the all-Ukrainian student strike that was key to the Orange Revolution. Prior to the revolutionary events, PORA informed and mobilized the public about the elections and the potential of election fraud. During the second half of 2004, PORA conducted national grass-root information, education and mobilization activities using "hand to hand" and "door to door" methods. In the absence of independent mass media, PORA volunteers became a key source of independent and alternative information for Ukrainian citizens. From March 2004 until January 2005, PORA distributed 40 million copies of print materials, involved in its work 35,000 permanent participants and an even larger number of regular supporters. PORA activists conducted more than 750 regional pickets and public actions, organized 17 mass rallies with more than 3,000 participants, set up the tent camp on Khreshchatyk in Kyiv (1,546 tents and more than 15,000 "residents") and 12 other tent camps across Ukraine. The official campaign web site (www.pora.org.ua) was among the five most popular web sites in Ukraine in the run-up to and during the Orange Revolution.

PORA was a special phenomenon. Actors of civil society in Ukraine were, for the first time, able to exert influence on the political process, thereby, creating preconditions for the building of a new political nation. Boris Nemtsov, member of the Federal Council of the Russian Union of Right Forces, said that "for the first time in world history, within such a short period of time, (PORA) managed to solve organizational and educational tasks of fantastic complexity: to create an efficient management structure, to involve and train thousands of activists, to mobilize the whole society, and first of all young people, for the active protection of their civil rights".[1]

This chapter presents an overview of factors underlying the emergence and development of PORA as a mass civic initiative, including a comprehensive description of the formation and development of the campaign, the main phases of its activity and analysis of the organizational and methodological principles key to its success. In doing so, the chapter will focus on what came to be known as Yellow PORA, not treating the related but distinct Black PORA.[2]

Post-Independence Ukraine and Democratization

In 1991, Ukraine seceded from the Soviet Union and subsequently established itself as an independent state. Rare among post-Soviet states, it managed to avoid interethnic conflicts and civil war. On December 1, 1991, Leonid Kravchuk was elected the first president of Ukraine. In 1994, he was replaced by Leonid Kuchma, who remained the head of the Ukrainian state for two terms, leaving office in 2004.

Since 2000, Ukraine has registered considerable economic growth. "In the course of the last four years, the average annual economic growth rate was 7.3 percent, industrial production increased by 16 percent and export volume, by 28 percent".[3] The country possesses a developed network of oil and gas pipelines, depositories and refineries and an advanced electrical power grid. Ukraine is also a part of an important Eurasian transport corridor. In early 2000, a team of reformers, led by Prime Minister Viktor Yushchenko and First Deputy Prime Minister Yulia Tymoshenko, entered government. They initiated reforms to curb the shadow economy and implemented a range of actions to improve living standards. Specifically, arrears in wages and pensions were largely paid off.

During this reform period, Ukraine declared its aspirations for European integration. This new approach triggered optimism in society and stimulated business and social activities. Steady economic growth and booming business characterized the period. However, the growing and influential middle and upper middle class of entrepreneurs and young professionals were becoming increasingly dissatisfied

---

1 Boris Nemtsov, speaking at the ceremony marking the completion of PORA activities on January 29, 2005.

2 Influenced by Serbia's OTPOR and Georgia's KMARA, Black PORA advocated a more spontaneous and decentralized approach, aimed at directly discrediting the Kuchma government.

3 From the speech of Anders Aslund in the House of Representatives of the U.S. Congress, Washington, DC, on May 12, 2004. The full text of this speech can be accessed on the following website: http://artukraine.com/buildukraine/uafuture1.htm.

with the clearly corrupt and authoritarian tendencies of the incumbent government and their cronies, the all powerful Ukrainian oligarchs.[4]

The success of the reformers threatened the interests of financial, political and criminal clans and a year after it had come to power, on April 28, 2001, the reform-oriented government was dismissed. Viktor Yushchenko pledged: "I go in order to return".[5] This led to the rise of a democratic opposition led by the ex-prime minister, whose successful reform policy guaranteed him significant support among citizens. By the beginning of 2002, the opposition had grown into an influential political force. The political bloc Our Ukraine subsequently won the parliamentary elections in March 2002. However, President Kuchma suppressed the parliamentary opposition and created a pro-presidential majority held together by fear, blackmail and bribery. The differences between these power blocs were increasingly characterized by principled social priorities and geopolitical orientations: for or against liberal democracy, a market economy and Euroatlantic integration.

Ukraine officially declared its aspiration to Euroatlantic integration and its intention to join the European Union and NATO in 2002. However, during President Leonid Kuchma's term of office (1994 to 2004), foreign policy was distinguished by a "multivectorial"[6] doctrine, in other words, by the absence of clear foreign policy priorities. The essence of the multivectorial approach was the constant and uneasy weaving of a course between Moscow and the European Union and policymaking on the basis of temporary political configurations. Most statements by Kuchma claiming the need for European integration were declarative in nature and were not accompanied by any real action. Nevertheless, given its geopolitical location and human resource potential, Ukraine remains key to Euroatlantic security. The geopolitical significance of Ukraine even increased after the expansion of the European Union on May 1, 2004, when it became an immediate neighbor of several European Union member states.

By 2004, Ukraine was characterized by increasingly authoritarian tendencies, with fundamental freedoms and the rights of its citizens at risk or openly violated. Society had lost trust in the former communist nomenclatura that had been in power since independence in 1991. The regime was highly oligarchic, dominated by three main groups distributed regionally, controlling huge economic and political resources, in particular, close relations with various parliamentary factions, the president and law

---

4 Anders Aslund, "The Ancien Regime", in: Anders Aslund and Michael McFaul (eds.), Revolution in Orange: the Origins of Ukraine's Democratic Breakthrough (Carnegie Endowment for International Peace, Washington, DC, 2006), pp. 23-26.

5 Interview with Viktor Yushchenko, The Ukrainian, September 10, 2004. The full text of this interview can be accessed on the following website: http://www.yuschenko.com.ua/ukr/present/Mass_media/1125/.

6 See Viktor Zamyatin, "One Vector", Day newspaper, April 27, 2004, http://www.day.kiev.ua/13495/ and Andriy Okara, "Ukraine Is Focusing", Day newspaper, July 5, 2005, http://www.day.ua/139829/.

enforcement agencies.[7] Civil society was becoming increasingly radicalized in the wake of government harassment and the repression of critical nongovernmental organizations. A particularly popular method was the fabrication of tax violations and subsequent tax swoops. The aim of such activities was clearly to discredit openly critical elements of civil society in the eyes of the public at large.

In light of the above situation, it was clear that the decision about which way Ukraine would go would be made at the 2004 elections. The main contenders for the presidency were opposition candidate Viktor Yushchenko and the government backed Prime Minister Viktor Yanukovych. Yanukovych was the former governor of the Eastern region of Donetsk, and had served as prime minister since November 2002. While in the eyes of public opinion Yushchenko represented the voice of "clean" government, the incumbent was understood to be the Donetsk oligarch's choice. Noteworthy is that in Ukraine it was common knowledge that Yanukovych had served three and a half years in jail for assault and robbery.

The Development of Civil Society as an Effective Opposition Force in Ukraine

Since independence in 1991, civil society has undergone a dynamic transformation. At the beginning of the 1990s, numerous NGOs started to emerge. However, they developed and acted separately. According to official statistics, at the beginning of 2003, there were more than 30,000 NGOs in operation. Most of these operated in regions with highly developed infrastructure, like Kyiv, Dnipropetrovsk and Donetsk, or in areas with cultural and intellectual potential, such as Lviv and the Autonomous Republic of Crimea, where the Crimean Tatar minority is active.[8]

With each successive electoral campaign, and the increasing authoritarianism of the regime becoming evident, a new breed of civil society organization developed: the civic organization dealing directly with electoral politics, its transparency and oversight.[9] Such organizations were frequented by young people who did not want to join a political party (in their perception corrupt and self-serving) for the very reason that they were concerned for the further development of the democratic process. These organizations developed valuable experience of information, education and monitoring. This period was also marked by considerably improved cooperation between representatives of the civic sector. The emergence of influential NGO

7 Anders Aslund, "The Ancien Regime", in: Anders Aslund and Michael McFaul (eds.), Revolution in Orange: the Origins of Ukraine's Democratic Breakthrough (Carnegie Endowment for International Peace, Washington, DC, 2006), p. 9, op cit.

8 For further information in this concern, please consult the following websites: www.ngoukraine.kiev.ua and www.civicua.org.

9 Nadia Diuk, "The Triumph of Civil Society", in: Anders Aslund and Michael McFaul (eds.), Revolution in Orange: the Origins of Ukraine's Democratic Breakthrough (Carnegie Endowment for International Peace, Washington, DC, 2006), p. 26.

coalitions and large-scale cooperation programs that encompassed many diverse projects facilitated this. The largest NGO coalition, called Freedom of Choice, was founded in 1999. Other influential platforms included the Coalition New Choice 2004 and the Committee of Voters of Ukraine.

The development of civil society as a strong and coherent actor in the years preceding the 2004 breakthrough was underpinned by a number of factors. In particular, economic growth and the development of a prosperous middle and entrepreneurial class, with access to technology and, thereby, independent media and interested in the business and social opportunities represented by political reform (including the prospect of increased foreign direct investment), encouraged social claims for civic liberties. Further, this burgeoning middle class became discontented with the obvious abuses of power taking place among the political and economic elites and their shameless personal enrichment. The worsening suppression of independent media and the scandalous disappearance and presumed murder of Heorhiy Gongadze, founder of the independent web newspaper *Ukrainska Pravda,* on the order of high-level government officials, were particularly worrisome for many ordinary citizens. As these various claims fell on deaf governmental ears, civil society became their channel for articulation and with time, increasingly politicized and radicalized.[10]

This development culminated in the launch of a complex program of cooperation among actors in the civic sector aimed at ensuring free and fair presidential elections that was launched under the banner of the "Wave of Freedom" campaign in early 2004. It included a series of information, education and monitoring projects. The implementation of this campaign became part of a democratization strategy coordinated by different organizations, including the formal democratic opposition, with the ambition of ensuring the influence of civil society on the political development of Ukraine and to cement the country's democratic and Euroatlantic choice.

The "Wave of Freedom" campaign included many projects aimed at public monitoring of campaign finances and the drafting of voter lists prior to the elections, including "hotline" information resources covering the elections, training for commissioners of polling stations, international public monitoring of voting at polling stations abroad and a large-scale public and voter information and education campaign called PORA.

PORA: It's Time for Change!

PORA was a civic campaign whose aim was to ensure the democratic election of the president of Ukraine in 2004 in free and fair elections through the provision of

---

10 Anders Aslund, "The Ancien Regime", and Michael McFaul, "Conclusion – The Orange Revolution in Comparative Perspective", in: Anders Aslund and Michael McFaul (eds.), Revolution in Orange: the Origins of Ukraine's Democratic Breakthrough (Carnegie Endowment for International Peace, Washington, DC, 2006), pp. 9-27 and pp. 165-195, op cit.

independent information to citizens about the election results and the recording of violations of the electoral process. PORA functioned as a united initiative of hundreds of NGOs, involving large numbers of volunteers, and implemented dozens of projects. PORA included elements of monitoring, information, education and public protest. In doing so, PORA functioned within the larger framework of the "Wave of Freedom" campaign. Despite being informed by the experiences of international partners, PORA was driven and supported mainly by domestic Ukrainian actors across society.

The main aim of PORA, based on the principles of openness, nonpartisanship, responsibility, volunteering and the priority of public interests over corporate ones, was to ensure conditions for the democratic development of Ukraine, including the realization of complex reforms, the formation of transparent power structures and the reiteration of the country's Euroatlantic choice, during the 2004 presidential elections.

The most important strategic goal of the campaign was to ensure the conduct of free, fair and transparent elections for the president of Ukraine that would bring to power a candidate genuinely supported by Ukrainian citizens. PORA did not campaign for any presidential candidate in particular. A key principle was that the people of Ukraine should decide for themselves who their president should be. In addition, PORA members considered the conduct of a democratic election as the first step to improving the situation in relation to respect for freedom of expression and the media, the elimination of deeply rooted corruption and the implementation of urgently needed economic reforms.

The priority tasks of the campaign included the creation of an alternative mechanism for delivering objective information about the course of the electoral campaign and the positions of individual candidates directly to citizens in all regions, the increase of voter turnout among those electoral groups that support democratic development, national priorities and Euroatlantic integration, mobilization of the society for the protection of their democratic rights and freedoms (particularly, in case of a falsification of election results or other illegitimate actions by the authorities).

The management of PORA was to a large extent provided by experienced activists and leaders of both the student movement created in the early 1990s and the All Ukrainian Public Resistance Committee Za Pravdu! (For Truth). Students constituted the majority of PORA activists, which is explained by the fact that students are the most educated and well-informed social group, with a high level of solidarity, thanks to student mobility and the intensive use of new information and communication technologies. The fast dissemination of information was crucial to the campaign's functioning. In those areas where higher educational institutions do not exist, students of the professional and technical schools, gymnasiums, lyceums and even schools joined PORA's activities.

In the final stage of the electoral campaign, representatives of small and medium sized enterprises became involved. Representatives of the Ukrainian middle class were not only a source of financial and other resource support, but they were ready to get involved in activities to ensure the elections were free and fair.

As a broad civic movement, PORA united a diverse range of people in terms of age, social standing and ideological position. Campaign activists ranged from adherents of rightist nationalistic movements across the political spectrum to anarchists. Most of the activists were characterized by three fundamental features: a strong commitment to the ideas and principles of democracy, determination to stand up for those principles, even under the conditions of harassment and repression inflicted by the authorities, and belonging to the post-Soviet generation. The mentality of most PORA's members was not shaped by Soviet ideology and was free of the fears, prejudices and apprehensions inherited from the Soviet period that prevented many members of older generations from participating in the protests. In fact, the typical PORA activist was male, 18 to 20 years of age and a student in his first or second year of university.

More than 80 public organizations from different regions, mostly member organizations of the Freedom of Choice Coalition, expressed their readiness to lend support to the campaign and a "declaration about support for the nationwide information and education campaign PORA" was signed by representatives of those organizations in the period from March to April 2004. Members of the largest all-Ukrainian youth organizations, including the Christian-Democratic Youth of Ukraine, the Union of Ukrainian Youth, *Zarevo*, Young *Prosvita*, the Association of Law Students, as well as student organizations in the universities and institutes of higher education, joined the newly formed campaign.

The organizational structure of PORA was built on a model of horizontal network management. The core element of the structure was the so-called *Riys* or regional mobile group. These provided information and education to the voting public in a given region and comprised of between 10 and 15 volunteers each. Approximately 400 *Riys* formed a network whose activities reached an estimated 25 million citizens. *Riys* acted in circumscribed territories called *Kusches*, whose population they addressed. 78 *Kusches* covered the entire territory of Ukraine, with each addressing a population of approximately 500,000 people and reflecting specific regional, social and cultural profiles.

The organization of the work of the *Riys* groups was the main task of the coordination center. It was responsible for elaborating the information strategy of the campaign, coordinating the actions of regional units, organizing the production and distribution of printed materials and consulting with partners. The coordination center also dealt with contacts with the regions, the elaboration of the program of the campaign, the creative dimension of informing the public, public relations, international cooperation, security of communication and information systems, legal aid and safety of activists (given harassment by the government), fundraising and financial management, and finally organizational support and logistics.

In addition, the campaign council brought together influential public figures, representatives of the business community, politics, state and international structures and was in charge of making important strategic decisions and securing political support for the campaign. The constituent assembly of the PORA campaign, with the participation of 70 regional leaders, took place from April 14 to 18, 2004, in Uzhhorod.

In order to achieve resource stability and efficiency, PORA's coordination center developed a decentralized system of financial and resource management. With the help of the campaign's main partners, a scheme was developed that diversified the financial sources and resource supply of individual activities and projects. This scheme helped to decrease the risk of resource concentration. The campaign's initial funding was supplied by the founders of PORA themselves. These funds were used to organize activities, to develop information support and print materials. Training of activists was supported by small grants provided by the German Marshall Fund of the United States, Freedom House and the Canadian International Development Agency (in total, approximately US$ 130,000). It is noteworthy that this sum is rather minimal in comparison to the overall amount of financial support from the international community received by similar movements in Serbia and Georgia.

Entrepreneurs from all over Ukraine provided the bulk of resources needed to conduct PORA activities during the presidential elections. A significant proportion of these had been directly involved in the student movement of the early 1990s. The support was provided in kind, including free production of publications, provision of communications and transportation, etc. It is estimated that the value of this in-kind support exceeded US$ 6.5 million. In cash, PORA spent US$ 1.56 million. More than 60 percent of these resources were spent during the Orange Revolution for the organizational needs of tent camps, transport, food, etc.

The development of PORA's approach was inspired by the nonviolent student movement's participation in the struggle for independence at the beginning of the 1990s, the experience of the Ukraine without Kuchma movement and of the activities of the All Ukrainian Public Resistance Committee Za Pravdu! (For Truth) of 2000 and 2001.

Their methods included hunger strikes, demonstrations, rallies, picketing and other kinds of strike action. The methods developed by the student movement in the areas of volunteer network development, of establishing strike committees in universities and of staging protest actions proved effective during the electoral campaign in 2004. The basic form of mass protest action (tent camps in the capital and other cities) also has its origins in the student protests of the 1990s.

In the run-up to the 2004 elections, it became increasingly clear that Ukraine had significant problems of democratic development (widespread corruption, violations of human rights and persecution of independent mass media). In this context, protest initiatives re-emerged in the activities of the All Ukrainian Public Resistance Committee *Za Pravdu!* (For Truth), established in the upsurge of mass social and political resistance to the Kuchma regime in 2000 and 2001. The protests were triggered by the disappearance and presumed assassination of the opposition journalist, Heorhiy Gongadze, editor in chief of the Internet site *Ukrainska Pravda*, in September 2000, and the sabotage of the murder investigation by the authorities. The authorities then used mass repression against participants of the protests.

In the process of the preparation and implementation of PORA's campaign, the experience of Ukraine without Kuchma, Revolt Ukraine! and the All Ukrainian Public Resistance Committee *Za Pravdu!* (For Truth) were thoroughly analyzed. Concerned with avoiding hierarchy and maintaining horizontal relations with participants, neither the Ukraine without Kuchma movement nor the All Ukrainian Public Resistance Committee *Za Pravdu!* (For Truth) realized the importance of centralized coordination. An overall lack of strategic planning and weak organizational capacity led to certain executive functions not being performed and to a lack of supervision. The promotion of a positive image of these movements towards the international community was also lacking. Ukraine without Kuchma did not clearly identify itself as a movement based on the principle of nonviolent resistance. Several clashes with police caused a lot of people to turn away from the movement. The All Ukrainian Public Resistance Committee *Za Pravdu!* (For Truth), on the other hand, suffered from excessive politicization. Many of its members were also members of political parties, which did not enhance the committee's legitimacy in the eyes of the public.

Unfolding the Campaign

In accordance with the campaign's goal and tasks, the plan of action was divided into two main stages. Stage one included the implementation of various information and education actions aimed at increasing voter turnout, counteracting censorship and supplying voters with objective information about the electoral campaign, the programs of the individual candidates, voter rights and the necessity of their protection in the case of violations. Stage two envisaged the organization of mass protests to protect the results of the elections, in the case of election fraud.

In March 2004 the principle elements of the campaign's graphic line, its name (PORA) and its logo were developed. PORA means the same in Ukrainian and Russian, which is very important in a bilingual country. Besides, PORA can be used both as a noun (in the sense of "the time has come") and as an imperative with an appeal for action (time to think, time to choose, etc). Yellow was selected as the main campaign color, with the additional usage of black and red.

The web site of the campaign was established at www.pora.org.ua and served not only as a source of information, but also for coordination among regional departments. This website became, and remains, one of the five most popular political Internet sites in Ukraine. A system of immediate dissemination of information by SMS was also put in place and proved to be important. On March 9, 2004, the campaign concept was officially presented on www.hotline.net.ua – "Everything about Elections".

One of the first public actions of PORA, and one of its most significant, aimed at ensuring free and fair mayoral elections in the Transcarpathian town of Mukacheve on April 18, 2004. These elections were held under the scrutiny of international organizations, in particular, the Organization for Security and Cooperation in Europe (OSCE). Nevertheless, representatives of the incumbent authorities considered them a kind of rehearsal for the upcoming presidential elections in October 2004 and applied an arsenal of the most brutal methods of obstruction: intimidation of voters, physical clashes, disruptions at polling stations and the theft of ballots. Despite the clear victory of the other candidate, the pro-regime candidate, Ernest Nuser, was announced victorious.

In close cooperation with the representatives of the Freedom of Choice Coalition, PORA activists worked as observers and carried out public surveys on voting day. After clear indications of vote falsification in favor of Ernest Nuser, the campaign mobilized the town's inhabitants to protect their rights and to put pressure on the local authorities. Residents of a tent camp distributed brochures including copies of the protocols of the district election commissions, the results of the parallel vote count and exit polls conducted by independent NGOs.

On May 8, PORA activists addressed Ernest Nuser with an open letter urging him to step down and apologize to the inhabitants of the town. The following day a second open letter about the events in Mukacheve addressed to Prime Minister Viktor Yanukovych was issued. By May 11, PORA had gathered more than 7,000 signatures from Mukacheve residents in support of its actions. The same day picketers organized a satiric public action "Time for dry crackers", which involved the preparation of a prison diet for the head of the Mukacheve territorial election commission, Yury Peresta (responsible for the election fraud). The diet was handed over to Ernest Nuser. At the end of May, PORA activists started picketing the Transcarpathian oblast administration.

In Kyiv, PORA organized an exhibition called "MUKAcheve of democracy" (in Ukrainian this is a play on words: *muka* means pain or torture) at the premises of the National University of Kyiv-Mohyla Academy, in which photos of disrupted polling stations, broken windows and chairs and fights with gangsters were displayed. On June 1, PORA hung the campaign's flag from the gallery during the parliamentary hearings that were devoted to the investigation of crimes committed during the Mukacheve elections.

With these actions, PORA succeeded in forcing the illegally proclaimed mayor to resign. This success inspired the drafting of the PORA Manifesto, the basic ideological document of the campaign, outlining its main principles, including continued commitment to the struggle to establish genuine democracy in Ukraine. This manifesto proclaimed: "Freedom is the highest value and must be protected".

PORA also gained useful experience during the monitoring of elections in the agrarian Poltavska oblast in Central Ukraine (June 20, 2004), the important Southern city of Odessa (May 30, 2004), and in the industrial town of Vakhrusheve in Eastern Ukraine (July 11, 2004). During these elections, communication between mobile group leaders, monitoring of voter lists, access to information, observation of electoral commissions, control of the use of administrative resources, monitoring of the vote and the organization of mass protests were tested. A key element during this phase was the testing of different formats of information and education activity, such as the "hand to hand" and "door to door" methods that also proved effective for increasing voter turnout in the OK '98 campaign in Slovakia.

In August 2004, PORA played an active part in the Sumy Revolution, in which university students in the Northern town of Sumy started mass actions to protest against the unjustified and illegitimate merger of several local universities and political pressure being exerted on them by the authorities. On August 7, 2004, against the backdrop of indiscriminate arrests of Sumy students, PORA restated its determination to protect student rights in accordance with Ukrainian law and international standards. The same day, participants of the PORA training camp that was taking place in Eupatoria joined Sumy students marching on Kyiv.

Training played an important preparatory role before the active phase of the campaign was launched. From August 1 to 8, 2004, a training camp entitled *"PORA pochynaty!"* or "Time to begin!" was organized in the Crimean town of Eupatoria for more than 300 regional campaign leaders. The intensive lecture and interactive workshop program covered important skills for activists and regional leaders, including internal organizational issues, external interaction of the campaign with diverse target groups and methods of organizing of protest actions.

September 2004 marked the final consolidation of a stable network of 72 regional centers including around 150 mobile groups all over Ukraine. In the following months, the mobilization of volunteers continued and resulted in the registration of more than 30,000 people.

The information strategy of the campaign comprised five main phases aimed at individual issues deemed crucial for legitimate and democratic elections, including dissemination of objective information about the electoral campaign and the programs of the individual candidates, mobilization of voters to participate, explanation of voter rights, information about criminal liability in case of breaches of the electoral law and public appeals for mass protest, if needed.

September and October 2004 was the key period for the realization of the information and education components of PORA's campaign. The first phase of information campaigning, "It's time to stand up" had already started in August and primarily addressed students and young people with an appeal to join PORA as volunteers. The materials produced during this phase were distributed primarily in the student environment: universities, student dormitories, through the network of youth organizations and during the training camp in Eupatoria.

In the beginning of September 2004, the second element of the campaign entitled "It's time to think" was launched, with the purpose of providing voters with information about the presidential elections, voter rights, and the candidates for the presidency and their programs. Diverse forms of publication, leaflets and stickers were distributed "door to door", in public transport and using other creative methods. Information was also disseminated through Internet and electronic mail.

By the beginning of October 2004, PORA activists started to implement two further phases of the information campaign. "It's time to vote" aimed at increasing turnout among citizens at the forthcoming presidential elections. PORA used a range of techniques including concerts, civic activities and printed materials to reach different segments of the population, and especially young people. At the same time a preventive action called "It's time to control" aimed at preventing election fraud, began. This phase addressed personalized letters to the representatives of local authorities, heads and members of the election commissions and members of law-enforcement bodies, informing them about their individual legal liability for any violations of the electoral law. In cooperation with the Freedom of Choice Coalition, PORA organized a nationwide monitoring of voter lists. This drew the attention of the voting public to manipulations of voter lists during the electoral campaign. Further, PORA conducted a nationwide action on September 29, 2004, in which appeals to handle the elections in a fair manner were delivered to 225 territorial electoral commission (TEC) members throughout Ukraine.

One of PORA's key activities in this period was to discredit those mass media that systematically spread biased and distorted information. Actions included the distribution of stickers with the logos of five well-known Ukrainian media (the TV channels *UT-1*, *Inter*, *1+1* and the newspapers *Fakty* and *Segodnia*) sporting the slogan "They lie". A series of actions near the offices of TV stations ("It's better to chew than speak", "Kill the TV within yourself", and others) were also conducted.

PORA distributed print materials to the most remote cities and localities. This became an extremely powerful instrument for overcoming the information blockade and ensured that even citizens of the most isolated parts of the country could make an informed choice. Despite distortions in coverage, leading TV channels covered PORA actions, impressed with the unusual character and courage of PORA's activities. Laughter was an important tool in the struggle against the regime. For example, PORA activists organized a theatrical performance called "Egg Relatives", alluding to an incident in which the Prime Minister, Viktor Yanukovych, was pelted with an egg in front of government buildings in Ivano-Frankivsk on October 4.

On the whole, within the framework of the six information phases of the campaign ("Time to stand up", "Time to think", "Time to vote", "Time to win", "Time to understand – they lie" and "Vote or you'll lose"), 37 different types of printed materials, with a general circulation of around 40 million copies, were published and distributed nationwide. The English version of the PORA website and regular news mailing played an important role in establishing and maintaining contact with international partners and supporters. It not only provided people outside Ukraine with the latest PORA news, but also generated international support for the movement, such as the "Letter of Freedom and Solidarity" that was signed by more than 560 people from 29 countries. In addition, a special newsletter about Ukrainian civil society in the 2004 presidential elections, under the title "Times of Change" was regularly mailed to hundreds of recipients in the United States and Europe.[11]

State Reaction

Intimidated by the impressive scale of PORA activities and the elusive character of its mobile groups, the regime launched an unprecedented wave of repression against its leaders and activists, as early as October 2004. This persecution culminated in the fabrication of a criminal case in which PORA was accused of acts of terrorism.

At a press conference on October 14, 2004, PORA announced an initiative to draft a "Black List" of state officials engaged in acts of repression against PORA activists, students and members of other public organizations, and known to be engaged in violations of the constitutional rights and freedoms of Ukrainian citizens. On October 15, 2004, PORA's offices in Kyiv were searched. State militia found explosives on the premises. A criminal case against PORA was launched. Activists were charged with the "organization of illegal military units" and the "organization of terrorist acts". This was followed by searches at the offices of the Freedom of Choice Coalition, the apartments of the leaders of the campaign and the detention and interrogation of more than 150 PORA activists. Fifteen criminal cases, with accusations ranging from forging money to rape to the illegal possession of weapons and explosives, were fabricated against PORA activists in different regions of Ukraine. More than 300 persons involved in PORA activities were detained before the first round of the presidential elections.

PORA responded with a series of actions under the title "We are not terrorists". Namely, on October 18, 2004, PORA activists chained themselves to the independence

---

11 The archive of all newsletters published can be accessed at www.pora.org.ua.

monument in Kyiv. PORA condemned the authorities' attack on democratic rights and freedoms, addressing NGOs, political parties and international organizations with a call for solidarity, which was signed by the Freedom of Choice Coalition of Ukrainian NGOs, the Ukrainian Helsinki Group on Human Rights, several well-known Lviv authors, Amnesty International, representatives of the international community as well as many Ukrainian citizens. Amnesty International called the jailed PORA activists "prisoners of conscience". The result of these actions was to shatter any remaining illusion on the part of the Ukrainian voting public concerning the possibility of holding free and fair elections. After October 21, 2004, PORA transformed from an information and education campaign into a civic campaign aimed at organizing the active protection of the election results, with a central focus on "direct action" including the staging of mass protests.

The attempt of the authorities to associate PORA with acts of terrorism was a serious challenge for the campaign. Maintaining the campaign's legitimacy with the voting public was crucial. For this reason, student activity was upgraded and made more visible. In Ukraine, the public perception of students is generally positive. PORA chose to create strike committees in educational establishments throughout Ukraine. These later played a crucial role in the context of the Orange Revolution.

A Civic Movement with a Difference

According to Nadia Diuk, "the most striking aspect of the Orange Revolution was the level of mass participation – not only in Maidan – but also the millions who followed events by watching *Channel 5*, listening to *Radio Era* or hearing from friends and relatives in Maidan".[12] One would be forgiven for taking this fact for granted and flippantly underestimating the achievement that this mass mobilization actually represents. The eventual success of this revolution hinged on the success of PORA and its partners to trigger the mobilization. The movement had much in common with its predecessors in other countries.[13] Nevertheless, PORA also demonstrated some uniquely Ukrainian features. A further discussion of both the similarities and differences of PORA with other movements is warranted at this point.

PORA was created as an independent and nonpartisan initiative. Nonetheless, the successful pursuit of its activities required frequent communication with representatives of diverse political forces. Already during the mayoral elections in Mukacheve, PORA cooperated with the leading candidates to ensure free and

12 Nadia Diuk, "The Triumph of Civil Society", in: Anders Aslund and Michael McFaul (eds.), Revolution in Orange: the Origins of Ukraine's Democratic Breakthrough (Carnegie Endowment for International Peace, Washington, DC, 2006), pp.69-84, op cit.

13 See Pavol Demeš and Joerg Forbrig, "Pora – 'It's Time' for Democracy in Ukraine", in: Anders Aslund and Michael McFaul (eds.), Revolution in Orange: the Origins of Ukraine's Democratic Breakthrough (Carnegie Endowment for International Peace, Washington, DC, 2006), pp. 85-102, op cit.

fair elections. During the presidential elections, PORA permanently informed the candidates' campaign headquarters about its activities and updated them about the results of its election monitoring. However, PORA did not engage in election campaigning for any particular candidate for the presidency.

After the results of the first round were announced, PORA publicly declared that it was clear the incumbent regime was determined to maintain power through the manipulation of the presidential elections in favor of its candidate, Viktor Yanukovych. In response, PORA launched direct actions aimed at protecting free and fair elections, and starting from October 15, 2004, these activities were coordinated with the coalition of democratic forces *Syla Narodu* (Strength of the Nation), which included Viktor Yushchenko's party Our Ukraine, the Socialist Party of Ukraine, and the coalition led by Yulia Tymoshenko. Those political forces worked together with PORA and some other civil movements (including *Studentska Khvylia* [Student Wave], *Chysta Ukraina* [Clean Ukraine]) within the framework of a plan of action that focused on ensuring the publishing of the legitimate election results and the preparation of mass protest actions in case of election fraud. Hence, close cooperation between PORA and the political forces of the opposition began only after the first round of the elections. This cooperation was based on partnership, but did not include the integration of organizational structures or resources.

Given the nongovernmental and nonpartisan status of the PORA campaign, a broad range of Ukrainian NGOs, international organizations and democratic movements in other countries, in particular in Central and Eastern Europe, were counted among its partners. Although PORA received only modest resources from international and foreign partners, their experience, solidarity and political support did much to strengthen the campaign and its role for the democratic process. The administrative structure and human resources of PORA largely derived from the qualified staff and organizational resources of existing nongovernmental organizations, in particular those belonging to the Freedom of Choice Coalition. Cooperation with the small group of independent media helped to publicize PORA activities. The information service "Hotline" (www.hotline.net.ua), an Internet-based newspaper called *Ukrainska Pravda* (www.pravda.com.ua), *Channel 5*, *Radio Era*, and the newspapers *Ukraina Moloda* and *Vechyrny Visty* played an important role in getting the campaign message out to the people.

On the international level, and among similar foreign movements, the experiences of the Slovak '98 campaign, *Solidarność* (Solidarity) in Poland and FIDESZ in Hungary turned out to be the most valuable. The grassroots OK '98 campaign succeeded in increasing the traditionally low voter turnout in Slovakia, thereby, securing the peaceful transition of power from the Mečiar government to that of democratic forces, using, in particular, activities in favor of voter mobilization, voter education and prevention of election fraud. PORA organized its own strategy around these three pillars. Key figures of the OK '98 campaign were instrumental in training

PORA activists at the training camp in Eupatoria and others contributed to the development of the public information strategy of the campaign. Further, and similar to Polish *Solidarność*, PORA was oriented towards the development of a broad public movement and made significant use of networked strike committees. The partner movements of PORA included ZUBR[14] and other democratic organizations in Belarus. ZUBR signed a declaration of partnership with PORA on March 9, 2004. Representatives of these movements, along with many young activists from other countries, took part in the events of the Orange Revolution.

The experiences of OTPOR in Serbia and KMARA in Georgia were less applicable in Ukraine. The postmodern, carnival character of the Ukrainian revolution, its principle of pacifism and the absence of aggression are key differences to the events in Serbia and Georgia. Nevertheless, PORA used some of the creative elements, logos and symbols of those movements (for example, the clock was borrowed from the logotypes of the Serbian campaign *"Gotov je!"* [He's finished!]).

Nonetheless, PORA was especially designed for the Ukrainian context, taking into account the specifics of Ukraine's social and political situation including its size and population, administrative, cultural and geographical particularities, international and regional factors, resources and partnerships

The Uniquely Ukrainian Dimension of PORA

The conditions under which the realization of PORA's civic educational initiative, and especially under which the organization of mass protest actions took place, were very complex and diverge significantly from the cases of similar civic movements in other countries. They demanded the development of specific and context appropriate techniques and formats of information, education and protest activity.

In particular, several conditions of the Ukrainian reality should be emphasized. First, Ukraine has a very large territory (603,700 square kilometers) and population (47 million). It required considerable effort to cover the whole country with information, education and mobilization activities. The well-developed regional structure of the campaign significantly increased the autonomy of the regional centers and hampered attempts to put obstacles in the campaign's way. Second, a relatively small share of the Ukrainian population resides in the capital city Kyiv (just four percent), in comparison to Belgrade (the capital of Serbia) or Tbilisi (the capital of Georgia), in which more than 30 percent of the respective populations live. Under such circumstances, events aimed only at Kyiv residents, would not gain nationwide support.

Third, the historical, social and cultural heterogeneity of the Ukrainian population has led to significant differences in the level of development, social situation and

---

14 ZUBR is a youth pro-democracy movement in Belarus (www.zubr-belarus.org).

linguistic preferences of its diverse regions. As a result of Russification, spanning long periods of Ukrainian history, the prevalent language in Eastern and Southern Ukraine is Russian rather than Ukrainian. This language factor had to be taken into account in the elaboration of print materials. History also had to be taken into account. Due to Soviet propaganda, the leader of the Organization of Ukrainian Nationalists, Stepan Bandera, a hero for many Western Ukrainians, has an ambiguous position in the eyes of the population of Eastern Ukraine. So, while in other parts of the country, his picture was used for a sticker campaign, in Eastern Ukraine a neutral image of Che Guevara was chosen.

Fourth, domestic peculiarities in the development of democratic rights and freedoms were also significant. When speaking about freedom of speech or freedom of the press in Ukraine, it is necessary to point out that the level of access to the independent mass media differed widely between different regions of Ukraine. The constant interruptions to broadcasting by *Channel 5* meant that access to independent information was very limited. Internet information was available only to the approximately 6 million Ukrainians that have Internet access. The lion's share of Internet use is concentrated among residents of Kyiv and other major cities, where civic protest and opposition were the most determined.[15]

Last, the considerable interference of Russia in Ukraine's electoral process cannot be neglected. Several visits of President Putin of Russia to Ukraine before the presidential elections, as well as his extension of premature congratulations to Yanukovych after the run-off demonstrated the major interest of Russia in the electoral campaign and its results. The attempts by Russia to influence the results of the elections in Ukraine and the intention of the Russian-backed candidate to introduce dual Ukrainian–Russian citizenship represented a real threat to Ukrainian independence.

The main task of PORA, therefore, consisted of communicating a sense of the strategic importance of the presidential elections for the future direction of the country to all parts of Ukrainian society. It was crucial for the electorate to understand the need for radical change.

Conclusion

Among the main challenges and obstacles that PORA encountered during its emergence, development and activities, the most significant and problematic were internal problems within the civic sector and the absence of sufficient coordination and communication between members of the diverse civic movements and their leaders and even competition between them. This was to a great extent overcome

15 Adrian Karatnycky, "Ukraine's Orange Revolution", Foreign Affairs, vol. 84, no. 2 (March-April 2005), pp. 35-52.

with the creation of powerful NGO coalitions, the realization of the "Wave of Freedom" campaign and through the cooperation of PORA with friendly civic movements such as *Studentska khvylia* (Student Wave), *Chysta Ukraina* (Clean Ukraine) and *Znayu* (I know). Information and communication technologies also contributed positively to this process. Regretfully, competition remains a problem of the third sector in Ukraine, even after the Orange Revolution.

PORA had to take into account the absence of independent mass media, a factor common to many authoritarian regimes. All hope for the dissemination of objective information rested with the campaign itself. The establishment of direct contact with voters, through "door to door" campaigning and activities in the regions, were crucial to the campaign's success. Even negative publicity in the mass media (independent or not) is useful, if handled correctly (immediate refutation of erroneous or false accusations, for example). Repression against PORA was also a serious problem, as it endangered the capacity of the campaign to fulfill its mission. Effective counteraction was possible due to the elaborate regional structure and the use of decentralized management. This prevented the paralysis of the campaign when its leaders were attacked. A further challenge was the absence of sufficient financial resources.

PORA was able to overcome these obstacles as a result of a number of its specific features. The highly developed regional structure enabled fundraising from many representatives of small and medium sized enterprises at the regional level and ensured that the campaign would not collapse if its national leaders were imprisoned. The activities of the campaign helped to create a "presence" in every corner of the country, which functioned as a powerful alternative means of communication with citizens. The intensive use of modern technologies, and in particular Internet, email, SMS communication and mobile phones, was crucial, helping to instantly spread information about ongoing abuses during the elections and how to participate in protests, and alternative information to that published in the regime-controlled media.

During the twelve months of its existence, PORA's campaign became a pillar of Ukraine's new democracy: a community of people from different generations, professions, social and geographical backgrounds and even espousing diverging political views, united in their faith in a free, just and democratic future for Ukraine. It became a genuine prototype for civil society development and after the completion of its activities its transformation led to the creation of a number of civic organizations and political initiatives.

The Civic Party PORA[16] is a new political party that was founded by several former PORA activists in the aftermath of the Orange Revolution. Despite a delay in the registration of the party and after a few months of legal wrangling in court, the

---

16 http://pora.org.ua/eng/.

party won a case against the justice ministry and was registered with the possibility to take part in the parliamentary and local elections in 2006. The constituent assembly of the Civic Party PORA took place in Kyiv, on January 12, 2005. This new political party has become a new force on the Ukrainian political scene and has the ambition to present an alternative to established figures in Ukrainian politics. Civic Party PORA took part in the parliamentary and local elections held on March 26, 2006, forming a coalition with the liberal party "Reform and Order" and fielding the famous heavyweight boxer, Vitaliy Klichko, at the head of the joint electoral list. Gaining 372,931 votes (1.47 percent), the party did not achieve the minimum to be elected to parliament. But, taking into consideration the limited time for its electoral campaign, it managed a remarkable success in the local elections. 361 representatives of the Civic Party PORA were elected to local councils at different levels.

A further organization that has been created in the aftermath of the campaign is the International Democracy Institute (IDI). This is a nongovernmental institution that aims at supporting democratic processes in Central and Eastern Europe, by bringing together the knowledge and experience of democratic movements in the region, facilitating exchange between civic activists and experts and at building Ukraine's regional leadership in the field of democracy assistance. IDI's priority countries include Belarus, Russia, Azerbaijan, Kazakhstan and Moldova.

Finally, a range of nongovernmental organizations have emerged from the campaign (among them the NGOs Civic Campaign PORA and *Nova PORA*) and aim at furthering the accomplishments of the campaign and at becoming watchdogs of democracy in Ukraine. The priority spheres of activity of these NGOs include the fight against corruption, public information, voter education, election monitoring and the promotion of Euroatlantic integration.

Chronology

March 9, 2004
The civic campaign PORA and its concept are publicly launched on the website www.hotline.net.ua.

April 14 – 18, 2004
Campaign activities begin with a first seminar for 70 regional leaders in Uzhhorod.

April 18, 2004
The campaign's methodology is tested during municipal elections in Mukacheve. After the falsification of the election results, PORA activists start protest actions that finally lead to the resignation of the illegitimately declared winner of the elections.

April 27, 2004
The official website of PORA is launched at www.pora.org.ua.

May – July, 2004
Practical tests of the campaign's methodology continue during interim elections to the *Verkhovna Rada* (parliament) in Odessa (May 30) and in Poltavska oblast (June 20), and during municipal elections in Vakrusheve and Luhansk oblast (July 11).

August 1 – 8, 2004
A training camp entitled *"PORA pochynaty"*, or "Time to begin", is organized for more than 300 PORA activists in Eupatoria, Crimea.

August 7, 2004
PORA supports the protest actions of students in the town of Sumy against the illegitimate merger of local universities and later joins a march of Sumy students on Kyiv.

August 1 – November 21, 2004
The PORA campaign goes nationwide. The first of several stages of the campaign, "Time to stand up", begins. Over the next months, the stages "Time to think", "Time to vote", "Time to win", "Time to understand–they lie" and "Vote or you'll lose" follow.

September 12, 2004
Municipal elections in the town of Zdolbuniv in Rivnenska oblast provide an occasion for the further testing of the PORA campaign methodology.

September 20 – November 21, 2004
As a preventive measure against election fraud, polling station commissioners are informed about their criminal liability in the case of any falsification of election results.

September 29, 2004

PORA conducts a nationwide action in which appeals to conduct the elections in a fair and democratic manner are handed over to members of all 225 territorial election commissions.

October 1 – 31, 2004

In cooperation with the Freedom of Choice Coalition, PORA conducts nationwide monitoring of the drawing up of voter lists and reveals irregularities in up to 10 percent of all cases.

October 14, 2004

PORA announces its initiative to create a "Black List" of state officials and employees implicated in repression against PORA activists, students and members of other public organizations.

October 15 – 31, 2004

A wave of repression against PORA by state authorities ensues, including the fabrication of criminal cases, arrests of PORA activists, searches at the Freedom of Choice Coalition office and at the apartments of activists. PORA responds with a series of activities entitled "We are not terrorists".

October 20 – November 21, 2004

The "Orange Wave" is launched, in which the mass distribution of orange ribbons, scarves and clothes takes place. Strike committees are created in universities and institutes of higher education across Ukraine, with the aim of organizing mass protests by students in the case of electoral fraud.

October 21, 2004

PORA transforms from an information and education campaign into a civic campaign aimed at organizing the active protection of the election results, with a central focus on "direct action" including the staging of mass protests.

October 31, 2004

The first round of the presidential elections takes place and is observed by PORA activists.

November 1 – 21, 2004

The information campaign "Everyone for the protection of the elections" and "Vote, or you'll lose" is carried out.

November 6 – 21, 2004

Protests are launched against manipulations that took place during the first round of the presidential elections. A tent camp *PORADiy* is established on Kontraktova ploshcha near the National University Kyiv-Mohyla Academy.

November 21, 2004

The second round of the presidential elections takes place and is observed by PORA activists. That morning PORA activists block a bus leaving for Poltava carrying people intending to vote with absentee ballots. In the evening, a column of PORA activists marches from Kontraktova Ploshcha to Maidan Nezhalezhnosty.

November 22, 2004

A tent camp is set up on Khreshchatyk in central Kyiv. This camp is to become the epicenter of popular protest during the Orange Revolution.

November – December 2005

Protests are systematically broadened to include a blockade of the building of the presidential administration (November 24), tent camps near the *Verkhovna Rada* (November 28), the residence of outgoing President Leonid Kuchma (December 3) and the premises of other state authorities.

December 14 – 24, 2004

A motorcade entitled "Train of Friendship" travels 3,700 km across the Eastern and Southern regions of Ukraine to spread the "spirit of the Orange Revolution" and to advocate for unity and democratic development in Ukraine. Concerts, rallies and photo exhibitions are held.

December 26, 2004

The third round of the presidential elections takes place and is observed by PORA activists. Observers conclude that this time the elections meet international standards. Viktor Yushchenko wins with 51.99 percent of the vote.

January 23, 2005

The official inauguration of the legitimately elected president of Ukraine, Viktor Yushchenko, takes place in Kyiv.

January 29, 2005

An official ceremony is held to mark the completion of the civic campaign PORA.

PORA activists at a training camp at Eupatoria, August 2004.

PORA campaign sticker: "It's time to understand!". 1+1 state TV channel. "They are lying!".

"Don't be chicken!".

Protestor chained to a state building. Placard reads: "I am not a terrorist!".

PORA activists during a demonstration in Kyiv after the election fraud.

Protest during the Orange Revolution in Kyiv.

Security forces block the streets of Kyiv.

Tent city at Kreshchatyk in Kyiv. Thousands of Ukrainian citizens take up residence in the tent city as the protests snowball.

"PORA – Vanguard of Victory".

PART II: COMPARISONS

DIFFERENT AUTHORITARIANISMS, DISTINCT PATTERNS OF ELECTORAL CHANGE

Vitali Silitski

The sequence of democratic breakthroughs in postcommunist Eurasia, often referred to as color revolutions, has dramatically reshaped the political landscape in the region and has raised expectations that a contagious spread of democratic impulses will give rise to further democratic development. Unlike the revolutions of 1989 that brought liberal democracy to the Western rim of the former communist world, this new wave of democratic transitions has spread to far more culturally and geographically diverse polities from, Slovakia in Central Europe to Croatia and Serbia in the Balkans, from Georgia in the Caucasus to Ukraine in the Western CIS and finally to Kyrgyzstan in Central Asia. These events have cast grave doubt on the propositions of many commentators that civilization fault lines safeguard the region from democratic impulses and that parts of the region are inherently unfit for freedom and the rule of law.

The role of elections was pivotal in galvanizing all these democratic breakthroughs: from Slovakia to Georgia, people did not merely rise up against bad kings, they made and then defended a conscious choice in favor of democracy. The mix of self-organization, readiness for self-sacrifice and restraint shown by citizens, especially in the context of the more dramatic events that took place in Serbia, Georgia and Ukraine, was admirable. And, even in Kyrgyzstan, where the revolution was chaotic and violent, the situation settled down much faster than critics anticipated.

The victory of the political oppositions in securing electoral change, with the support of the nationwide civic movements analyzed in detail in this volume, re-opened avenues for democratic development in several countries. Ironically, they have also made postcommunist politics less democratic in some others. Most post-Soviet states unaffected by the wave of electoral revolutions recorded a regression on both political rights and civil liberties in 2005.[1] This deterioration is in many respects a

---

1 According to the Freedom House Nations in Transit survey, political conditions worsened in Azerbaijan, Belarus, Kazakhstan, Moldova, Russia, Tajikistan, Turkmenistan and Uzbekistan in 2005. Out of the "non-revolutionary" cases, only Armenia recorded a slight improvement. The situation in Kyrgyzstan also deteriorated, in spite of, or, as will be explained in this chapter, because of, the nature and dynamics of the "Tulip Revolution". Nations in Transit surveys for 2005 and 2006 are available online at http://www.freedomhouse.hu/nit2005.html and http://www.freedomhouse.hu/nit2006.html, respectively. For the methodology Freedom House uses to prepare its ratings, see: http://www.freedomhouse.org/template.cfm?page=35&year=2005.

direct consequence of the anxiety of surviving autocrats about the possibility of democratic contagion spreading to their countries and ousting them from power. As will be explained further in this contribution, not only do such leaders react to changes occurring elsewhere in the region, they also preempt them by doing away with opponents, restricting the activity of NGOs, criminalizing democracy assistance and targeting other potential threats, even though they are unlikely to effectively challenge authoritarian power in the near future.

As a result, the wave of change is visibly fizzling out. Elections in Moldova, Tajikistan and Azerbaijan in 2005 and in Belarus and Kazakhstan in 2006 have all ended with confirmation of the *status quo*, as the attempts of the oppositions to mount effective challenges were easily rebuffed. In more tragic circumstances, the bloody suppression of rebellion in the Uzbek town of Andijan in May 2005 confirmed the length to which some of post-Soviet incumbents will go to cling to power.

Given this general trend, the overthrow of President Askar Akaev in Kyrgyzstan following the rigged parliamentary elections in February 2005 stands out as a notable exception.[2] After all the setbacks and acts of repression that have occurred in the region following the Orange Revolution, the question "who is next?" seems to have become increasingly irrelevant. Instead, it is questionable whether further democratization can be realistically expected anytime soon and a more pertinent question seems to be whether or not the age of color-coded revolutions has, in fact, come to an end.

Unraveling Electoral Breakthroughs: Three Forms of Regime Change

While the future of further democratization in the post-Soviet space may be hard to predict, these initial considerations undoubtedly indicate that developments in countries that transit to democracy through elections do affect realities in countries that have not done so, so far. This being said, to understand the political prospects of the countries of the former Soviet Union that currently remain authoritarian and that move towards even more repressive forms of non-democratic rule, requires a reassessment of the factors and reasons that were conducive to the occurrence of recent democratic breakthroughs. This chapter seeks, through such a reassessment, to challenge some of the views that have become popular in the wake of the several color revolutions that have taken place and, particularly, since the Orange Revolution in Ukraine.

Take, for example, the widespread idea that recent democratic change represents a "wave" of revolutions. It is always difficult to determine causal links between

---

2 For an in depth analysis of the Kyrgyz case, see Vitali Silitski, "Beware of the People", Transitions Online, 31 March, 2005.

separate cases of transition to democracy. It is even harder to prove that these causal links are prime movers of transition.[3] Are the recent democratic revolutions in postcommunist Eurasia, then, a wave or, in a somewhat cynical definition of history, "just one damned thing after another?".[4] One can argue that the connection between the separate episodes of regime change in this particular sequence is evident and substantial. All of the recent revolutions have occurred in the era of Internet and mobile communications, of global media and of a highly versatile international civil society with regional networks of democracy activists. Today, inspirational images of people power, ideas and organizational know-how spread at the speed the newest technology can afford. Once "home" revolutions are completed, their organizers move on to new territories, share experience and train new cohorts of aspiring democracy activists. OTPOR in Serbia lent its expertise to KMARA in Georgia, PORA in Ukraine and Kel-Kel in Kyrgyzstan. The approach of IZLAZ 2000 in Serbia can be easily traced back to OK '98 in Slovakia and to the mass mobilization campaigns witnessed in Romania in 1996, or maybe even further back to the first-ever *electoral revolution*[5], which took place in the Philippines in 1986.

Yet, even if all these transitions are considered to be a part of a wave, it is obvious that there have been significant differences between the different cases of regime change, especially as regards the form in which they came about. Thus, elections in Slovakia in 1998 and Croatia in 2000 were *revolutionary* in their consequences, as both countries rid themselves of obvious authoritarian tendencies in political life and firmly put themselves on track towards liberal democracy and European integration. However, the events in these countries were not *revolutions*.[6] Instead, transition occurred in both cases through regular voting exercises conducted in a mostly free

---

3 Michael McFaul, "The Fourth Wave of Democracy and Dictatorship: Compromise and Non Cooperative Transitions in the Postcommunist World", World Politics, vol. 54, no. 2 (January 2002), pp. 212-244.

4 This expression is attributed, alternately, to Winston Churchill and Arnold Toynbee.

5 There are two ways to define electoral revolutions. One is procedural and refers to the situation where "the emergence of two groups claiming sovereign authority over the same territory and the subsequent attempt by the revolutionary victors to destroy the political and economic institutions of the ancien regime" and occurs as a result of contested elections; see Michael McFaul, "Refocusing American Policy toward Russia: Theory and Practice", Democratizatsiya, vol. 6, no. 2 (Spring 1998), pp. 326-246, quote: 331. The second, outcome-oriented, definition is given by Bunce and Wolchik, who consider electoral revolutions as voting exercises that "have had political consequences that have been far more significant for the future of democracy than 'normal electoral politics'"; see Valerie J. Bunce and Sharon L. Wolchik, "Defining and Domesticating the Electoral Model: A Comparison between Slovakia and Serbia", CDDRL Working Paper, no. 61, Stanford University, May 2006, p. 6. For the purpose of the present analysis, an electoral revolution shall be defined in procedural terms and refer to elections with revolutionary consequences, but without a revolutionary situation in process, as in the case of "transformative elections".

6 See definition by Michael McFaul in "Refocusing American Policy toward Russia: Theory and Practice", Democratizatsiya, vol. 6, no. 2 (Spring 1998), pp. 326-246, quote: 331, op cit.

and fair manner. The election results were credible and were accepted by all the contestants. One can call this mode of transition *transformative elections.*

The transitions in Serbia in 2000, Georgia in 2003 and Ukraine in 2004 to 2005 were *electoral revolutions.* Unlike transformative elections, they only began, but did not finish, with the victory of the opposition in the elections. Once the authoritarian incumbents tried to deny the victory of the opposition and to falsify the election result, the opposition mobilized and took to the streets. Electoral revolutions are, thus, two-step processes, combining regular electoral exercises with a popular uprising to overcome vote rigging and confirm opposition victory in a forceful, yet nonviolent, manner. Due to this duality, electoral revolutions are essentially legalistic: the legitimacy of the opposition power claim is derived from the institutions maintained by the authoritarian incumbents, whereas society is mobilized to make the system work according to its written rules. The legalism of electoral revolutions comes at a certain price, however. While it ensured that transitions were orderly and bloodless (the old regimes were automatically replaced by new leaders possessing legitimate authority to sustain order), it also validated the institutions of the old regime, thus, denying the victorious democrats a fresh start.

The regime change that took place in Kyrgyzstan in 2005 was exceptional and cannot be classified as either a transformative election or an electoral revolution. Rather, it can be more or less viewed as a revolution in the conventional sense. Although it was triggered by rigged parliamentary elections, the forces that were key to overthrowing the old regime (it was rural under-classes, rather than civil society and urban sophisticates who led the change) and the logic of mass mobilization (which began at the periphery, not in the capital) were different compared to electoral revolutions in Serbia, Georgia or Ukraine. No less importantly, as the opposition did not win the ballot, the "illegitimate" revolution created a power vacuum that resulted in violence and protracted political turmoil.

The Tulip Revolution may be considered the result of a collision between two conflicting trends engendered by the previous, more conventional, electoral revolutions. It can be said that forces of contagion (there is no doubt that the Kyrgyz opposition was invigorated by the examples of other successful revolutions, particularly that of Ukraine) unwound a bit faster than the forces of preemption. The Akaev regime was prepared for something similar to what happened in Ukraine (which he demonstrated by denying the opposition a meaningful result), but was at a loss when things developed according to a different, unwritten and more chaotic scenario. The irony of the turnaround in Kyrgyzstan is that most revolutionary in form, it was also the color-coded revolution that brought about the least revolutionary consequences, that is, any prospect for the establishment of a mature, liberal democracy.

This, however, demonstrates the limits of revolutionary contagion and the extent to which those limits are inherent to the dynamics of the process. The pattern of regime change is invented in countries with more favorable domestic pre-conditions. It does spread further by virtue of demonstration, as the discovery of the "recipe for change" empowers aspiring oppositions with a new repertoire of approaches and motivates them to challenge authoritarian power, even in their less favorable domestic circumstances. However, as "the cross-national impact of precedent increases, (...) it is joined with weaker and weaker local structural support for change."[7] When revolutions begin to be driven more by contagion than by the domestic conditions, they are increasingly characterized by "declining mass participation, more violence and less powerful democratic consequences."[8] In the end, local conditions prevail over the contagious spirit of change and they stifle the wave. Moreover, as episodes of regime change put surviving incumbents on alert, the tide can even be turned back.

Domestic Sources of Electoral Change 1: Unconsolidated Authority

The self-limiting nature of democratic contagion turns attention to the domestic factors conditioning transition to democracy. One obvious aspect is the institutions of the old regime. In fact, the degree of institutional openness to free and fair elections determined to the greatest extent the *form* (if not altogether, the fact) of transition by creating the minimum conditions for democratic challenges to entrenched power. Thus, democratic revolutions were only achieved through transformative elections if the integrity of the electoral process was not substantially violated by authoritarian incumbents. This was particularly the case in Slovakia, a country that even amidst the abuse of power and crackdowns on civil liberties by the national populist government of Vladimír Mečiar, maintained the integrity of the electoral process. As a result, when his party won fewer seats than necessary to form a government in September 1998, he simply bowed out and quit.

Politics were more restricted and the electoral process was more abused under the rule of President Franjo Tuđman in Croatia. In fact, with its Gaullist constitution, codified electoral rules advantageous to the ruling party, a record of electoral manipulation and attacks on political opponents, Croatia was a classical example of competitive authoritarianism, alongside countries like Ukraine, Russia and even

---

7 Valerie J. Bunce and Sharon L. Wolchik, "International Diffusion and Post communist Electoral Revolutions", Communist and Postcommunist Studies, vol. 39, no. 3 (September 2006), pp. 283-304, quote: 287.
8 Ibid.

Serbia.[9] However, Tuđman's death in late 1999, just a few months before the parliamentary elections, intervened conveniently to throw the regime built around the charismatic president into total disarray, disabling its machine of abuse and denying it a chance to win in a fair contest.[10]

Electoral revolutions, then, occurred in institutional environments that simultaneously combined both the logics of authoritarianism and democracy. Competitive authoritarian regimes were closed enough not to allow completely fair elections and sufficiently open to give the opposition a legitimate space for contestation. As a rule, incumbents did not possess total control over the institutions of state, local administrations and, in some cases, even the courts. This particular dualism was created by the way in which these hybrid regimes developed. After all, incumbents built their authority on electoral legitimacy and tried to present a semblance of democracy by admitting a certain level of contestation and a degree of transparency in elections. This allowed for the development of an opposition in parliaments and between elections. Eventually, these *nuclei* grew into forces capable of challenging incumbents.

The institutional duality of competitive authoritarianism was also replicated in state-society relations and allowed extensive and legitimate space for independent organization, social autonomy, civil society and independent media, including TV and radio broadcasting. Decentralization of power and influence was also achieved to varying degrees through economic means, as consolidated control was absent not only in politics, but in the business sphere, which secured domestic financial bases for the opposition.

Competitive authoritarianism worked smoothly to the extent that incumbents managed to validate their authority through partially controlled and manipulated elections. However, when they were no longer able to do so, the ploy failed and paved the way for democratic change. In these moments of crisis, the dualism of competitive authoritarian rule played in favor of the opposition. Partially decentralized authority hampered attempts to cover up vote rigging and to crack down on popular protest. Independent media, particularly electronic media, mobilized people onto the streets. And, the significant independence of parliaments and courts ensured legal solutions to political crises, which incumbents were then compelled to accept.

---

9 Competitive authoritarianism refers to political regimes that, while falling short of democracy, "also fall short of full-scale authoritarianism. Although incumbents in competitive authoritarian regimes may routinely manipulate formal democratic rules, they are unable to eliminate them or reduce them to a mere façade (...) As a result, even though democratic institutions may be badly flawed, both authoritarian incumbents and their opponents must take them seriously"; see Stephen Levitsky and Lucan A. Way, "The Rise of Competitive Authoritarianism", Journal of Democracy, vol. 13, no. 2 (April 2002), pp. 51-65, quote: 53f.

10 Even while Tuđman was alive, the opposition had a commanding lead in the polls. Not only did his death accelerate events, the ruling HDZ proved unable to put forward a candidate capable of competing with the opposition nominee, Stipe Mesić; see Fisher and Bijelić in this volume.

Unconsolidated power in competitive authoritarian regimes also had social roots. Many of these regimes were "pluralistic by default". The multitude of social, cultural, economic and political cleavages in these societies ensured that politics was fragmented and power dispersed, simply because no single force or individual could grab it all. These societies lacked both the homogeneity that would allow for the emergence of primitive *sultanistic* rule, as well as an overarching democratic political culture of consensus and compromise. On the one hand, such divided polities play into the hands of the incumbents, by giving them a ready social base and a ready sense of purpose to "protect" their loyal following from dangerous "others", such as pro-western liberals, nationalists or a combination of the two. On the other hand, a divided polity also means that the opposition can mobilize those social forces left behind by the incumbent power-holders.

Domestic Sources of Electoral Change 2: Leadership and Hegemony Advantage

Yet, institutions alone do not pre-determine political outcomes. Regime change can only occur once the social demand for political change is firmly in place and once a credible and sufficiently united democratic opposition with a leader capable and worthy of election has emerged. The emergence of social demand is not simply and exclusively determined by the deterioration of economic conditions, unbearable poverty and public resentment of corruption among those in power. While the voting publics in Belgrade, Tbilisi and Kyiv were truly angered at their leaders' ongoing excesses, they were equally prone to repeatedly vote down democratic candidates in similarly dire, if not worse, economic circumstances throughout the 1990s.

Discussions about the supply side of the equation, or the availability of effective democratic agency, often place emphasis on the mobilization of public protest by groups, such as OTPOR in Serbia, KMARA in Georgia or PORA in Ukraine. Without a doubt, these groups played an important part and an indispensable role in the democratic transitions in those countries. They demystified the regimes and unmasked their primary weaknesses, including fear of their own people and especially of young people. The members of these groups motivated their parents to become active and they rallied crowds for the post-election protests. However, youth movements did not win the elections *per se*. They only helped to defend victories achieved by democratic politicians.

The experience of Belarus confirms that civil society, without the existence of a strong political opposition and without a credible opposition leadership, is essentially powerless. It can mount a strong moral challenge to the dictator, but not a political one. In 2001, when the opposition campaign for the presidential elections tried to steer towards the Serbian scenario of an electoral revolution, Belarus could boast its own replica of OTPOR, called ZUBR (Bison). There also existed a rather sophisticated and reasonably well-organized NGO campaign geared towards voter mobilization. Yet, Belarus was nowhere close to developing the powerful opposition movement that, for example, the Democratic Opposition of Serbia was. No credible opposition leader was available to lead the movement, as did Koštunica in Serbia, Saakashvili in Georgia or Yushchenko in Ukraine. And, of course, the institutions of Lukashenka's power had already been fully consolidated to the extent necessary to deny any degree of fairness in the elections. The failure of the political opposition also doomed civil society to failure. History repeated itself in many respects during the March 2006 presidential elections. Although the opposition achieved a high degree of unity and conducted a vigorous campaign, its challenge for power was rather feeble and unconvincing to society. Mass protests that erupted after election day on March 19, 2006, surprised many observers with their initial size and determination. However, opposition leaders had little idea how to manage and direct these protests, since they were unable to declare victory for their candidate, Aleksandar Milinkievič, and thus, to set objectives for the protest. A spontaneous and disorganized action by civil society, it quickly fizzled out and was easily put down by the authorities.[11]

If considering the opposition, two political advantages have been critical for ensuring democratic change in the most recent cases of transition to democracy. The first is *leadership advantage*.[12] Electoral revolutions, in particular, require a combination of various factors, including opposition leaders who can, with equal success, win votes and rally crowds to street protests, two tasks that are hard to combine. Milošević might have been bankrupt by 2000, but no one except Koštunica could beat him (and he needed Zoran Đinđić's help to rally the streets and neutralize Milošević's henchmen). Kuchma annoyed and antagonized Ukrainians in both the country's East and West, but without Yushchenko, the Orange Revolution against Kuchma's chosen successor would have had little chance of even starting (and it might not have ended as it did without the flair and determination of his then second in command, Yulia Tymoshenko). And, it is even harder to imagine the Rose Revolution in Georgia without the persistence and charisma, the risk-taking and the ability to make impossible decisions that was demonstrated by Mikheil Saakashvili (who also had a key lieutenant to manage the revolution backstage, the late Zurab Zhvania). After all, he managed to organize the ouster of Shevardnadze in the context of parliamentary elections, in which the office of the president was not even at stake.[13]

---

11 For more on the March 2006 presidential elections in Belarus, see Vitali Silitski, "Belarus: Learning from Defeat", Journal of Democracy, vol. 17, no. 4 (October 2006), pp. 138-152.

12 Leadership advantage refers to the electoral and mobilizational capacities of the democratic opposition usually dependent on the appeal, charisma and (or) organizational skills of its leader.

13 Of course, this description somewhat simplifies the leadership factor. In all three cases of electoral revolution, there were tandems between popular leaders (Koštunica, Saakashvili and Yushchenko) and effective opposition managers (Đinđić, Zhvania and Tymoshenko).

The opposition's leadership advantage in all these electoral revolutions was nicely complemented by the complacency of the incumbents. Milošević sincerely believed he could win 70 percent of the votes and he even amended the constitution to arrange for direct presidential elections. Shevardnadze admitted after his downfall that he could not imagine youngsters shouting at him, let alone overthrowing him. By contrast, Kuchma and Yanukovych were alert to the risks. However, even they considered their task easier than it actually was, as a strong vote for the incumbent prime minister in the East and unlimited administrative control of Eastern provinces suggested that, if necessary, electoral fraud would be easy to organize and could be relatively limited in scale. That logic eventually proved disastrous, as widespread election rigging in one region proved to be just too obvious.

The second important factor that ensured the opposition's domination in the electoral politics of unconsolidated autocracies was the occurrence of a remarkable shift in *hegemony advantage* in favor of the opposition.[14] Hegemony has been crucial in all the recent democratic breakthroughs for one simple reason. All of the discussed countries were formerly parts of multi-ethnic federal states (Czechoslovakia, Yugoslavia and the Soviet Union). The collapse of communism ushered them into the era of independent national development, at the beginning of which authoritarian politics could be justified by the necessity of state- and nation-building. The ability of the opposition to equate, or at least reconcile, the notion of the nation with democracy was a crucial factor in denying legitimacy to authoritarian politics and their protagonists. Overall, the shift in hegemony advantage "undermined incumbent capacity and facilitated opposition mobilization even when civil society was weak."[15] The recovery of hegemony advantage was facilitated wherever incumbents claimed democratic credentials and tried to develop positive relations with the West, thus, engaging in policies and discourses that legitimized democratic opposition and civil society.

In those countries that experienced democratic breakthroughs through transformative elections, one could easily cede some ground to the Huntingtonian argument,[16] as it was hardly possible for Slovakia and Croatia to indefinitely justify authoritarian rule by pointing at the democratic West as a civilizational enemy. The picture was radically different in Serbia, where the anti-western overtones of Serbian nationalist mythology provided seemingly solid foundations for the authoritarian rule

14 Hegemony advantage can be understood as the capacity to connect the political agenda to identity. A position gains hegemony advantage if it manages to formulate identity in anti-incumbent and, moreover, anti-authoritarian terms. This term is closely connected to and inspired by what Lucan Way defined as "anti-incumbent identity"; see Lucan A. Way, "Authoritarian State Building and the Sources of Regime Competitiveness in the Fourth Wave: The Cases of Belarus, Moldova, Russia and Ukraine", World Politics, no. 57 (January 2005), pp. 231-61.

15 Ibid, p. 232.

16 Here, reference is made to the concept of civilization and the connection made by Samuel T. Huntington between western culture and the spread of democracy in his 1998 book, "The Clash of Civilization and the Remaking of World Order".

of Milošević.[17] His downfall is widely associated with the disenchantment of Serbs with nationalism. Following the catastrophic consequences of the defeat in Kosovo in 1999, Milošević failed to maintain the trust of the nationalists, that is, those who had initially entrusted him with the establishment of a Greater Serbia. But, it is also important to note that the opposition was increasingly successful in merging nationalism with democracy.

In both Georgia and Ukraine, the shift in hegemony advantage was an unexpected consequence of the semi-authoritarian incumbents' own policies of self-legitimization, state building and their strategies for securing international legitimacy and foreign assistance. This had a particularly profound impact in Ukraine. The failure of the first attempt at democratization in the early 1990s was significantly conditioned by the fact that, in the context of electoral competition, pro-western Ukrainian nationalists were at a numerical disadvantage in comparison to profoundly Sovietized, Russified and "Creolic" political and cultural forces in the Eastern and Southern parts of the country.[18] The ideological hegemony of nationalism in Ukraine was gradually strengthened during the 1990s, as the Ukrainian national revival was supported by incumbents who found it an acceptable solution for legitimizing their own status as a ruling elite in the independent state.[19] With this came an endorsement of the fundamental political and ideological content connected to the national discourse, as well as legitimacy for democracy promotion, cultural exchanges and a variety of training and education programs for both students and government officials. Young Ukrainians not only grew up in an independent Ukraine and were educated in the Ukrainian language, but they were also equipped with a different quality of education, skills, worldview, aspirations and habits of the heart as compared with their parents and grandparents.

Nationalism was a mixed blessing for prospects for democracy in Georgia, which experienced a brief and tragic period of homogenizing authoritarian nationalism under Zviad Gamsakhurdia in 1990 to 1991.[20] Georgia's pro-western orientation under Shevardnadze was partly a by-product of the dependency of the entire country on foreign aid in the aftermath of the civil war, as much as of the government's

---

17 Moreover, for most of Milošević's rule, the opposition tried to challenge his nationalist credentials rather than the foundations of the regime's practical ideology, thus, only strengthening the hegemony advantage of the incumbent.

18 This term is used by Ukrainian academics to identify "Russified" segments of the society that maintain a political rather than ethnic allegiance to the respective independent states. See Mykola Ryabchuk, Dvi Ukrainy: realni mezhi, virtualni vijny (Kritika, Kiev, 2003).

19 See Timothy Garton Ash and Timothy Snyder, "The Orange Revolution", New York Review of Books, vol. 52, no. 7 (April 28, 2005).

20 According to Charles Fairbanks, "[t]he independence movements that triumphed in both Georgia and Azerbaijan at the beginning of the 1990s understood themselves as democratic breakthroughs. Nationalism fueled the early democratic movements and then immensely complicated their successful institutionalization"; see Charles Fairbanks, "Georgia's Rose Revolution", Journal of Democracy, vol. 15, no. 2 (April 2004), pp. 110-124, quote: 111.

efforts to minimize Russian encroachments on Georgian sovereignty and territorial integrity.[21] This resulted in policies that furthered space for rhetoric, discourses and practices favoring the eventual rise of a strong democratic opposition.[22] Shevardnadze's retreat into authoritarianism in the last years of his rule put him on a collision course with the democracy promotion community. Remarkably, he joined Milošević and Lukashenka in evicting the Soros Foundation from Georgia. Authoritarianism led him to adopt a harder-line rhetoric and, thus, only to destroy his own credibility, while boosting that of the democratic opposition that advocated a clear choice in favor of democracy, the rule of law and Europeanization.

Overall, the importance of identity and hegemony emphasizes the cultural dimension of the observed democratic breakthroughs. But, unlike more traditional arguments that tend to define countries as "fit" and "unfit" for democracy because of cultural legacies, culture is here not understood in such rigid terms. Indeed, culture may change in a relatively short period of time to create pre-requisites for democratic transition. In the case of recent democratic breakthroughs, it was the younger generations that, unlike their parents and grandparents, grew up in the context of independent statehood and were exposed to political pluralism, democratic ideas, western education and free media, that eventually tipped the balance in favor of the forces of democracy.

Reversing the Tide:
Preemption and the Authoritarian Internationale

In light of these considerations, the recent democratic changes in Eurasia can be considered to be path dependent. It is important that all recent breakthroughs happened in polities that already possessed a substantial degree of political and social pluralism. However, it is noteworthy that most of today's remaining former Soviet states do not possess the basic social and political features seen in competitive authoritarian systems. Authority is usually firmly concentrated in the hands of the president, with representative institutions serving largely as window-dressing. Centralized control over wealth (particularly natural resources) helps to maintain a fair degree of social cohesion, because it makes it easier to pursue redistributive policies. Kazakhstan and Putin's Russia, as much as Belarus, represent examples of the effective use of social policies to secure public acceptance of authoritarian politics. Elites are extensively monitored and purged so as to prevent

21 In Georgia, Russia was widely viewed as the sponsor of Abkhaz and South Ossetian separatism and as a direct threat to the country's independence.

22 "The Georgian and Azeri elites have been almost unanimous in their desire for a fresh start in at least outwardly western forms. Accordingly, both countries have multiple parties, media nominally free of censorship (Georgia even has more than two television networks) and the rest of the panoply of western institutions"; see Charles Fairbanks, "Georgia's Rose Revolution", Journal of Democracy, vol. 15, no. 2 (April 2004), pp. 110-124, quote: 111, op cit.

the rise of internal opposition and to establish prohibitively high costs for defection into opposition. Independent media either do not exist or are restricted to the print media and forced into self-censorship.

In these regimes, political competition, even when it officially exists, is hardly meaningful. Central Asian presidents, in particular, have enjoyed a long tradition of extending their rule through referenda rather than elections. The political opposition is either banned (as in Turkmenistan and Uzbekistan) or faces severe limits to the available space for genuine competition (as in Russia and especially Belarus). The most prominent and charismatic opposition leaders may face imprisonment on trumped-up charges (commonly made just ahead of elections), character assassination by regime-controlled media or even attempts at outright elimination. The lack of transparency in the electoral process is a rule that has few exceptions.

In more benign cases, the incumbents reshape the political arena to present themselves as the most respectable choice out of what is available to voters. In Tajikistan, for example, an Islamist party is the only visible contender to the dominant party of President Emmomali Rakhmonov. In Russia, the employment of administrative and media resources has framed the political arena so as to leave President Putin and the pro-regime United Russia Party competing in the field with only the communists and ultra-nationalists, both of which are also *de facto* manipulated by the Kremlin.

Furthermore, some of the surviving post-Soviet autocracies lack the versatility or social structure conducive to democratic change. Central Asian states, in particular, remain rural and impoverished societies, where an urban-youth social coalition, a factor that has been significantly conducive to democratic breakthroughs elsewhere, is unlikely to form. Kazakhstan is the exception in this particular instance, but as an oil-based economy, it has other and specific barriers to democratic change. In Russia, the younger generation favors an authoritarian president as much as, and even more so than, the rest of society.[23] The Kremlin uses this fact to organize loyalist youth groups with the clear goal of crowding out and preventing the emergence of an opposition youth movement.

Likewise, there are considerable obstacles to formulating political discourses that would wrench the hegemony advantage away from incumbents. Authoritarian nationalism in Russia takes the form of an official moral doctrine that denounces democracy as western treachery and, more recently, as an attempt to spread terror.[24]

---

23 See, for example, the findings of the Moscow-based VCIOM center, testifying that Putin's policies are highly popular with young people. Available online at http://www.wciom.ru/?pt=41&article=861.

24 Remarkably, President Putin, when addressing the nation in the aftermath of the terrorist attack in Beslan, blamed the country's lack of security and exposure to terror on the break-up of the Soviet Union. He also used the tragedy as a justification for the further tightening of his grip on power by abolishing the direct election of provincial governors.

Lukashenka in Belarus successfully battles democratic- and nationally-minded opposition by imposing a slightly modified Soviet ideology and symbolism, which still has broad popular appeal. In Central Asia, the moral base for the opposition is often provided by Islam, which allows the incumbents, whether rightly or wrongly, to score legitimacy points by presenting themselves as bulwarks against international terrorism inside the countries themselves, in Russia and even in the West. Clearly, such social environments do not favor democratic change.

Preemptive measures come on top of already reinforced authoritarian rule. Revolutionary contagion carried advance knowledge about the threats facing incumbents and likely targets to be taken care of before the conditions for regime change matured sufficiently at home for revolution to get off the ground. Moreover, one also has to take into account autocratic contagion, or the "copycat effect".[25] This refers to when legislation or practices introduced by the regime in one country are copied by others and introduced with the aim of preventing the spread of democratic activism. Not all the attacks against political opponents throughout the former Soviet Union unleashed in 2005 and 2006 were directly prompted by the Orange Revolution, as many of these actions can be considered part of "business as usual" in an autocracy. Nevertheless, many of them were prompted by a sense of the "anti-revolutionary".

Moreover, it is obvious that the autocrats across the region employ remarkably similar strategies to combat democratic contagion.

Removal of political opponents from the political arena

The most notorious examples of the preemptive harassment, arrest and jailing of political opponents have occurred in Azerbaijan, Belarus and Kazakhstan. A major opposition party was banned in Kazakhstan in 2005, where new legislation, making it virtually impossible to establish new political parties (by demanding that they have 50,000 members before applying for registration), was also passed.[26] Belarus introduced new legal regulations severely restricting activities of opposition parties by changing housing regulations so that it has become impossible for local party chapters to rent premises, leading to the deregistration of more than 300 opposition party branches nationwide.[27]

Restriction of political competition by changing electoral laws

The new electoral law adopted in Russia in 2005 has raised the threshold for entering the parliament from five to seven percent, severely impeding the chances of smaller independent parties not controlled by the Kremlin to enter parliament. Changes

25 See Carl Gershman and Michael Allen, "The Assault on Democracy Assistance", Journal of Democracy, vol. 17, no. 2 (July 2006), pp. 36-51, quote: 40.

26 See Kazakhstan report in Nations in Transit 2006. Available at http://www.freedomhouse.hu/nitransit/2006/kazakhstan2006.pdf.

27 See Belarus report in Nations in Transit 2006. Available online at http://www.freedomhouse.hu/nitransit/2006/belarus2006.pdf.

to the electoral law in Belarus in October 2006 have placed new restrictions on election observation and opposition campaigning.

Disruption of independent election monitoring

On the eve of its parliamentary elections in February 2005, Moldova expelled scores of international observers. In February 2006, the Belarusian KGB arrested the leaders of the largest election monitoring NGO (Partnership) on charges of terrorism and running an illegal organization, effectively terminating its activity.

Restriction of the activities of independent civil society and assaults on democracy assistance

The adoption of a new NGO law in Russia in December 2005, significantly impeding the activity of civil society and restricting its access to funding abroad, was openly justified by the necessity to prevent a Ukraine-style electoral revolution in Russia. Even tighter restrictions on NGO activities were introduced in Kazakhstan (under the guise of anti-terrorism laws) and particularly in Belarus, where the activity of organizations that have failed to obtain official registration has become punishable by up to three years in prison. New laws in Belarus also prohibit foreign assistance to support election monitoring or activities advocating foreign "interference into the internal affairs of Belarus" (implying, among other things, human rights advocacy).[28] New regulations in Tajikistan restrict the contact of foreign diplomats and media with representatives of the domestic NGO sector. Branches of international NGOs had been forced to close down in Uzbekistan.[29]

Attacks on independent media and Internet censorship

Opposition press almost entirely disappeared from news stands and subscription catalogues in Belarus just months before the presidential elections in March 2006. The remaining media outlets affiliated to the anti-Putin opposition in Russia have been tamed by lawsuits and forced ownership changes. Scores of journalists reporting for foreign media have been arrested or expelled in Uzbekistan.[30] Censorship of the Internet has been practiced in several CIS states and discussion of joint efforts for controlling the Internet emerged at the CIS Summit in December 2005.

Preemption by imitation

Last but not least, surviving authoritarians have learned to combat electoral revolutions, not only by preemptive strikes against opposition leaders, NGOs, independent press and electoral observers, but also by deploying henchmen, surrogates and loyal media. They have learned, for example, how to convince the public that claims of vote fraud are themselves fraudulent. They have also practiced

---

28 See Belarus report in Nations in Transit 2006. Available online at http://www.freedomhouse.hu/nitransit/2006/belarus2006.pdf, op cit.

29 See Uzbekistan report in Nations in Transit 2006. Available online at http://www.freedomhouse.hu/nitransit/2006/uzbekistan2006.pdf.

30 Ibid.

the bussing-in of loyalists to central squares to stage counter-demonstrations against post-election protests.[31] They have founded and promoted youth movements with "anti-revolutionary" agendas and have co-opted artists and singers in the same way as the democratic revolutionaries have. In brief, they disguise anti-revolutionary activity by making it look revolutionary. President Nursultan Nazarbaev of Kazakhstan went so far as to run a "color-coded" campaign for his re-election in December 2005. A similar pop-culture approach to combat contagion, although without color-coding, was taken by Belarus' Alyaksandr Lukashenka in the run-up to the March 2006 presidential elections.

Preemptive authoritarianism is not a new phenomenon in the region, but recent developments have brought with them a significant increase in attacks on the political opposition and civil society. The success of Ukraine's Orange Revolution, in particular, has demonstrated that the spread of democracy and, by extension, the replacement of incumbent elites, can happen in the former Soviet Union. It convinced Eurasian autocrats that even the mere presence of elements of pluralism, such as independent NGOs and the offices of western democracy promotion organizations, could be a long-term threat.

Preemptive authoritarianism is rapidly gaining an international dimension. The actions of the Putin government in relation to the revolutionary events in Ukraine are exemplary of this trend. Russia discharged an unprecedented range of political, financial and information resources to prevent the victory of the democratic opposition, with the aim of imposing not only a pro-Russian leader, but also a Russian (Putin)-style system.[32] In the aftermath of the Orange and Rose Revolutions, the Kremlin made efforts to undermine the newly democratized states, launching a series of trade blockades and "gas wars" and demonstratively supporting the opposition. In the case of Georgia, Russia has long supported separatist groups threatening the territorial integrity of the country. Economic conflicts were unequivocally presented to the Russian public as reprisals against regimes that dare to democratize and attempt to move out of the Russian orbit. Kremlin-controlled media go out of their way to scare the public with images of gloom and deprivation in post-revolutionary states, spreading the fear of contagion to society.

31 Several such "drill rallies" were organized in Moscow in 2005 by the pro-Putin youth movement "Nashi". Kremlin spin-doctors later confirmed that these were meant to show the opposition that its protests could be stopped not just by the police, but also by ostensibly "private" and "spontaneous" violence.

32 Besides the pre-election visit and de facto campaigning for the pro-regime candidate, Putin gave his blessing to the vote rigging by twice congratulating Yanukovych on his "victory". Yury Luzhkov, Mayor of Moscow, publicly endorsed the secessionist attempts of pro-Yanukovych Eastern regions; see Jan Maksymiuk, "Analysis: Will Ukraine Split In Wake Of Divisive Ballot?", Radio Free Europe/Radio Liberty, November 30, 2004. Top Russian officials, including Duma speaker, Boris Gryzlov, warned against opposition accession to power; see "Compromise in Kiev, Confrontation Abroad", The Economist, December 10, 2004. The amount of Russian spending on the Yanukovych campaign has been estimated as high as US$ 300 million; see Jackson Diehl, "Putin's Unchallenged Imperialism", The Washington Post, October 5, 2004, p. A19.

Although it failed in Ukraine, Russia is fully committed to the protection of its CIS partners from the spread of democracy. The former head of the Russian security council and current CIS Executive Secretary, Vladimir Rushailo, explicitly declared that the "replacement of ruling elites by means of political technologies is a threat to all CIS states and to Russia in particular".[33] The electoral observation missions of the Organization for Security and Cooperation in Europe (OSCE) came under Kremlin attack for "interference" in the Ukrainian elections,[34] and, one year later, in Belarus, for "instigating mass disorder".[35] The Kremlin pressed for the OSCE to relinquish its monitoring activities and even threatened to block the organization's finances if it failed to do so.[36] Missions of election observers from the CIS countries have been dispatched to elections across the region in ever growing numbers with the clear aim of denouncing western and opposition monitoring efforts as falsified or ideologically motivated.

Nevertheless, Russia appears to be more successful in helping authoritarians survive than in exporting autocracy to more competitive environments, like Ukraine. In the run-up to the 2006 presidential elections in Belarus, Russian security forces duplicated Lukashenka's propaganda, declaring that plots by western powers to oust the Belarus strongman had been uncovered. The Russian city of Smolensk was pressured into refusing to print independent Belarusian press. Furthermore, the Kremlin has not hesitated to repatriate political opponents of CIS strongmen who have sought shelter and political asylum on Russian territory.

The growing financial power of this petro-state also means that Russia is capable of spending more to pursue the anti-revolutionary agenda abroad. In 2005, the Russian parliament established for the first time its own funding program for "civil society" groups both in Russia and abroad. In an attempt to clone western democracy promotion institutions, it engages increasingly in funding media, recruiting politicians and even in funding political parties in the near abroad.[37]

A further indication of the internationalized dimension of the Authoritarian Internationale is the Shanghai Cooperation Organization, comprising China, Kazakhstan, Kyrgyzstan, Russia, Tajikistan and Uzbekistan (with observers including Belarus and Iran). The regional economic and security cooperation group redefined

---

33 "Vladimir Rushailo ispugalsya Gleba Pavlovskogo", Charter '97 News, January 13, 2005.

34 Ronald Eggleston, "OCSE Election Monitoring Criticized by Russia", RFE/RL Newsline, April 21, 2005. Available online at http://www.rferl.org/featuresarticle/2005/04/f08f6c6a-6848-4ea3-b6aa-28097ea1e560.html.

35 http://www.apn-nn.ru/event_s/21531.html.

36 Vladimir Socor, "Moscow Defying OSCE on Democracy Front", Eurasia Daily Monitor, November 4, 2004. Available at http://www.jamestown.org/edm/article.php?volume_id=401&issue_id=3130&article_id=2368797.

37 See Ivan Krastev, "Democracy's 'Doubles'", Journal of Democracy, vol. 17, no. 2 (July 2006), pp. 56-62, and Carl Gershman and Michael Allen, "The Assault on Democracy Assistance", Journal of Democracy, vol. 17, no. 2 (July 2006), pp. 36-51.

itself as an instrument of collective defense against the spread of "unwanted" political and economic influence on the region (also protecting it from foreign "meddling" on issues of human rights protection),[38] and has adopted its own "anti-terrorist" policies that, in fact, facilitate the extradition of political opponents from one member to another.[39]

The Authoritarian Internationale is, thus, not restricted to Russia's activities in the CIS or to the CIS itself. China's communist authorities are concerned, as "the fall of post-Soviet authoritarian regimes has raised the uncomfortable specter of a Chinese popular uprising".[40] In response, the Chinese government tightened controls on international NGOs, reportedly sent researchers to Eastern Europe to assess the role of pro-democracy NGOs and to propose counter-measures and have pressured foreign companies to provide better tools for controlling and monitoring the Internet.[41] Chinese dissidents directly associate this new crackdown on free speech with the impact of color-coded revolutions elsewhere.[42]

China is also likely to emerge in the near future as a major source of financial assistance and foreign aid, which can be used by autocratic governments (including those in the post-Soviet space) to relieve domestic tensions and enforce their repressive capabilities. Besides China, Venezuela and Iran have enhanced their presence in the post-Soviet space, using their oil wealth to pursue investments and purchase weaponry. They have most likely also learned some political lessons from recent transitions.[43]

Conclusion: What Is Next?

For now, the surviving post-Soviet autocrats seem to be well-entrenched in power, well-educated, well-organized and well-endowed with resources to protect the *status quo* in the region in the foreseeable future. Paradoxical as it may sound, it is the dynamics and the violent nature of the Tulip Revolution in Kyrgyzstan (even though its outcome was by no means democracy), as well as the horrific images of

---

38 "'Authoritarian Internationale' Leads Anti-Democratic Backlash", Democracy Digest, vol. 3, no. 1 (March 31, 2006); available online at http://www.civnet.org/journals/democracy_digest_3_1.html.

39 http://ru.iras.ir/rendermodule.aspx?SelectedSingleViewItemID=1175&ModuleID=348&rendertype=print.

40 Ying Ma, "Democracy Slow Boat to China", Asia Wall Street Journal, February 15, 2006.

41 The Chinese authorities have reportedly sold their Internet control technology to Belarus; see "'Authoritarian Internationale' Leads Anti-Democratic Backlash", Democracy Digest, vol. 3, no. 1 (March 31, 2006), op cit. Available online at http://www.civnet.org/journals/democracy_digest_3_1.html.

42 Yongding, "China's Color-Coded Crackdown", Foreign Policy, October 18, 2005.

43 A study group similar to one discharged by the Chinese was reportedly organized by the government of Iran. Author's communication with Abbas Milani, fellow at the Hoover Institution, Stanford University.

the slaughter in Andijan, that should be a warning against new complacency among surviving autocracies in Eurasia. The electoral revolution, after all, is not the only possible mode of regime change. The restriction of political competition and growing repression may win incumbents some extra time in power, but may eventually cost them much more than the electoral revolutions cost their colleagues, one of whom, Viktor Yanukovych in Ukraine, not only survived his own downfall, but has already managed to return to power as a democratically elected leader.

Electoral revolutions were facilitated by political and social environments that contained a fair amount of openness and pluralism. The dynamics of post-electoral transitions may well be determined by the absence of these elements of liberty. Consolidated autocracies still suffer from fundamental flaws, including the extreme personalization of power, severity of repression, a tendency to block societal inputs to the government and, last but not least, a determination of incumbents to cling to power, indefinitely. Inevitably, at least some such regimes will face violent overthrow, simply because there will be no other way out for those who want change and once the pressure for change reaches a critical level.[44] Alternative modes of leadership change, such as succession crises, do not promise to be smooth and violence-free either. Only the least personalized and least repressive autocracies are likely to have a chance of transition in a smooth manner.

The sobering implication of the non-electoral character of possible future transitions is that, when not underwritten by a strong and organized opposition and civil society, they are very unlikely to generate democracy. Nevertheless, it is wanton repression that will eventually cost autocratic leaders their rule, rather than any tricks by the democracy promotion community or the actions of so-called "terrorists".

However, active democracy promotion in Eurasia remains something of an uphill struggle. Its presence and financial resources are increasingly unwelcome in the region. The knowledge and expertise accumulated as a result of the recent sequence of successful democratic breakthroughs will be hard to apply to new and more repressive environments. The scenario of the electoral revolution, a revolutionary development in itself just a few years ago, is now well-studied by incumbent autocrats and their security apparatuses. And, while consolidated authoritarianism, bolstered by preemption, denies the possibility of a peaceful, nonviolent transfer of power, democracy promotion institutions are hardly fit (and hardly supposed) to promote actors and develop strategies that employ violence. Rightly or wrongly, the reality of who the "opposition" is, particularly in Central Asia, will pose democracy promotion institutions ethical and other dilemmas about engaging with political Islam.

---

44 A thorough discussion of how repression by the state can provoke revolutionary movements can be found in: Jeff Goodwyn, No Other Way Out: States and Revolutionary Movements, 1945-1991 (Cambridge University Press, Cambridge, 2001).

Against this background, new democratic breakthroughs in the former Soviet Union seem to be a distant prospect. Effective democracy promotion will require not only the continuation of the involvement of international NGOs in the region, but also firm political commitment and support from western democracies. First, democratic change badly needs to develop a more positive image among the voting public in the region, especially as it is routinely presented in surviving autocracies as banditry or as utterly chaotic. Further, those countries that have recently achieved electoral change cannot be left to languish by their democratic neighbors. Instead, democratic consolidation needs to be supported and encouraged, as a positive post-revolutionary experience in these countries may inspire their neighbors in the region.

Secondly, wherever possible, the West must apply systematic political leverage to ensure at least basic respect for free and fair electoral processes and the autonomy of civil society and the independent media in the region. The consequences of further ignoring Russia's slide into authoritarianism will be catastrophic, given its central role in organizing collective defense actions against democratic developments in Eurasia. If even more damaging incidents are to be avoided in the future, it needs to be made clear to the Kremlin that the benefits of engagement with the West are contingent upon certain conditions. Those should include a greater degree of political freedom inside the country and more restraint in the provision of support for the survival of hardliners in the post-Soviet space.

Finally, and regarding the democracy promotion community, it is in urgent need of significantly updating the focus of its fieldwork. On the one hand, the expertise accumulated pre-1989 may be increasingly relevant in relation to current repressive environments, which compare more to repressive state socialism prior to 1989 than to pseudo-democratic post-communism since. Activists need to learn how to continue their work and spread their message when there are fewer and fewer legitimate and legal means to do so. Democracy assistance should no longer just be generous. It must be smart and needs to offer strong intellectual input and practical support in an effort to put democrats just that little bit ahead of the learning curve of autocratic rulers.

Democracy assistance has to be continued. The promotion of responsible and civilized democratic agency is an indispensable investment in the future of the Eurasian states, especially given the fact that extrication from the current authoritarian condition is likely to be accompanied by violence and incivility. Only then will the promise held by recent democratic breakthroughs also come true for those post-Soviet societies where democracy still seems to be a distant and uncertain prospect.

CIVIC ACTION AND DEMOCRATIC POWER SHIFTS: ON STRATEGIES AND RESOURCES

Pavol Demeš and Joerg Forbrig

After the collapse of communism in 1989, Central and Eastern European countries embarked on a path of political and social reform that has been full of unpredictable difficulties and unforeseen outcomes. One of the challenges facing several postcommunist countries was the emergence of neo-authoritarian tendencies that first halted, and soon started to reverse, reforms towards basic standards of democracy, human rights and the rule of law. In the countries where this occurred, including Slovakia, Croatia, Serbia, Georgia and Ukraine, strong and charismatic leaders began to systemically change young democracies, centralizing power, and ultimately engaging in the suppression of political opponents and critical voices, albeit to varying degrees.

Although histories and circumstances of the individual countries differ considerably, there are a number of striking similarities between how neo-authoritarian regimes emerged and, more importantly, how they were defeated. Firstly, all five countries are young states that came into being after the breakup of larger and multi-ethnic entities (Czechoslovakia, Yugoslavia and the Soviet Union). Initially, nation- and state-building took precedence over democracy-building, a fact easily exploited by autocrats to justify their authoritarian policies as being in defense of the nation. Secondly, although considerably authoritarian in nature, these regimes maintained a number of core democratic institutions and processes, including multiparty systems, elections and constitutions, and they declared adherence to European and international standards. Finally, all these countries experienced democratic breakthroughs that followed very similar patterns, involving broad-based and concerted civil society efforts around parliamentary or presidential elections that aimed at ensuring a democratic ballot in process and outcome. These breakthroughs ultimately resulted in democratically elected (and minded) governments taking office.

This form of democratization represented a novelty in Central and Eastern Europe. In 1989, political change occurred (in part) as a result of massive, but largely unexpected and unplanned, protests. By contrast, more recent democratic changes coincided with elections, included the conscious mobilization of citizens and were helped by concerted efforts of organized civil society. The engagement of numerous nongovernmental organizations, civic initiatives, youth groups and election monitors has been acknowledged by many as critical, as has the unity and commitment of pro-democracy political parties, their agreement on political tactics and strategies, and crucially, on who should lead them. At the same time, this role of civil society has triggered a variety of criticisms, ranging from undue interference in democratic politics to the "importation of revolutions" by foreign funding agencies.

This chapter wishes to address aspects of the strategy and resources civil society involvement in electoral breakthroughs involved in Slovakia, Serbia, Croatia, Georgia and Ukraine. It will also try to address some of the common criticism of civil society in this regard. The chapter begins with a brief look back at the development of civil society in postcommunist countries since 1989 and continues with a more detailed overview of the strategic approach taken by civic initiatives in their pre-election campaigns and activities. This is followed by a discussion of the resources available to civil society, including foreign funding. Concluding this chapter is a brief overview of some of the main similarities and differences of civil society engagement in the context of breakthrough elections in the five countries under consideration.

Civil Society in Postcommunist Countries since 1989

Civil society organizations play an indispensable role for the vibrancy of democracy. Among other functions, they sensitize society to pressing domestic and international issues, build cohesion within communities, help citizens to articulate their beliefs and interests, exercise control over those holding political power and provide social services. In the five countries covered here, as well as in Central and Eastern Europe more broadly, civil society structures were able to develop freely only after 1989, as communist regimes in the region did not permit voluntary organizations, in the real sense of the term, to exist and function. Following the collapse of communism, a massive revival of civic association took place, under the newly gained conditions of freedom of expression and assembly, of religious belief and practice and of cooperation with counterparts in the democratic world. This expressed itself in the proliferation of civic associations, foundations and other forms of nongovernmental organization and activities witnessed in the region since 1989.[1]

This upsurge in civic initiative and self-organization was accompanied by an enormous learning process. People in these countries gained new skills, in areas such as creating and developing sustainable and independent organizations, making strategic plans and building partnerships, fundraising from domestic and foreign sources and recruiting volunteers. With the effective achievement of their goals in

---

1 Comparative information on the development of civil society in Central and Eastern European countries can be found in the NGO Sustainability Index published by the United States Agency for International Development (USAID), the annual Nations in Transit report compiled by Freedom House and the Civil Society Index by Civicus.

mind, civil society organizations started to create coalitions, umbrella organizations and networks, taking advantage of advances in information and communication technologies to facilitate their cooperation, within and across borders. With the emergence of training and resource centers for civil society, a new professional field opened up, providing civic actors with the opportunity to learn from the example of local and international counterparts and trainers. Very quickly, thus, civil society organizations became "schools of democracy" for independent and active citizens, who associated the new democratic state with the decentralization of power, the rule of law, the protection of human rights, media freedom and independence and justice. Through their activities in civil society organizations people learned to appreciate these values, engage in their strengthening and mobilize in their defense.

An important part of this learning process was interaction with international partners. Quickly after 1989, an intensive transfer of expertise and resources between established western and emerging postcommunist democracies began. In the course of the 1990s, such transfers also developed between more and less advanced transition countries. Partnerships developed in numerous areas of civic initiative. Fellowship and scholarship programs provided civic activists and citizens, more broadly, with the opportunity of learning from the experience of advanced democracies. Financial support was mobilized on a massive scale by private foundations and public agencies in Europe and North America, which provided resources that were not available locally, supporting the full spectrum of civic activities from humanitarian, social, educational, environmental and cultural projects to politically more sensitive advocacy activities in fields such as human and minority rights, the fight against corruption and monitoring of government agencies and political actors.[2] Indeed, there has been hardly any democracy assistance program that did not include civil society as a specific target for support.

Civil society, a previously unknown realm of social life, had to generate acceptance and support for its activities among the citizenry. This was relatively easy in some areas, such as social welfare, education, leisure and charity, where civic organizations provided services, or environmental protection and the preservation of cultural heritage that are hardly controversial. In other fields, however, public acceptance was much harder to achieve. Organizations and activities challenging public policy, aiming at the control of political and economic power or expressing critical positions towards government and political actors found it more difficult to establish legitimacy in the eyes of the public and the governing elites. For many, any such form of advocacy on the part of civil society was unacceptable, as the public domain was understood as the preserve of state agencies, political parties and, to some extent, the media. Disagreement reached far into civil society itself, as civic

---

2 There are few comprehensive studies of democracy assistance. For U.S. support, see Thomas Carothers, Aiding Democracy Abroad: The Learning Curve (Carnegie Endowment for International Peace, Washington, DC, 1999); for European assistance, see Richard Youngs (ed.), Survey of European Democracy Promotion Policies 2000-2006 (FRIDE, Madrid, 2006).

activists debated the "politicization" of NGOs and their legitimacy to engage in the public sphere. A typical argument was that those wishing to get involved in politics should join political parties.

These questions gained in relevance as independent civic organizations found themselves increasingly at odds with the semi-authoritarian politics of governments in Slovakia, Serbia, Croatia, Georgia and Ukraine. Civil society's capacity to act as a watch-dog of political power and to mobilize protest against its abuse did not escape the attention of ruling political elites. Consequently, governments attempted to silence the civic sector by introducing legislation to limit the space available for its activities, by curtailing its financial and resource base, by orchestrating scandals to discredit civil society organizations and activists in the eyes of the public and, in an attempt to crowd out critics, by providing material and other forms of support to pro-government organizations. These measures posed a considerable challenge to civic organizations in the five countries, forcing some to wind up, and pushing others to withdraw from open engagement in public affairs. At the same time, however, government hostility had an integrating effect on civil society that was actively searching for ways to effectively counteract the pressure to which it was subjected.

Civic Action for Democratic Elections: Key Strategic Features

Towards the end of the 1990s, democratic backsliding and semi-authoritarianism in the five countries under consideration intensified. Democratic institutions were manipulated, state apparatuses abused and propaganda increased. Physical violence was employed against political opponents. Perpetrators did not have to fear prosecution for violations of the law, as the justice systems were largely under the control of government. Politics and business became closely intertwined, as representatives of these regimes and entrepreneurs supporting them were involved in illegal, often criminal, activities. The interest of incumbent regimes and their cronies in maintaining power was self-evident.

Ironically, semi-authoritarian leaders and their supporters realized that if they wanted to maintain their grip on power, they would have to legitimize it through the electoral process by being seen to win a majority of the votes. In preparing for elections, these regimes relied on the support they knew they could muster from some segments of the population, the fear and apathy of others, and ever increasingly, on their ability to rig elections in their own favor. At the same time, however, elections were also potentially a moment of regime vulnerability. Even if not entirely free and fair, limiting political competition or manipulated, elections still presented an opportunity for pro-democracy forces, including civic groups, to appeal to the population for support and to contest the legitimacy of governments. And as the democratic breakthroughs in the five countries would eventually demonstrate, the regimes were wrong to underestimate their own vulnerability in the context of elections. Much taken by surprise, the regimes found themselves ousted. Pressure was exerted by the democratic opposition and the citizens, activated through nationwide information and mobilization campaigns launched by civil society in the run-up to elections. Across the five countries, these campaigns had several key characteristics in common.

Grass-roots activism

Until this most recent series of democratic breakthroughs, there was little tradition of self-organized citizen action in the electoral process in the countries concerned. The prevailing wisdom among politicians and the public at large was that citizens should indeed have the right to vote for their elected representatives, but that it was the role of the state to organize the electoral process, in which political parties would have the opportunity to compete for a political mandate. Civil society was faced with the difficult task of challenging and changing this deeply embedded tradition.

At the outset, this involved an important psychological test. Civic activists had to realize that they could contribute to meaningful political change and that they had every right to enter the electoral arena and develop independent civic activities to ensure free access to information and the fairness of the electoral process, even (or especially) in situations where governing elites openly violated the written and unwritten rules. Once this key psychological barrier had been overcome, the NGO community had to develop new communication skills to be able to engage voters, governmental and political institutions, media and donor agencies, for all of whom the experience was rather new. In each of the countries considered in this book, it was a small group of NGOs active in the areas of civic education, human rights, policy analysis and advocacy that started this process, which eventually snowballed to involve many different kinds of civil society groups from a wide variety of fields.

Civil society representatives realized that they would only be able to have an impact on the course of the elections if they developed comprehensive nationwide efforts to mobilize and inform voters and to monitor the electoral process. These civic efforts typically consisted of one or several national mobilization-information campaigns (for example, OK '98 and "Rock the Vote" in Slovakia, GLAS 99 in Croatia, IZLAZ 2000 and OTPOR in Serbia, KMARA in Georgia, PORA and *Znayu* [I know] in Ukraine) and numerous local, issue based, projects, which targeted specific age or interest groups. The core assumption of these campaigns, and of individual campaign projects, was that properly informed voters would make the right choice, in favor of democracy and against authoritarianism.

Information was provided in a variety of ways. Humor was used to break down the fear of getting involved in anything political that gripped large segments of society, and with great success, as these civic campaigns attracted numerous volunteers, especially young people, who distributed campaign materials, organized concerts and meetings with voters, and other public activities. Creative imagery was developed, including logos, symbols and slogans that provided for clear campaign identities. It was especially important that these campaigns be understood as distinct from those of political parties. Hence, rather than using portraits of politicians, typical for party-political campaigns, they used images of the citizen, clocks with the dial set at five minutes to midnight, open hands or defiant fists, slogans emphasizing change and the importance of the individual vote in elections. The creativity, professionalism and impact of these civic campaigns often surpassed the pre-election efforts of well-established political parties.

A small group of highly specialized NGOs carried out monitoring projects, assessing government performance, voting procedures and media coverage of the elections and the candidates. Important examples of such domestic monitoring NGOs were *Občianske oko* (Civic Eye) in Slovakia, GONG (Citizens Organized to Monitor Elections) in Croatia, CeSID (the Center for Free Elections and Democracy) in Serbia, the International Society for Fair Elections and Democracy in Georgia and the Committee of Ukrainian Voters.[3] Closely related were media monitoring projects, such as the qualitative and quantitative media analyses carried out by MEMO '98, first in Slovakia and later in other countries of the region. These monitoring activities usually attracted a lot of media attention, both domestically and internationally, and the results were often included in the final reports of international election monitoring agencies, including the Organization for Security and Cooperation in Europe (OSCE).

One striking characteristic of governance in the civic campaigns under consideration is that they managed to achieve a high degree of cooperation and efficiency, despite the fact that they were run by nonhierarchical, decentralized and mostly small-scale entities without much previous experience of election-related activities. The large national campaigns established *ad hoc* coordination groups, which developed links with local branches or cooperating voluntary organizations. Special attention was paid to building networks among independent projects in order to minimize duplication and achieve synergy. Activists organizing projects within the campaigns had to overcome many logistical and organizational obstacles, including occasional tensions between various groups involved over tactics, strategies and even issues of public prestige. In Serbia, Georgia and Ukraine, additional difficulties arose when governments started to attack activists and declare their activities illegal. Underground techniques had to be developed, mastered by youth groups like OTPOR, KMARA and PORA.

Nonpartisanship

The aim of a political party's pre-election campaign is to mobilize the largest number of voters possible to vote for their candidates, thereby, ensuring they get into power.

---

3 In 2001, these and further groups founded the European Network of Election Monitoring Organizations (ENEMO).

To ensure that this key democratic political process takes place in accordance with the constitution and the appropriate legislation on elections, state institutions are charged with organizational arrangements for elections. Political parties use their members, professional agencies and volunteer supporters to help them inform the voting public about the programs and profiles of their candidates.

A key feature of the pre-election civic campaigns covered by the cases in this book is that they were developed independently of the competing political parties. These campaigns were activities carried out voluntarily by NGOs and civic groups in order to help citizens to better understand their rights, provide them with objective information about the elections and make sure that state institutions fulfilled their obligation to ensure that candidates would compete according to democratic rules. They did not aim to garner support for any particular political leader. The election materials they developed and distributed, and the activities they organized, were clearly distinct from those prepared by the political parties.

At the same time, and despite their emphasis on independence from any particular political party, these campaigns naturally influenced the political space, by contesting the authority and legitimacy of the incumbent and non-democratic regimes, which tried to monopolize the public sphere. Hence, these campaigns were, inevitably, anti-incumbent in character, stressing as they did the necessity of change and demanding good governance. It was also a key assumption of each of these campaigns that the higher the voter turnout, the better the chances for democratic candidates and parties to do well in the elections. All analyses pointed to the fact that key democratically-minded constituencies and a large number of first-time voters (educated, young, city dwellers) would not turn up at the polls without special efforts to mobilize them.

Under normal circumstances, such civic initiatives would not have been needed. In many ways, these campaigns responded to and compensated for the deficiencies of democracy in the countries under consideration, such as an almost complete lack of objective information provided by free and independent media, the marginalization and even suppression of the political opposition, the absence of an independent judiciary and the clear partiality of the public service. In the absence of these democratic checks and balances, an alternative mechanism had to be found to ensure fair competition between political rivals and independent oversight over the political process.

Nevertheless, and despite their nonpartisan identity, these pre-election civic efforts had to be coordinated, at least for some very practical purposes, with the democratic oppositions. For example, when civic activists organized meetings with voters in various localities around the country, they needed to know if party rallies had been scheduled for that place and time. In addition, and in one crucial respect, the civic and political actors had one important goal in common, that of abolishing semi-authoritarian rule in their country. In the case of Slovakia, for example, the creation of a "democratic round table", consisting of elements of the democratic opposition, trade unions and NGOs, proved to be an effective means of coordinating those common steps that were necessary. The huge protest movements that rallied in the aftermath of rigged elections in Serbia, Georgia and Ukraine are also excellent examples of effective coordination between political and civic actors.

Nonviolence

An important characteristic of the planning and implementation of these civic campaigns was their strict adherence to the principle of nonviolence, even though there was no guarantee that semi-authoritarian regimes, once challenged by civic campaigns, would act with restraint and refrain from harassment, scandal-mongering, and even, outright brutality against civic activists and ordinary citizens. For the campaigns, respect for the rule of law and ethical behavior were crucial and activists received training in how to avoid confrontation and how to behave during a police interrogation. They associated themselves with the long history of nonviolent political struggle, inspired by those led by Mahatma Gandhi and Martin Luther King and drew parallels with the peaceful dismantling of communism in 1989. Youth groups in Serbia, Georgia and Ukraine, in particular, were inspired (and instructed) by practical manuals for nonviolent action, such as Gene Sharp's "From Dictatorship to Democracy".[4]

In addition, civic activists were careful to consult with think tanks, policy analysts, media specialists and legal experts on human rights issues. Where necessary, such NGOs provided legal and human rights support to activists imprisoned or indicted for their involvement in the campaigns. Human rights violations of various kinds and attacks on civic activism were carefully monitored and publicized through independent media, Internet and other channels, to both domestic and international communities. The fact that semi-authoritarian regimes would resort to using force against their own citizens played a significant role in discrediting them in the eyes of their own citizens and the international community.

Adherence to the principle of nonviolence was especially important during the mass protests that took place after the election fraud in Serbia, Georgia and Ukraine, during which the atmosphere often grew extremely tense. State security forces were deployed in large numbers to face down protesting citizens and there was always the risk that standoffs would turn ugly. In these situations, the sophistication and courage of the activists was remarkable and contributed to the fact that these democratic changes happened without a single casualty.

---

4 In order to be more easily and broadly accessible to local activists, this book was widely translated into languages such as Serbian, Ukrainian and Russian.

Youth participation

In the democratic breakthroughs considered here, young people from 18 to 25 years of age played a special role, both as voters (many of them, first-timers) and as a highly engaged group demanding change, testament to which is that a chapter of this book is dedicated specifically to their participation. Some key items in this respect, nevertheless, are worth re-iterating.

The competing political parties, as well as the organizers of the civic campaigns, paid special attention to this age group. Young people are often thought to be less interested in the formal institutions and processes of democracy, such as political parties and elections. At the same time, they are often very sensitive to broader social and political questions, open to new approaches and interested in non-conventional, spontaneous and action-oriented forms of participation. Hence, they are a typical constituency supporting change in society. Public opinion research indicated that young people in the five countries could provide a strong support base for democratic forces, if only they could be mobilized to cast their vote, as well as to inspire other and older voters. If, eventually, very high voter turnout marked the elections in Slovakia (84 percent), Croatia (75 percent), Serbia (71 percent) and Ukraine (77 percent), this was not least due to the engagement of young people.

Moreover, young people were the central carriers and target group of several specialized and highly visible, election-related campaigns, including "Rock the Vote" in Slovakia, GLAS 99 in Croatia, OTPOR in Serbia, KMARA in Georgia and PORA (both yellow and black) in Ukraine. Large scale youth campaigns were especially effective in overcoming the fear of voters to get involved. They attracted young volunteers in high numbers, with a unique mix of creativity, positive attitudes, courage and action, and their logos and slogans became domestic brand names. Youth activists reached out to practically every corner of their countries, and made good use of modern information and communication technologies to extend their reach geographically and in terms of publics. For many young people, the civic campaigns around the elections were the moment that politics became "cool".

To an extent, though, youth groups departed from the principle of nonpartisanship. In more or less subtle ways, these groups named, blamed, shamed and poked fun at autocratic leaders and their abusive practices, through the production and massive distribution of leaflets, stickers, graffiti and other youth friendly materials. The Serbian campaign slogan *"Gotov je"* or "He's finished", developed and massively displayed by OTPOR activists, is an excellent example of the kind of approach taken. These campaigns were highly provocative to the regime and had a high impact on the public. Such approaches have been adopted as part of the standard practice of nonviolent resistance since, and they have influenced youth groups in Georgia, Ukraine and elsewhere.[5]

The role of young people in pressing for democratic change has been much appreciated, as is illustrated by a letter to PORA activists from the leader of the Orange Revolution and Viktor Yushchenko, who subsequently became the president of Ukraine: "I greet the young generation of citizens who, in difficult times, rose up for freedom and democracy in their country. I am proud of your courage, honor and your faith in your own strength to struggle and win. I saw the PORA flag among the others every day. This gave me and the resurgent people strength and confidence. During those days everyone knew that wherever PORA was there would be success and victory".[6]

Pro-democratic and pro-European orientation

In postcommunist countries, where citizens lack long-term experience with democratic political culture, populist politics found particularly fertile ground. Neo-authoritarian leaders supported democracy and the longer-term goal of European integration declaratively, at the same time as stressing the unique features of the domestic situation that set their countries apart from mature and stable European states and that continued to require "special measures". Using state media and a panoply of tried and tested propaganda approaches, such regimes effectively indoctrinated large segments of their own populations. Many people stopped believing that real change was possible, so disappointed were they that the promises made by the politicians during early efforts at democratization in the 1990s were not kept. Others were simply silenced by the regime, losing their livelihoods and positions for speaking out. Any criticism of the leadership or domestic opposition was interpreted as an attack on the nation and state. And, any criticism from foreign democratic governments or international organizations was rejected as ignorant of the domestic situation, as a threat or as interference. In such a situation, the possibilities for pro-democratic and pro-European political oppositions to get a fair chance at competing with the regime were extremely limited.

The emergence of the pre-election civic campaigns brought to the public sphere a new discourse, and with it the makings of a new political culture, by pointing especially to the central importance of citizens, their power and free will to choose the future course of their countries' development. The emergence of a voting citizenry that was well-informed, educated and not afraid became the key aim of all civic initiatives. Naturally, this shift was felt by the regimes as threatening, based as they were on

---

5 In follow-up to the events in Serbia and as testimony to the clear expertise developed by OTPOR in this domain, an international network of trainers and consultants working in the field of nonviolent resistance called the Center for Applied Non Violent Action and Strategies (CANVAS) was founded in Belgrade.

6 This letter addressed the participants of the closing ceremony of PORA in Kyiv on January 29, 2005.

the primacy and impunity of the strong leader and their national-populist discourses. And while governments were prepared for neutralizing political opponents through ersatz electoral competitions, they were not in the least prepared to face up to self-organized citizens demanding information, accountability, fairness, their right to choose their leaders and international oversight of the electoral process.

Throughout these campaigns a new form of patriotism, based on proud, active, citizenship, rather than the aggressive populist nationalism of the regimes emerged. Civic activists used the state flag and symbols, reclaiming them as positive and progressive images, as part of the symbolism of their campaigns. In stressing their desire to "return to Europe", these campaigns made the explicit link between the international isolation (even pariah status) of their countries and the policies of the incumbent regimes. This mobilized large segments of the population and when the breakthrough finally took place, it was felt not only to have been a victory for democratic political actors, but also as a victory of active citizens ready to engage as members of the wider democratic and European community.

The Resource Base of Civic Campaigns: NGOs, Volunteers, Media, Funding

These strategic features of civil society involvement reflect the genuine and homegrown character of recent electoral breakthroughs in Central and Eastern Europe. This is mirrored in the resource bases of these civic campaigns, which consisted of several major elements.

Firstly, civic campaigns emerged as joint efforts of existing civil society structures in the five countries. This cooperation was usually the result of a longer-term learning process, which led civic activists and organizations to the realization that the overarching goal to democratize their countries required concerted action, notwithstanding the pluralism of groups and views that are so characteristic of civil society. In some countries, these campaigns also developed from earlier experiences of NGO coalition building, as in the case of the *Tretí sektor SOS* (Third Sector SOS) campaign in Slovakia in 1996, the anti-war coalitions of NGOs in Croatia and Serbia or of the All Ukrainian Public Resistance Committee *Za Pravdu!* (For Truth) in 2000 and 2001. Important lessons from those earlier efforts included, for example, the implementation of principles of nonhierarchical and de-centralized coordination, a commitment to the far-reaching independence of participating NGOs and the creation of lean, but nevertheless, centralized coordination bodies.[7]

---

7 An interesting example of the nonhierarchical and decentralized nature of the campaigns is that they avoided using the term "leaders", using instead terms such as spokesperson or representative. In the egalitarian community of NGOs, this had important psychological implications.

On this basis, civic campaigns were eventually successful in attracting large networks of NGOs. As reported in the case studies, the OK '98 campaign consisted of 58 independent projects run by NGOs, while GLAS 99 in Croatia saw 35 civic groups unite in the Civic Coalition for Free and Fair Elections. Serbia's IZLAZ 2000 and Ukraine's PORA campaigns brought together more than 150 NGOs each. This provided these campaigns with country-wide infrastructure and reach, a strong presence in local communities, contacts on regional and local levels, knowledge of specific target groups and organizational capacities, such as office support, members and volunteers.

In contributing these organizational resources, individual NGOs were largely autonomous, bound only by very broad campaign parameters, including overall aims, key messages and imagery, which resulted from broad-based discussions among civil society representatives and participating organizations. In turn, the central coordinating bodies that were established for the campaigns focused on a few crucial functions, including the outreach of campaigns to media, donors and political actors.

This genuine grass-roots nature of civic pre-election campaigns is also reflected in their strong volunteer base, a second important resource. Although it is impossible to assess the scale of volunteer involvement precisely, estimates put volunteering within the Serbian IZLAZ 2000 campaign at over 25,000 people, while Ukraine's PORA is said to have benefited from the support of some 35,000 people. Youth groups, too, operated with larger numbers of volunteers. OTPOR in Serbia is estimated to have involved 20,000 activists and Georgia's KMARA is estimated to have mobilized some 3,000 activists.

These are remarkable figures for countries that many observers characterized as beset by apathy, a lack of interest in public affairs and widespread fear of regime retribution. Instead, these figures indicate the growing levels of dissatisfaction among citizens with the political and social situation in their countries and their increasing willingness to engage for change, especially among younger, urban and more educated segments. Thus motivated, volunteers became *the* central resource for civic campaigns, critical for their considerable scale and success in all stages, from the wide distribution of information materials and outreach to citizens to comprehensive election monitoring and mass mobilization during the elections.

A third critical resource for the civic campaigns was cooperation with and support from independent media. Although governments in the five countries had assumed control over most media, several radio and TV broadcasters managed to retain their independence. These included *TV Markíza* and Radio *Twist* in Slovakia, the radio station *B92* in Serbia, *Rustavi 2* television in Georgia, and in Ukraine, TV *Channel 5* and the *Era* radio station, in addition to a variety of print media and internet platforms in each of the countries.

Through these independent media, civic campaigns gained access to a mass audience. They ensured regular and objective reporting about the campaigns, important especially at times when state-controlled media launched attacks to discredit civil society groups. Some media participated directly in election-related projects, as in Slovakia, where TV and radio stations broadcast messages calling on citizens to cast their vote, while *Rustavi 2* in Georgia co-sponsored an exit poll that provided evidence of electoral fraud.

Lastly, financial support for individual campaign projects and the underlying organizational infrastructure involved in their implementation was important. Although NGOs participating in civic campaigns contributed considerable resources and while volunteers added important capacity, many costs could only be covered through direct funding. Since semi-authoritarian governments in the five countries made every effort to deprive civil society of domestic resources, financial support for the election-related activities of civic organizations had to come from foreign donors.

In Slovakia, the OK '98 campaign is reported to have received US$ 857,000 in financial support from foreign funders cooperating within the Donors' Forum, an association of Slovak, European and American foundations, including the British Know How Fund, the Carpathian Foundation, Civil Society Development Foundation (operating with EU Phare funding), the Charles Stewart Mott Foundation, the Children of Slovakia Foundation, the Dutch Embassy, the Foundation for a Civil Society, the Fund of Canada, the German Marshall Fund of the United States, the Jan Hus Educational Foundation, the Open Society Foundation and the United States Information Service.

The GLAS 99 campaign in Croatia had two main funders, the United States Agency for International Development (USAID) and the Open Society Institute (OSI). Additional resources came from the National Endowment for Democracy, Freedom House and the Charles Stewart Mott Foundation in the United States, from the European Commission, the British Know-How Fund, the Westminster Foundation for Democracy, and a variety of western embassies.

Serbia's IZLAZ 2000 adopted the Slovak model of a Donors' Forum, which was composed of the Canadian International Development Agency, the Fund for an Open Society, the Know How Fund of Great Britain, the Dutch and Swiss Embassies in Belgrade, the German interest section in Belgrade and the German Marshall Fund of the United States.

Much smaller amounts of foreign funding were received by KMARA in Georgia and PORA in Ukraine. KMARA reports funds received totaling US$ 175,000 and largely provided by the Open Society Foundation. PORA reports foreign funding totaling

US$ 130,000, provided by Freedom House, the German Marshall Fund of the United States, and the Canadian International Development Agency.[8]

These funding levels and partners represent those that provided funding directly to the five exemplary civic campaigns documented in this book. Other groups and campaigns, such as OTPOR in Serbia or *Znayu* in Ukraine, and a broad range of individual election-related projects and civic organizations in the five countries are likely to have received further financial support from assistance agencies in Europe and the United States.

Nonetheless, these funding levels remain relatively modest and hint at the comparably minor role played by foreign financial support for the emergence and success of civic campaigns aimed at democratic electoral change in Central and Eastern Europe. Contrary to widespread suspicions of "revolutions imported by foreign agencies", democratic change and the civic campaigns that contributed to them were largely homegrown developments that relied first and foremost on impulses and resources from within, in particular individuals, civic groups and society at large.

Adapting and Transferring Civic Campaigns

Many of the strategies, techniques and resources employed by civic campaigns were relevant for all five countries covered by this book, and key elements of these, such as civic advocacy, electoral information and communication, monitoring and mobilization of protest, have been applied in other parts of the world before and after.[9] This should not, however, lead observers to the conclusion that some form of tool box or recipe book exists for ousting semi-authoritarian regimes through electoral change. As was the case for the ouster of communism in Central and Eastern Europe at the end of the 1980s, these more recent democratic breakthroughs, and the civic campaigns that helped to bring them about, were conditioned by a set of political, social, economic and psychological conditions that were particular to each society. It was to these more specific circumstances of postcommunism, and of each individual country, that civic activists had to tailor their civic campaigns.

In so doing, they benefited from significant intra-regional learning processes. Civic activists from Bulgaria and Romania inspired their Slovak colleagues who, with

8 Foreign funding represented a fraction of the expenses of the PORA campaign, which reports total expenditures of over US$ 6.5 million, of which US$ 1.56 million were received in direct financial support largely from local sources, while the remainder was contributed in kind; see Pavol Demes and Joerg Forbrig, "Pora – 'It's Time' for Democracy in Ukraine," in: Aslund, Anders, and Michael McFaul (eds.), Revolution in Orange: the Origins of Ukraine's Democratic Breakthrough (Carnegie Endowment for International Peace, Washington, DC, 2006), pp. 85-101.

9 See for example, National Democratic Institute, How Domestic Organizations Monitor Elections. An A to Z Guide (National Democratic Institute, Washington, DC, 1995), and Robert Norris and Patrick Merloe, Media Monitoring to Promote Democratic Elections (National Democratic Institute, Washington, DC, 2002).

OK '98, pioneered large-scale civic pre-election campaigns and went on to train and support activists in other countries in the region and beyond, as did OTPOR veterans in Georgia, Ukraine and elsewhere, later.

In so transferring experiences, adaptations to the specific circumstances of each country were necessary. Slovakia, for example, clearly had the most favorable political and social conditions, and the most advantageous international environment, of the five countries examined in this book. With its comparably well-developed NGO community, a relatively liberal environment for political opposition and media, and close proximity to the West, it was comparably easier than in other countries to develop and successfully conduct civic campaigns.

By contrast, NGO leaders in Croatia and Serbia operated in a post-conflict situation. The Yugoslav wars had devastated the land as well as the minds of people. The incumbent regimes had only recently demonstrated their propensity to violence. As one Serbian democrat put it "Mečiar was Mother Teresa in comparison to Milošević". It required special courage, moral strength and commitment to the ethics of nonviolence, in addition to great effort, to introduce civic activism in this context. Campaigns like GLAS 99 and IZLAZ 2000 changed the political culture of their countries, as did OTPOR, with its very particular brand of nonviolent protest that played such an important role in ousting autocrats in Serbia and, subsequently, in other parts of the region and the world.

Georgia's KMARA benefited from previous experiences in Slovakia, Croatia and Serbia, but introduced election-related civic activism to the very different post-Soviet environment, additionally complicated by the legacy of a civil war, where regime change was always associated with violence and bloodshed. Young activists were able to overcome social apathy and made a special contribution to the Rose Revolution, sending political shockwaves across the post-Soviet space, signaling hope to hesitant democrats and issuing a warning to self-confident autocrats.

These signals were also received in Ukraine, vast in comparison with the four countries that had already experienced electoral change. Benefiting from these prior experiences, but adjusting them to Ukrainian conditions, the civic campaign developed prior to the 2004 presidential elections was the largest and most complex of all previous civil society efforts, and indispensable for the success of the Orange Revolution. The Ukrainian campaign not only brought about an unprecedented mobilization of citizens, engraved on the public memory in the image of the vast tent camp in downtown Kyiv, but was also based largely on resources generated locally.

In short, the specific political and social conditions in a given country, and the ability of civic leaders to adapt techniques successfully employed elsewhere accordingly, are as important as their skill in mustering the necessary resources for civic campaigns.

Conclusion

The democratic breakthroughs, marked by the electoral victories of pro-democracy candidates in the five countries, were more or less uniformly met with euphoria and enormous, although very often unrealistic, expectations of speedy progress on reform. Once the revolutionary enthusiasm subsided, however, political leaders and ordinary citizens faced the task of adjusting to the new reality, as did civic leaders now that their campaigns had been completed successfully.

In the aftermath of democratic changes, many civic leaders were asked to join new national or local governments in varying positions of authority and influence. Some of the most influential youth activists believed that they could simply transform their campaigns into viable political parties. As both OTPOR and PORA activists had to learn, however, successful civic activism does not necessarily translate into equal success in the formal political arena.

Others chose to remain involved with civil society but they, too, had to re-evaluate their role in public life. If prior to democratic change, reality often presented itself in simple "black and white" terms, with the goal clearly defined and supporters and opponents clearly distinguishable, the situation became much more nuanced and complex under the new democratic conditions. For many, this has turned into a veritable test of their commitment to democratic ideals and of their ongoing resolve to press for reform.

Yet, whatever the difficulties encountered on the further road to democracy, one fundamental change has taken place in all five countries and that concerns the role of citizens in society. Citizens discovered the power they can have, and politicians were forced to accept that citizens have the right to, and are capable of, shaping the democratic process through their initiative and through independent civic organizations. Across these countries, it has become a natural ambition of civil society and the free media to closely monitor the performance of political leaders and public officials, locally and nationally. This continuing role of citizens and their organizations for the political modernization of their countries is the most important legacy of recent electoral breakthroughs to democracy.

YOUTH AND POSTCOMMUNIST ELECTORAL REVOLUTIONS: NEVER TRUST ANYONE OVER 30?

Valerie J. Bunce and Sharon L. Wolchik

Young people, particularly those with higher education, are often the segment of the population most threatening to the *status quo* of political regimes, whether these are democratic, authoritarian or somewhere in between. Youth protests in the United States and what was known as Western Europe in the late 1960s had their parallel in the role of students in the effort to create "Socialism with a Human Face", called the Prague Spring, in Czechoslovakia in 1968. Young people played a large role in the new social movements that developed in Western Europe in the 1970s and 1980s, including the Greens, women's liberation, gay and lesbian and anti-nuclear movements.[2] They also participated in large numbers in the mass protests and demonstrations that helped to bring down communist regimes in a number of countries of Central and Eastern Europe, in the demonstrations in the Baltic States and in the development of national movements that preceded the breakup of the USSR in 1991.[3] Indeed, young people in Slovenia, beginning in the late 1980s, played a critical role in challenging not just communism in Yugoslavia, but also the Yugoslav state, especially with respect to the power of the military. Their challenge, moreover, generated conflicts between the Slovenian and Serbian party leaderships. The Slovenian party eventually sided with the rebellious young people

The authors would like to thank the International Center for Non-Violent Conflict, the Smith Richardson Foundation, the Einaudi Center for International Studies, the Institute for the Social Sciences at Cornell University and the Institute for European, Eurasian and Russian Studies at George Washington University for their support of the project in which the research for this piece took place. The authors would also like to express their gratitude to Vlad Micic, Sara Rzyeva, Nancy Meyers and Melissa Aten for the research assistance they provided.

2 See Herbert P. Kitschelt, *The Transformation of European Social Democracy* (Cambridge University Press, New York, 1994); Joerg Forbrig (ed.), Revisiting Youth Political Participation (Council of Europe Publishing, Strasbourg, 2005); and Nils R. Muiznieks, "The Influence of the Baltic Popular Movements on the Process of Soviet Disintegration", Europe-Asia Studies, vol. 47, no. 1 (1995), pp. 3-25.

3 For the role of young people in these various cases, see Mark R. Beissinger, Nationalist Mobilization and the Collapse of the Soviet State (Cambridge University Press, New York, 2002); Christian Joppke, East German Dissidents and the Revolution of 1989: Social Movements in a Leninist Regime (New York University Press, New York, 1995); Tomaz Mastinak, "From Social Movements to National Sovereignty", in: Jill Benderly and Evan Kraft, (eds.), Independent Slovenia: Origins, Movements, Prospects (St. Martin's Press, New York, 1994), pp. 93-112; John Glenn, III, Framing Democracy: Civil Society and Civic Movements in Eastern Europe (Stanford University Press, Stanford, 2001); and Padraic Kenney, A Carnival of Revolution: Central Europe 1989 (Princeton University Press, Princeton, 2002).

and embraced, first, their liberal political agenda and then, very soon thereafter, the struggle for an independent, as well as democratic, Slovenia.

In many of the new democracies that emerged in the postcommunist region, however, the political role of young people decreased rather abruptly after the end of communism. Thus, despite the fact that young people's attitudes towards the effort to recreate democratic polities and market economies and to return to Europe were generally more favorable than those of older citizens,[4] most rather quickly returned to their studies or professions after the first free elections. Others took advantage of the many new opportunities to increase their qualifications by studying abroad, entered training programs in private businesses, took entry-level jobs with multinational firms that opened branches in the region or started their own businesses. Still others became active as leaders in the burgeoning nongovernmental sector. Thus, only a minority of those who were active took up politics as a vocation, running for parliament or working for the emerging political parties. Efforts by former student leaders to call their elders to account, as in the "Thank You, Now Go" campaign that marked the tenth anniversary of the Velvet Revolution in Prague, were typically short-lived. After the novelty of the early competitive elections, in fact, young people were generally less likely to vote than older people, a pattern that, it should be added, is common in western liberal democracies.[5]

The main exceptions to this pattern of decreased political activity occurred in those countries in which early efforts to create democratic polities stalled or were temporarily derailed (Slovakia, Bulgaria, Romania) or those in which semi- or competitive authoritarian regimes replaced communist leaderships, only to be toppled in turn by citizens' campaigns organized around elections, commonly referred to as electoral revolutions (Serbia, Ukraine, Georgia). As will be shown, young people played important roles as actors in and objects of these campaigns. Although the forms their activism took, their relationship to the "older" opposition in both political parties and the NGO sector and their importance to the success of the campaigns differed, young people contributed to each of the democratizing elections analyzed in this volume.

As these authors have argued on previous occasions, both the development of the electoral model of change and the events that led to the replacement of semi-authoritarian leaders by the opposition or a democratic opening were influenced

4 Samuel H. Barnes and János Simon (eds.), The Postcommunist Citizen (Erasmus Foundation and Institute for Political Science, Hungarian Academy of Sciences, Budapest, 1998) and Ulrich Beck, Democracy without Enemies (Polity Press, Cambridge, 1998).
5 See Rafael López Pintor and Maria Gratschew, Voter Turnout Since 1945: A Global Report (International IDEA, Stockholm, 2002); Richard Rose, "Public Opinion in New Democracies: Where are Postcommunist Countries Going?", Journal of Democracy, vol. 8, no. 3 (July 1997), pp. 92-108; and Krzysztof Jasiewicz, "Sustainable Democracy in Post-Communist Europe: Public Attitudes and Elite Actions", Soviet and Post-Soviet Review, vol. 26, no. 1 (1999). See also the World Values Survey series, available at www.worldvaluessurvey.org.

in important ways by developments in other societies that had undergone similar processes of change.[6] Thus, as the other essays in this volume and earlier works by these authors indicate, the strategies and tactics for using mass mobilization of citizens in the context of an election campaign, together with unity of the political opposition, to oust semi-autocratic leaders, were tried out in the Romanian and Bulgarian elections of 1996 and 1997 and first fully articulated in the postcommunist world in the OK '98 campaign in Slovakia that ousted Vladimír Mečiar in 1998. The model was next used in Croatia and Serbia in 2000,[7] Georgia in 2003[8] and Ukraine in 2004,[9] as well as Kyrgyzstan in 2005.[10] This process of diffusion, which was facilitated by a number of features that postcommunist countries in this region share, including a highly educated population, a legacy of noninvolvement of the military in politics and a common set of problems created by the previous system,[11] also involved the direct transfer of knowledge and experience by "graduates" of earlier cases who shared their perspectives and who helped to train and advise activists in the later ones.

Diffusion of strategies and techniques was also evident in the actions of young people. Supported in many cases by funds provided by outside actors as well as by their own governments, young activists of the Slovak OK '98 campaign influenced developments among young people in Croatia and Serbia. OTPOR, the youth group that played a critical role in ousting Slobodan Milošević in Serbia, in turn played a particularly important role in carrying information about strategies and techniques to young people in other cases, like KMARA in Georgia and PORA in Ukraine.[12] Young activists also provided real life object lessons, through their own experiences and

---

6 See Bunce, Valerie J., and Sharon L. Wolchik, "Favorable Conditions and Electoral Revolutions", Journal of Democracy, vol. 17, no. 4 (October 2006), pp. 5-18; Bunce, Valerie J., and Sharon L. Wolchik, "International Diffusion and Postcommunist Electoral Revolutions", Communist and Post-Communist Studies, vol. 39, no. 3 (September 2006), pp. 283-304.

7 Sarah Birch, "The 2000 Elections in Yugoslavia: The 'Bulldozer' Revolution", Electoral Studies, vol. 21, no. 3 (September 2002), pp. 499-511; Florian Bieber, "The Serbian Transition and Civil Society: Roots of the Delayed Transition in Serbia", International Journal of Politics, Culture and Society, vol. 17, no. 1 (Fall 2003), pp. 73-90.

8 Zurab Karumidze and James V. Wertsch (eds.), Enough: The Rose Revolution in the Republic of Georgia 2003 (Nova Science Publications, New York, 2005); Jonathan Wheatley, Georgia from National Awakening to Rose Revolution: Delayed Transition in the Former Soviet Union (Ashgate, New York, 2005).

9 Lucan Way, "Ukraine's Orange Revolution: Kuchma's Failed Authoritarianism", Journal of Democracy vol. 16, no. 2 (April 2005), pp. 131-145; Taras Kuzio, "From Kuchma to Yushchenko: Ukraine's 2004 Elections and 'Orange Revolution'", Problems of Post-Communism, vol. 52, no. 2 (March-April 2005), pp. 29-44.

10 Erica Marat, The Tulip Revolution. Kyrgyzstan One Year After (The Jamestown Foundation, Washington, DC, 2006).

11 See Valerie J. Bunce and Sharon L Wolchik, "Favorable Conditions and Electoral Revolutions", Journal of Democracy, vol. 17, no. 4 (October 2006), pp. 5-18. op cit.

12 Giorgi Kandelaki, Rose Revolution: A Participant's Story (U.S. Institute of Peace, Special Report, November 2005).

success, of the role that hope and a sense of possibility could play in activating apathetic and alienated citizens.[13]

This chapter will focus on some of the factors that conditioned the participation of young people in electoral revolutions in the countries addressed by this volume and on the impact of young people's participation not only during, but after.[14] Key issues addressed include the relative importance of young people in the developments that led to the victory of the opposition in the elections, their relationship to older NGO and opposition leaders, the process by which young people became radicalized, the tactics and strategies used and the impact of new technologies on young people's actions. Underlying factors that influenced young people's involvement and the legacy of these periods of intense involvement of young people for the political process are also addressed.

Youth: How Important?

In these authors' earlier discussions of this issue, it has been argued that the role of youth in both initiating and supporting the citizens' movements that produced political change varied considerably in the cases under examination. In Slovakia and Croatia, young people were part of broader civic campaigns to, in the first case, oust Mečiar, and in the second, defeat the party of the deceased nationalist leader, Franjo Tuđman. Thus, young Slovaks were important participants in activities such as the "March through Slovakia" that brought the opposition's message to voters in towns and villages across the country, as well as in citizens' meetings with political candidates. They also contributed to the campaign by making and distributing flyers and leaflets in an effort to inform citizens and to get-out-the-vote. One of their more visible actions was called "Rock the Vote" (*Rock volieb*), that included a series of rock concerts and public performances designed to appeal especially to young voters.[15] Young people were also an important target group of the broader citizens' campaign. Survey research sponsored by the International Republican Institute (IRI) showed very clearly that young voters would be far more likely to vote for the

---

13 These authors have analyzed the role of youth in the electoral revolutions in Slovakia, Serbia and Georgia in some detail in a previously published article. See Valerie J. Bunce and Sharon L. Wolchik, "Youth and Electoral Revolutions in Slovakia, Serbia and Georgia", SAIS Review, vol. 26, no. 2 (Summer-Fall 2006), pp. 55-65.

14 Ibid.

15 Interview with Šarlota Pufflerová spokesperson for the OK '98 campaign, Bratislava, May 1999, Interview with Pavol Demeš, Washington, DC, Bratislava, May 1999. Please refer to Marek Kapusta, Rock volieb '98 Campaign-Report on Activities and Results: A Case Study (Foundation for a Civil Society, Bratislava, 1998); Martin Bútora, Grigorij Mesežnikov, Zora Bútorová and Sharon Fisher (eds.), The 1998 Parliamentary Elections and Democratic Rebirth in Slovakia (Institute for Public Affairs, Bratislava, 1999); and Preliminary Report. Slovakia, 1999, Civil Society and Governance (Comparative Research under the Auspices of the Institute of Development Studies, University of Sussex, 1999), for examples of overviews treating the OK '98 campaign more broadly.

opposition coalition than for Mečiar's party. The get-out-the-vote campaign, thus, put a great deal of emphasis on energizing and mobilizing young, particularly first-time, voters. At the same time, although young people were clearly an important part of the campaign, they were not its leaders. Rather, they were one part of a broader campaign organized and led by older activists in the well-organized NGO community. Members of radical student organizations at the universities, including *Odbojová mládež* (Youth Resistance), participated in some of the activities of OK '98, but they did not formally join the campaign, in part because their activities, which included staging provocations at meetings of Mečiar's Movement for a Democratic Slovakia (HZDS), were seen as too radical by some of the leaders of OK '98.

The role of young people was very similar in the Croatian campaign of 2000. Identified as a reservoir of electoral support for the opposition, young voters were one of the main targets of the get-out-the-vote campaign in Croatia. They also participated in significant numbers, as did their counterparts in Slovakia, as election monitors and helped get the message of older activists out to the broader public. *Gradjani organizovano nadgledaju glasanje* (Citizens Organized to Monitor Elections) or GONG, played an important role in training and organizing the participation of young people as election monitors.[16] The campaign to mobilize young voters was also a major part of GLAS 99, discussed in depth in another chapter of this volume. Young people and others involved in the campaign directed at youth made use of a variety of humorous slogans, ads and pamphlets, in order to juxtapose the outdated and stodgy ways of the regime and the youthful, modern, forward thinking of the citizens' campaign. As in Slovakia, however, young people were a secondary or supportive force in actions organized by the broader NGO community and the political opposition. This role reflected, in part, the fact that the "older" opposition remained politically engaged throughout the transition period.

Young people took more of a leadership role in the remaining cases examined. There is little doubt that OTPOR was the driving force in the ouster of Milošević in Serbia. That organization played a pivotal role, first, in challenging Milošević's power by organizing both college-age and even much younger youth throughout Serbia, mocking the regime, courting the Serbian Orthodox Church and pressuring the older opposition actors to form large and durable political alliances. Once early elections were called in summer 2000 and Milošević unexpectedly put his name on the ballot, OTPOR was central in the campaign to register voters, get-out-the-vote, monitor the elections, and more generally, to discredit the regime through humor and street theatre. When Milošević attempted to steal the election, large numbers of OTPOR

16 Interview with Alan Vojvodic, Zagreb, June 2005.

activists, who had been trained in techniques of nonviolent conflict,[17] participated in the short, but important, street protests that forced Milošević to cede power.

In Georgia, where the movement for change was much smaller in general, KMARA, the youth organization modeled on OTPOR, and its leaders, were in the forefront of the movement.[18] Indeed, they accompanied Mikheil Saakashvili (who had once been a minister in the government) when he led protesters to parliament, challenging not just the results of the parliamentary election in late 2003, but also President Eduard Shevardnadze's right to remain in office. In addition, many of Saakashvili's most important allies were young leaders of important NGOs, such as the Liberty Institute and the Georgian Young Lawyer's Association. As in Serbia, young activists in Georgia coordinated their activities with the older opposition and with NGO leaders. This said, however, OTPOR was distinctive in maintaining its autonomy and functioned more as a primary instigator of the process of change than as its "assistant".

Young people were also central to the process that brought about the victory of Yushchenko in Ukraine in 2004. As the chapter on PORA in this volume demonstrates, students, many of whom had been active in earlier student campaigns in the 1990s, accounted for most of PORA's activists. Part of the broader civic campaign aimed at educating and mobilizing voters and ensuring free and fair presidential elections, PORA proved to be the critical actor in organizing mass protests in anticipation of the falsification of the first round of the presidential election.[19] Young people also participated in the pre-election campaign and post-election protests as members of other NGOs including *Studentska khvylia* (Student Wave), *Znayu* (I know), the Freedom of Choice Coalition and the Committee of Voters of Ukraine.[20]

As this brief review illustrates, young people and their organizations also had varying relationships to other actors in the events described by the case studies in this book. Although activists in OTPOR and PORA worked closely with other elements of the opposition and NGOs, they retained a great deal of autonomy. OTPOR, in particular, remained skeptical of the motives of the organized political opposition, in part because of its track record. While active, the Serbian opposition was relatively internally divided, and on occasion some leaders collaborated with the

---

17 One of the central resources for training in nonviolent resistance was Gene Sharp's From Dictatorship to Democracy; available online at http://www.aeinstein.org/organizations/org/FDTD.pdf.

18 See Valerie J. Bunce and Sharon L. Wolchik, "Youth and Electoral Revolutions in Slovakia, Serbia and Georgia", SAIS Review, vol. 26, no. 2 (Summer-Fall 2006), pp. 55-65., op cit.

19 See Nadia Diuk, "The Triumph of Civil Society", in: Anders Aslund and Michael McFaul (eds.), Revolution in Orange: The Origins of Ukraine's Democratic Breakthrough (Carnegie Endowment Press, Washington, DC, 2006) and Taras Kuzio, "Ukraine Is Not Russia: Comparing Youth Activism", SAIS Review, vol. 26, no. 2 (Summer-Fall 2006).

20 See Taras Kuzio, "Ukraine Is Not Russia: Comparing Youth Activism", SAIS Review, vol. 26, no. 2 (Summer-Fall 2006), op cit; Taras Kuzio, "Everyday Ukrainians and the Orange Revolution", in: Anders Aslund and Michael McFaul (eds.), Revolution in Orange: The Origins of Ukraine's Democratic Breakthrough (Carnegie Endowment Press, Washington, DC, 2006).

regime. Moreover, OTPOR members were strongly influenced by two developments distinctive to Serbia: the remarkable 88-day protests in 1996 to 1997 that placed considerable pressure on the regime to accept the results of the local elections and to allow oppositions to take office and the harsh crackdown, soon thereafter, on the power of local governments and the autonomy of universities.[21] What is important to recognize, therefore, is that by the second half of the 1990s repression had increased significantly in Serbia. Both youth and the older opposition were primary targets. KMARA activists in Georgia, who were far less numerous than those involved in OTPOR or PORA, worked more closely with established NGOs and with the political opposition, particularly, Mikheil Saakashvili. Moreover, the Georgian political setting was less harsh than that in Serbia, especially regarding regime control over the media. In Croatia and Slovakia, students were active primarily as part, and as objects, of an overall strategy devised by others.

Strategies and Tactics

One of the interesting aspects of the role young people played in the electoral revolutions under consideration is the fact that, despite their leadership, or lack thereof, and despite the many ways in which their situations differed from one country to another, their strategies and tactics were quite similar. Thus, most young leaders and organizations in the countries considered chose nonhierarchical forms of organization and nonviolent techniques.[22] With few exceptions, young activists adhered very closely to the idea that they could only win converts and overcome the apathy and alienation of the population, particularly among youth, by eschewing violence and relying on persuasion, organization and planning and on the power of example. Many were trained in techniques of nonviolent conflict, including most notably those set out by Gene Sharp.[23] They were aware of the resources the regimes could muster against them and generally chose nonviolent methods of exposing the incumbent leaderships' deficits. The participation of young people in the storming of the parliament in Belgrade in Serbia and of the White House in Tbilisi in Georgia, along with the role that young people played in the spontaneous protests that broke out in Bulgaria early in 1997, may be seen as partial exceptions to this rule, but it was only in Kyrgyzstan that the end of the old regime resulted in violence.[24]

---

21 Mladen Lazić (ed.), Protest in Belgrade: Winter of Discontent (Central European University Press, Budapest, 1999); Vladimir Ilić, OTPOR: In or Beyond Politics (Helsinki Committee for Human Rights in Serbia, Belgrade, 2001).

22 U.S. Institute of Peace, Strategic Non-Violent Conflict: Lessons from the Past, Ideas for the Future (U.S. Institute of Peace Special Report, May 2002).

23 Ibid.

24 In this case, the end of the Akayev government led to protestors taking over the Southern half of the country and organizing demonstrations against the results of the parliamentary elections. This created a power vacuum that allowed widespread looting to take place.

However, and as the chapters in this volume and other studies illustrate, there were clearly also differences between the actions undertaken by young people that reflected the particular circumstances in which they found themselves and national traditions. Thus, PORA activists in Ukraine adopted an organizational strategy that reflected both previous experiences from the student movements of the 1990s and the country's large size, as well as symbols that could resonate with populations in different parts of the country.[25] However, they also relied very heavily on many of the same strategies and techniques used in earlier electoral revolutions, as well as in earlier struggles against communism in Central and Eastern Europe and the Soviet Union. As in the actions of young people against the regime in Poland in the 1980s,[26] humor and ridicule played a large role in the actions of all of these groups, and symbols and actions that depicted the old regime as powerless and outdated, as well as corrupt and detrimental to the country's future, were common. Posters, flyers and t-shirts were used in all of these sometimes only half jokingly called "t-shirt revolutions", as were street theatre, rock concerts and other events designed to rouse citizens from their apathy and create the sense that change was not just possible, but also desirable. The slogan in Serbia, "*Gotov je*" (He's finished), was typical of the kind of succinct and very effective appeal young people made to the public in order to challenge authoritarian leaders. Also typical was a pattern of establishing direct contact with potential voters.

Young activists also relied on new technologies and new media. This emphasis, which reflects the greater degree of comfort that young people have with cell phones, text messaging and various aspects of the Internet, ranging from email to web sites, was particularly evident in the Ukrainian case, where PORA activists and leaders made great use of cell phones to keep in touch with each other and to coordinate their activities.

Underlying Factors

One struggle any analyst of episodes of "contentious politics" faces is how to reconcile explanations that privilege structure with those that focus on agency. In other words, the question to be answered concerns the extent to which it is necessary to focus on the structures of political opportunities, in this case for youth activism, and to which extent the analysis should focus on more contingent decisions and actions by those involved. One of the puzzles in looking at the role of youth is how to explain why

---

25 See Vladyslav Kaskiv, Iryna Chupryna and Yevhen Zolotatiov, "It's Time! PORA and the Orange Revolution in Ukraine" in this volume; Nadia Diuk, "The Triumph of Civil Society", in: Anders Aslund and Michael McFaul (eds.), Revolution in Orange: The Origins of Ukraine's Democratic Breakthrough (Carnegie Endowment Press, Washington, DC, 2006), op cit.

26 See Padraic Kenney, A Carnival of Revolution: Central Europe 1989 (Princeton University Press, Princeton, 2002), op cit.

sizeable numbers of young people in the countries concerned became politically active in the late 1990s and early 2000s.

To some degree, of course, young people were influenced by the same factors as their elders. As outlined in greater detail elsewhere,[27] there were important differences in the circumstances under which electoral revolutions occurred and these differences might have been influential on the extent to which youth became involved, as well as on their strategies and tactics. These are particularly evident if one looks at the degree of repressiveness of the old regime, whether indicated by control over the media, willingness and capacity to control elections, limits on civil liberties and political rights or the use of violence to punish both potential and real enemies. From this vantage point, cases of electoral revolution may be understood as ranging from Slovakia at one end of a spectrum of repression to Serbia and Kyrgyzstan, at the other. Here, it is important to note, for example, that 1,700 members of OTPOR were taken into police custody prior to the 2000 election in Serbia, and during the electoral campaign, the police repeatedly raided OTPOR offices, seizing their equipment and bringing volunteers in for questioning.[28] Georgia and Croatia, at the time of their revolutions, fell in the middle of this continuum, while Ukraine fell closer to Serbia and Kyrgyzstan. Just as important are differences in the size and autonomy of civil society. Here, we can (roughly) array cases from the most developed civil society in Slovakia to the least developed in Kyrgyzstan, with the remaining cases, in fact, skewed more towards the Slovak end of the continuum. Put simply, therefore, the level of repression did not predict civil society development all that well, which testifies, among other things, to the importance of civil society and its long-term development for electoral revolutions. In addition, cases varied in the state of the economy, the country's aspirations, or lack thereof, to join Euroatlantic institutions and the extent to which the existing regime had experienced significant defections by supporters, whether among politicians or the police and security forces.

However, there were also a number of similarities between these cases that, in the end, proved to be more important. Thus, in all of the cases examined, the old leader or regime was vulnerable, whether because of economic failure, international isolation, corruption or perceived governance fatigue. It is striking in the Georgian case, for example, how widespread the perception was among young people and leaders of the liberal opposition that Shevardnadze was tired, distant and, as a result, unlikely to defend his power, even when, as in 2003, he was not up for re-election. That he failed to re-assemble his governing party, once it began to dissolve during and after

27 See Valerie J. Bunce and Sharon L. Wolchik, "Youth and Electoral Revolutions in Slovakia, Serbia and Georgia", SAIS Review, vol. 26, no. 2 (Summer-Fall 2006), pp. 55-65, op cit; "Electoral Breakthroughs in Postcommunist Europe and Eurasia: How Do We Explain Successes and Failures?", unpublished manuscript.
28 Vladimir Goati, "The Nature of the Order and the October Overthrow in Serbia", in: Ivana Spasić and Milan Subotić (eds.), R/evolution and Order: Serbia After October 2000 (Institute for Philosophy and Sociology, Belgrade, 2001), pp. 45-57.

the local elections and that he gave up trying to reign in the media in response to popular protests, both of which prefaced by several years the pivotal elections of 2003, communicated to all those dissatisfied with his rule that he lacked the will and the means to remain in power.

Elections, furthermore, provided a very useful focus for youth activities in that they were a very visible, important, but time limited, event. They required specific actions, they required short bursts of political engagement, they provided a clear opportunity for individuals to register their concerns and they had an end-point that provided a clear measure of the regime's political support. Moreover, elections, far more than other aspects of democratic life, are understood in the public mindset as the measure of democracy, which is why even authoritarian leaders feel compelled to hold them regularly, even if not allowing them to be conducted in full freedom. As with older activists, youth in these countries were also influenced by a transnational network of outside actors that supported and encouraged and, in some cases, even initiated, their activities.

What is interesting here is that electoral breakthroughs, and youth participation in them, occurred in what scholars of political opportunity structures call both high and low opportunity regimes and in systems with high and low capacity governments.[29] As the diffusion of the strategies and techniques used in electoral revolutions in the postcommunist world illustrates, perceived political opportunities may be equally or more important than actual opportunities.[30] In some ways, this is not surprising. There are many cases outside this region where crackdowns on political protests have fed, rather than frustrated, subsequent rounds of political mobilization.[31]

A related question concerns the process by which young activists became politicized or radicalized enough to become active in the public sphere. As argued on earlier occasions, some young people who became active in the electoral revolutions appear to have followed a route that was very common during the 1960s in the United States and Western Europe. Thus, some activists first became involved in public life or protest in connection with issues that affected their status as students or young people directly. Several of the leaders of PORA, for example, had participated in student movements in Ukraine in the early 1990s. Similarly, the founders of OTPOR were veterans of student protests in 1996 and 1997 against the Milošević regime,

29 See Mark R. Beissinger, Nationalist Mobilization and the Collapse of the Soviet State (Cambridge University Press, New York, 2002); Doug McAdam, Sidney Tarrow and Charles Tilly, "Comparative Perspectives on Contentious Politics", in: Mark Lichbach and Alan Zuckerman (eds.), Ideals, Interests and Institutions: Advancing Theory in Comparative Politics (Cambridge University Press, Cambridge, 2006).

30 See Valerie J. Bunce and Sharon L. Wolchik, "Youth and Electoral Revolutions in Slovakia, Serbia and Georgia", SAIS Review, vol. 26, no. 2 (Summer-Fall 2006), pp. 55-65; "Favorable Conditions and Electoral Revolutions", Journal of Democracy, vol. 17, no. 4 (October 2006), pp. 5-18, op cit.

31 Ronald Francisco, "After the Massacre: Mobilization in the Wake of Harsh Repression", Mobilization: An International Journal, vol. 9, no. 2 (June 2004), pp. 107-126.

and the very founding of OTPOR took place in reaction to his efforts, beginning in 1998, to restrict university autonomy. Youth activists in Georgia, Croatia and Kyrgyzstan, on the other hand, as well as many young activists in Slovakia, first became engaged to protest or change the policies or the personnel of the national government.[32]

Some of the factors that appear to have influenced young people's decisions about getting involved are also similar to those that have led to higher levels of youth activism in other settings. These include an unpopular regime that adopted policies young people did not like, youthful idealism and enthusiasm coupled with the perception that a great deal was at stake for them if change did not occur and, in some cases, previous experiences with mobilization around issues related to student life. In many of the cases under consideration, moreover, long-entrenched authoritarian regimes left young people with virtually no hope for economic opportunities and those who could leave often did. This was a clear pattern in post-independence Serbia, Georgia and Ukraine.

Other factors that contributed to the mobilization of young people were peculiar to the postcommunist setting. Whatever differences there were in the economic or political situations young people faced prior to the electoral revolutions, their societies faced numerous common economic and political problems because they were postcommunist societies. Young people grew up in countries in which the old structures that had molded and limited their parents' lives no longer existed. This factor created both benefits and drawbacks for young people. On the negative side, the end of communism created a great deal of uncertainty in all areas of life and, for certain groups in the population, particularly in countries such as those discussed here, in which there was not a radical and sustained break with the past, a fair degree of hardship. These effects were often compounded by disruption and disillusionment caused by the transition and the actions of less than scrupulous political leaders and citizens alike. On the other hand, many young people, particularly those in urban areas and at universities, had had far more extensive opportunities than their parents' generation to travel abroad or, at the very least, to be exposed to the broader world via television and the Internet. The yearning, as some expressed it, to live in a "normal" country, with easy access to both the material and cultural goods of advanced industrial societies, led some young people to make the link between their own life situations and the semi-autocratic or backsliding regimes in power in their countries. Many young people were, thus, tired of the limited possibilities they faced at home and became active because they wanted to register their dissatisfaction with the impossibility of obtaining a decent job and the lack of opportunity for professional advancement because the regime had failed to undertake real economic reform and was corrupt or with the threat of

---

32 See Valerie J. Bunce and Sharon L. Wolchik, "Youth and Electoral Revolutions in Slovakia, Serbia and Georgia", SAIS Review, vol. 26, no. 2 (Summer-Fall 2006), pp. 55-65, op. cit.

being isolated from the "West" and stuck in a "grey zone" of countries, because their political leaders engaged in illiberal actions, as was the case in Slovakia, or would not comply with the international community's demands for cooperation with the international war crimes tribunal, as was the case in Croatia and Serbia. Perhaps the bitterest pill for young people in Serbia to swallow was that their country was bombed by NATO in 1999.

The facility of young people in using new modes of communication such as the Internet, cell phones and text messaging, also helped to spread youth activism. The impact of this factor was particularly evident in the Ukrainian case, where the regime exercised tight control over the media, yet where the role of an Internet newspaper, *Ukrainskaya Pravda,* in reaching young citizens was enormous. Similarly, coordination among the various units of PORA and the organization of protests on Maidan would have been difficult, if not impossible, to achieve without ready access to cell phones. Young activists learned a great deal about developments in other parts of the world, including those in which there had been previous electoral revolutions, from Internet sites, which also served as a means of internal communication.

Efforts to reform and expand civic education are another factor that may have had some influence on the mobilization of young people in several of these postcommunist states. Although the extent of such efforts and the ability of activists to pursue them free of interference from the regime varied considerably across the region, the adoption of democracy as an official norm was accompanied in all by an effort, be it only skin deep, to educate citizens to take an active part in civic and political life. Even in a country such as Slovakia, which experienced a brief but important break with the past and a short period of rapid movement toward democracy before Mečiar became the dominant political figure, such efforts were controversial and often faced both political and bureaucratic obstacles. In more authoritarian settings, such as Croatia under Tuđman and Serbia under Milošević, there was far less leeway for such education and political interference was far greater. In fact, in these cases, the regime had become more intrusive over time. But, in all, there was at least official recognition of the rights of citizens to be involved in the political process and to have their voices heard, and in all, there were at least some of the trappings of democracy. Research on young people indicates that many are alienated from the political system, as well as from those in power. However, as the first generation in this region to have been raised almost entirely in the postcommunist era, young people can be expected to have been more open than their elders to calls to abandon their passivity and take an active role in shaping their own future through participation in elections and civic campaigns. The format of the civic movements that developed (loose coalitions of citizens organized nonhierarchically) may also have been far more appealing to young people than membership in a political party or other forms of "politics as usual".

The availability of experiences and models of electoral change and the support provided by transnational networks for democracy promotion are final factors that influenced the politicization of young people in the cases examined. Young people who had participated in the earlier electoral breakthroughs were prominent among those who traveled to share their experiences and strategies with others in semi-authoritarian states. Whether it was leaders of MEMO '98 or Civic Eye in Slovakia in 1998 or of OTPOR or CeSID, the key organizations in Serbia in 2000, young activists helped inspire as well as train other young people in techniques of nonviolent conflict, media and election monitoring and get-out-the-vote strategies. Given the similarity in age and experiences, young "graduates" were powerful examples of the rewards of overcoming passivity and getting involved in public life.

Conclusion: The Longer-Term Impact on Civil Society and Politics

The mobilization of young people in the context of the electoral breakthroughs examined might have been expected to lead to a major and durable increase in the participation of young people in the political process. There is some evidence that, in certain cases, participating in the get-out-the-vote campaigns and protests did serve as a "school of democracy" with lasting effects. But, this occurred only in some cases and only for some groups. The youth organizations that formed to lead or participate in the electoral breakthroughs have had different fates.

Some young activists suspended their distrust of parliamentary politics and formed political parties. The effort by some of OTPOR's leaders to do this failed, as their party gained less than two percent of the vote in the December 2003 parliamentary elections. Similarly, the efforts of one fraction of PORA to turn popular support during the Orange Revolution into votes failed, with the political party PORA also gaining less than two percent of the vote in the March 2006 parliamentary elections. KMARA no longer exists as an organization, although some of its leaders have been successful individually as advisors to the current Georgian leadership. Most of the young leaders who emerged during these episodes of civic awakening, however, have followed the path of most of their supporters, which is to say, they returned to their studies or began careers as lawyers, doctors, professors or in other professions.

But, some have also taken a different route. Most clearly evident in the activities of several of OTPOR's leaders, but also in the work of some PORA activists and young people who participated in the OK '98 campaign in Slovakia, some have continued to work as organizers and activists, this time in other countries. With support from their own and other governments and various international organizations, these young people have founded think tanks or have joined existing groups that allow them to share their expertise with activists attempting to change regimes in Belarus and other countries, including in Central Asia. For these activists, participation in the campaigns that led to leadership change in their countries has had a lasting impact.

The impact of these experiences on the political behavior and attitudes of other young people does not appear to be as lasting, however. Studies of youth in Croatia, for example, have found that there were greater differences in the voting preferences among young people in 1999, just prior to the 2000 elections, than in 2004. Many young people have also simply reverted to their generally passive political role. Thus, voting levels among young people, as well as more active forms of youth involvement in politics, were once again far lower than those of older groups in the population.[33] NGO leaders in Ukraine note the generally higher levels of interest of young people in politics since the Orange Revolution, but it remains significant that they did not turn out in sufficient numbers during the parliamentary elections in March 2006 to prevent the victory of Yanukovych forces.

The decline in political activity and interest among young people may reflect disappointment with the outcome of the electoral breakthroughs. In Serbia, high levels of youth alienation reflect, in part, the continuing inability of the government to make significant progress on combating corruption, reforming the economy and settling state border questions. Another factor may also be at play here, however, particularly in those cases in which the breakthrough has led to sustained progress towards creating democratic political life and international recognition of the change of direction of the country. Thus, some young people may have retreated from active political involvement because they felt that their country was on the right track and that they had the luxury of following the path many young people choose in stable societies, which is to focus on their private lives by completing their education, establishing careers and, in some cases, beginning families.

Whether this withdrawal from the politics of campaigns and protest is a sign of success or failure of the governments that came to power after the breakthroughs in question and the impact of their experiences on the political values and attitudes young people later hold is, however, a matter for further investigation.

---

33 Institut za drustvena istrazivanju, Mladi Hrvatski i europska integracija (Zagreb, 2005).

THE ECONOMY AND DEMOCRATIC CHANGE: THE MISSING LINK?

Robin Shepherd

In some quarters, it was once an article of ideological faith that the relationship between economic and social conditions and the prospects for revolutionary change was self-evident. In the old jargon of Marxist discourse, changes to the political "superstructure" were always pre-determined by tectonic shifts at the economic "base". Indeed, not so very long ago in the countries surveyed in this book, totalitarian systems of government, inspired by such ideological precepts, explicitly forbade serious discussion about alternative ways of trying to understand the currents of political change that shape the course of history.

These days, however, economic determinism, especially the kind propounded in Marxist-Leninist ideology, has gone out of fashion. It has been replaced by a profound recognition that crudely reductionist systems of analysis are simply unable to cope with the sheer complexity of the social and political organism. No one disputes that the economy plays *some* role in influencing political change. But, economic factors, which appear to have played key roles in the chain of cause and effect leading to revolutionary change in one country often turn out to have been less significant, or indeed absent, in others. Moreover, economic factors do not exist in isolation from other factors at play. The urge to revolt against a particular system of government is derived from a variety of psychological impulses that are usually impossible to disentangle from one other.

By way of brief illustration, consider Ukraine prior to the Orange Revolution. In that country, and at that time, many oppositionists would cite their horror at the fate of murdered opposition journalist Heorhiy Gongadze as a key motivation for wanting to bring down the Kuchma regime. But, they would do so alongside concerns about corruption in privatization, the presence of political censorship, their outrage at social injustice and many other issues. No single factor existed in isolation from the others.

At the other end of the ideological spectrum from Marxian determinism, there is, of course, a wide body of thinking, which holds that there is a firm link between democracy and the market economy. A privatized economy, it is held, disperses power throughout society in such a way that political authoritarianism becomes less and less tenable. It provides a social dynamic improving the chances for democratic breakthroughs and enhancing democratic consolidation, once those breakthroughs have been made.

There is undoubtedly much that is worthwhile in this kind of argumentation. But, the experience of more than two-dozen postcommunist countries over the last decade and a half or so must surely make its exponents pause for thought. Russia, for example, is a largely privatized, market economy. Yet, few would claim that democracy under the Putin administration has become stronger as a result. Slovakia and Poland, both now members of the European Union, have been among the best economic reformers in the postcommunist world in recent years. That did not stop populists and nationalists gaining footholds in power following recent elections.

With such thoughts in mind, what follows is not an attempt to breathe life into the rotting corpse of economic determinism, however that may choose to express itself. Instead, this chapter attempts to round out the discussion of revolutionary events in the postcommunist world by surveying the broad economic conditions prevailing in the countries under consideration prior to political change and by looking selectively at some economy related issues which appear to be most relevant. Crucially, it also flags some of the dangers of imposing western ways of understanding the relationship between economics and politics onto countries whose political cultures and basic economic infrastructures are very differently constituted. What matters in terms of the role of economics in a potentially revolutionary situation, after all, is not how outside observers view things, but how they are perceived by the actual agents of change, the people in the countries themselves.

Economic Dynamics Prior to Democratic Change

There are few revolutions in recent history, which illustrate the paucity of the connection between overall economic performance and the impulse towards political change than the Orange Revolution in Ukraine at the end of 2004. During that year, figures from the European Bank for Reconstruction and Development (EBRD)[1] put real growth in gross domestic product in the country at 12.1 percent. In the five years since 2000, yearly growth never fell below 5 percent and averaged 8.4 percent. Gross average monthly earnings rose at a rate of almost 28 percent. Inflation stood at 9 percent and the official unemployment rate was 3.5 percent. To say the least, therefore, the economic cycle hardly disfavored the Kuchma regime.

Such impressive macroeconomic indicators, however, can be misleading. Economic growth figures, it should be remembered, merely offer a picture of the way in which an economy is performing relative to itself over time. In western economies with high income levels, high growth rates are usually expected to produce a "feel good" factor with positive consequences for political incumbents. High growth in

---

1 All economic data in this chapter are taken from the Transition Reports of the European Bank for Reconstruction and Development (EBRD), available at http://www.ebrd.com/pubs/econo/series/tr.htm.

a developed economy means that a given population moves from a high absolute level of income in one year to an even higher absolute level in another.

The rules of the game for much lower income societies may, however, be very different and it is vital to bear this in mind if serious misjudgments are to be avoided. When one looks further into the economic situation in Ukraine, it is easy to see why. Gross domestic product per capita rose in Ukraine from the 2003 level of US$ 1,053, or approximately US$ 3 per person per day, to the 2004 level of US$ 1,374, or approximately US$ 3.75 per person per day. Strong growth rates, therefore, took place against what, by western standards, would be considered an extremely low base, yielding a rise in national income of just 75 cents per person per day.

The key point, then, is that headline growth rates, which look impressive to the outsider, may well be viewed very differently from inside the country. Indeed, this is a lesson, which ought to be borne in mind when trying to understand the dynamics of political economy in all relatively poor countries. For, even accepting the questionable assumption that high growth rates are evenly spread across all income groups in the population, they may still yield very small absolute gains. People on very low incomes may need to see a doubling or trebling in their purchasing power before they begin to feel that they are no longer poor. Double-digit growth rates that would create euphoria in Western Europe or in the United States may simply not be sufficient to overcome deep seated feelings of economic privation in other countries. Growth may be high, but discontent at the everyday reality of life in a low income country remains.

Similar observations may be made about the economic situation in the run-up to Georgia's Rose Revolution in 2003. Even a superficial glance at the most important economic indicators hardly reveals a depressed economy. Real economic growth in that year hit 11.1 percent and averaged 5.8 percent since 2000. Unemployment dipped from 11.9 percent in 2002 to 10.7 percent in 2003, while gross monthly earnings were rising at an annual average rate of 10.4 percent after rising 20.5 and 30.8 percent, respectively, in the two previous years. Inflation stood at 4.9 percent. In absolute terms, however, gross domestic product per capita in 2003 was just US$ 864, or approximately US$ 2.35 per person per day.

The overall situation in Serbia in 2000, the year that saw the removal from power of Slobodan Milošević, was more mixed. While growth, at 5.0 percent, was robust, the economy had declined by 15.7 percent in 1999, the year that NATO bombed the country over the Kosovo crisis. The country was also plagued by mass unemployment, which ended the year at a rate of 25.6 percent. For those in work, gross earnings were rising by more than 90 percent, though the annual inflation rate was over 60 percent. Gross domestic product per capita was just US$ 834 or approximately US$ 2.30 per day.

The ouster of Croatia's nationalist HDZ party in 2000 took place against an economic background of negative growth of minus 0.9 percent in 1999. Unemployment was 13.6 percent with gross monthly earnings rising at an annual rate of 10.2 percent and inflation of 4.2 percent. Gross domestic product was US$ 4,371 per capita, yielding an approximate level of US$ 12 per person per day.

For Slovakia, whose people charted a new political course after the overthrow of Vladimír Mečiar at elections in 1998, gross domestic product per capita was US$ 3,951 or US$ 10.8 per day. Gross domestic product growth was 4.0 percent with gross monthly earnings rising at an annual average rate of 8.4 percent, against an inflationary backdrop of 6.7 percent. Unemployment was 15.6 percent.

So much, then, for the basic economic background on the five countries under consideration in this volume in the period preceding radical political change. And, so much for any hope of establishing a pattern. All five countries exhibit widely differing growth rates, some spectacular, some robust, others more moderate, and only one (Croatia) demonstrates recession. In all cases, growth in earnings is positive, in some cases strong in others weaker, but in no case are real earnings declining. Unemployment is high in most cases, though not, if the figures are reliable, in Ukraine. Inflation ranged from a low of 4.2 percent in Croatia to a high of 60 percent in Serbia.

Perhaps the one thing that all the countries under consideration do have in common, however, is that regardless of growth rates, national income per capita was well below prevailing levels in Western Europe and the United States. The economic dynamics may, thus, be less significant to the ordinary citizen than the seemingly unchanging reality of ongoing social deprivation. Reservoirs of political discontent borne of feelings of relative or absolute poverty are not hard to find.

Perceptions: Corrupting Politics

But, it is not simply a question of the direct conditions in which people live. There are also the crucial questions of whether people believe that the rules of the game apply to all equally and whether they believe that everyone has a chance to improve their lot if they work hard and employ their abilities effectively. Difficult circumstances do not necessarily translate into social and political discontent. If belief that society is governed by meritocratic principles prevails, discontent is not inevitable. If, on the other hand, there is a general perception that the rulers and their cohorts have rigged the system in their favor and have unfairly or illegally appropriated property and wealth for themselves, it can have a deeply depressing effect on society.

The way in which public perceptions about economy and society intermingle with the political can be clearly seen, therefore, when considering the issue of corruption, possibly the number one gripe among all countries in the postcommunist world.

The perception of prevalent corrupt practices, after all, reflects on the reputation of political elites in a manner, which may do fatal damage to a regime's reputation.

All former communist countries started out on the path to reform with judicial systems and law enforcement agencies, which were totally beholden to the previous regimes. In communist countries, the rule of law was superseded by the rule of politics, which is to say that the ruling party always stood above the law and directed it according to its own whims. It was always, therefore, going to be difficult to establish good practices after decades in which judges, lawyers and policemen had been trained to think and act in a manner appropriate to a totalitarian environment. The problem was compounded tenfold, however, because of the urgent need for governments to privatize entire swathes of what had previously been a totally (or nearly totally) state owned economy. Examples of corruption in privatization are, of course, ubiquitous, which makes it extremely difficult to assess its importance in discrediting those regimes, which succumbed to a second wave of revolutionary activity. Nevertheless, the example of Slovakia, especially when seen in contrast with the Czech Republic, may be instructive.

Privatization began for both countries inside Czechoslovakia, which broke apart peacefully at the end of 1992. The federal government chose to use a highly innovative voucher system to implement the privatization of state property. The idea behind the voucher system was to sell off the country's assets without giving undue advantage to those who had done well out of communism, mostly the former political elite and black marketeers. Voucher books were sold at an affordable price to all citizens over the age of 18. The coupons they contained were used in bidding rounds. The greater the demand for a particular share, the more rounds and the more coupons needed to obtain one. As envisaged by its creators, the system was transparent, fair and contained built in mechanisms to prevent corruption, because people in positions of power had no obvious advantage over ordinary citizens. The mass voucher privatization process was launched in two rounds, the first of which took place before the Czech and Slovak Republics emerged as independent states on January 1, 1993.

Following the split, the Czech Republic went forward with the second phase of voucher privatization, while Slovakia, under the leadership of Vladimír Mečiar, cancelled it. The Mečiar government's motivation in canceling the second round of voucher privatization became crystal clear on March 15, 1994, when 27 direct sales of state enterprises to allies and friends of Mečiar's government were approved in one night. The most infamous case was that of the VSZ Košice steel mill, at that time the country's biggest company. It was sold to Alexander Rezeš, a close ally of Mečiar. Later that year, Rezeš became transport minister in Mečiar's government. In 1998, he managed the election campaign of Mečiar's party.

One major study of corruption in privatization in the former Czechoslovakia and its successor states concluded that in Mečiar's Slovakia, corruption had become "systemic" in nature.[2] The government had simply used the privatization of state assets to forge alliances with individuals that would become wealthy allies. Those allies would sometimes receive positions of state power and would always be expected to use their wealth to shore up the government that had helped them to gain both wealth and position. The era of crony capitalism had arrived. The sheer visibility of what Mečiar had been doing caused outrage among those sections of society that were not already loyal to the government and played an important role in energizing the opposition movement and giving it fertile ground on which to operate.

Once again it is helpful to set these events in their proper context. Back in the Czech Republic, a country which did not experience revolutionary change, ordinary citizens were far from satisfied with the way their own privatization process had, in the end, turned out. Among dozens of highly publicized cases, that of Jaroslav Lizner, the chief official heading the voucher privatization process and the boss of the Central Securities Register, who was caught red handed with US$ 300,000 in cash in a suitcase outside a Chinese restaurant in Prague, is probably the most notorious. He had taken the money to "broker" a deal between the TransWorld International company, a dairy called Klatovské Mlékárny and CS Fond. He was sentenced to seven years in jail (a sentence reduced to six on appeal) for accepting a bribe and abusing his office. A poll conducted in July 2004 found that 69 percent of the Czech population believed that bribery was used by companies to buy state property.

Nevertheless, the contrast between what has been described as "institutionalized" corruption, the corruption which was allowed to exist by ruling elites during the privatization process in the Czech Republic, but which was not actually intended, and the "systemic" corruption of Mečiar's Slovakia, which involved corruption being a matter of government policy, may have been significant.[3]

Ordinary Czechs certainly believed that the state, construed as referring to state officials in general, had not given them a fair deal during privatization. But, it was almost impossible for ordinary people in Slovakia not to see that Mečiar had created a crony network that was now financing his activities. The connection between corrupt practices and the highest state officials, such as the prime minister, was never as close as in Slovakia. In the end, that distinction illustrated the gaping gulf that had emerged between the style of the governments operating in the Czech Republic and Slovakia since independence. With Slovaks acutely aware of that difference, it is reasonable to surmise that it played no small part in motivating large sections of the

---

2 Quentin Reed, "Political Corruption, Privatization and Control in the Czech Republic: a Case Study of Problems in Multiple Transition", Doctoral Thesis, Oriel College, Oxford, September 1996.

3 Ibid.

population to revolt against Mečiar and to help Slovakia plot an entirely new course following elections in 1998.

Still, it remains difficult to draw broader conclusions. What applied in the particular cases of the Czech Republic and Slovakia may not be applicable elsewhere. Corruption in privatization was systemic in both Russia and Ukraine, two countries that also emerged as independent entities from the same federal state. Revolutionary change occurred in Ukraine. It did not in Russia.

To help illustrate the dangers of assuming too much about the importance of corruption, and of foisting western expectations on to peoples whose expectations of what constitutes normal behavior may be very different, it is perhaps useful to consider a counter example, a case where revolutionary change did not take place, despite widespread evidence of mass corruption.

Transparency International's 2005 corruption perceptions index[4] ranked Alyaksandr Lukashenka's Belarus in position 107 out of 159 countries surveyed, with a ranking of 2.6. In the index, a ranking of 10, the best possible ranking, is defined as "highly clean" while 0, the lowest possible score, is defined as "highly corrupt". Iceland had the highest score with 9.7, while Chad and Bangladesh tied for the lowest score at 1.7 each. This ranking puts Belarus in the same category as Ukraine and, among others, countries such as Zimbabwe and Eritrea. From a western perspective, the situation looks dire, indeed.

But, in terms of public opinion inside Belarus on the extent to which levels of corruption are viewed as "acceptable" or "unacceptable", it is helpful to contrast the situation prevailing in neighboring countries, which ordinary Belarusians frequently visit and, whose styles of government might reasonably be expected to resonate in the public consciousness. Russia was placed in 126th position with a score of 2.4. This is lower than Belarus, but not significantly. Ukraine, as has already been noted, scored the same. Poland, the biggest new EU member on Belarus' border, scored better but, perhaps surprisingly, not dramatically so. Poland came in 70th with a score of 3.4. Latvia ranked 51st with a score of 4.2, while Lithuania ranked 44th with a score of 4.8.

In other words, although Belarus scores very badly in terms of corruption when viewed from the global and especially western perspective, a rather different picture emerges when one sets corruption in a context, which has more immediacy to the Belarusian people. When one sets the problem of corruption in its regional context, it is perhaps easier to understand how many ordinary Belarusians and Ukrainians (as well as others in the region) fail to respond to a corrupt environment, which may

---

4 Transparency International's Corruption Perceptions Indices are, according to the organization itself, based on expert assessments and opinion surveys. Available at: http://www.transparency. org/policy_research/surveys_indices/cpi.

well be perceived locally as more or less normal, with the kind of horror western observers might expect or wish.

The Voice of Business and the Private Economy

Social deprivation and corruption offer examples of the kind of economic issues that might be expected to have negative consequences for incumbents. But, unless there is a space in society for oppositionists to bring such issues into the public domain, to link them in popular thinking with the practices of governments and to suggest how things could be different under a new regime, the prospects for political change are bleak. The role of the media, therefore, has been crucial. Consider the following brief survey.

In 2003, multimillionaire Ukrainian businessman, Petro Poroshenko, bought a small Ukrainian television station with low ratings and coverage extending to only limited sections of the population. A strong supporter of the opposition Our Ukraine grouping, Poroshenko gave the then opposition leader, Viktor Yushchenko, airspace to provide at least something of a counterweight to the blatantly biased state controlled and state supporting media. The importance of *Channel 5* and its ratings skyrocketed in the latter part of 2004, when it began broadcasting nonstop coverage of the crowds thronging the center of Kyiv to protest against the rigging of the presidential elections. All significant players in the Orange Revolution agree that without *Channel 5* the prospects for radical political change would have been severely limited.

In Georgia in 1994, businessman Erosi Kitsmarishvili co-founded and took a leading role in running the *Rustavi 2* television station, which originally began broadcasting from two rooms in a local hotel. Following years of attempts to shut it down and the assassination of high profile news anchor, Georgy Sanaya, in 2001, the station is credited with a pivotal role in the downfall of Eduard Shevardnadze in the Rose Revolution of 2003. In Serbia, with Veran Matic's *B92* radio station having been kicked off the airwaves, the Association of Independent Electronic Media (ANEM), which he also established, offered people in Serbia vital sources of information leading up to the ouster of Slobodan Milošević in October 2000. In the lead-up to radical change in Slovakia, private television and radio stations such as *TV Markiza* and *Radio Twist* (Slovakia), ensured that the overwhelming bias of the state media was effectively countered. In Croatia, *Radio 101*, which began operating under communism, emerged as a crucial hub for independent voices under the Tuđman regime, which controlled state television and radio, as well as three out of four national newspapers.

In all of these countries, it was never a question of whether authoritarian incumbents wished to suppress opposition voices. It was in the nature of the respective regimes to want to do so. And, they all tried. The real question was whether they had the means at their disposal to translate those wishes into practice. Presiding over economies, which had been mostly privatized in the early to mid-1990s, the Ukrainian, Georgian, Serbian, Croatian and Slovak authorities simply lacked the degree of control over society to prevent someone, somewhere, from getting enough of a foothold to use against them. There were too many people in these countries with enough financial resources for the authorities to stop all of them setting up a radio station here, a newspaper there or a television station somewhere else.

Something similar, of course, applies to the role of opposition-minded business people that funded civic groups and political parties in the run-up to elections. With the exception of Ukraine, where oligarchs, millionaires and billionaires were, in high profile cases, publicly identified with either the opposition or the incumbents, it is not easy, and may even be impossible, to establish a definitive list of precisely which people funded which political groupings. Lacking western style traditions of party financing, much that was done was covert and its extent and importance remains difficult to verify. Nevertheless, anecdotal evidence suggests that business people sympathetic to regime change had some role to play, at least at the margins, as the examples of Yulia Tymoshenko and Petro Poroshenko in Ukraine clearly illustrate.

The lessons that can be learned from such cases are far reaching and go to the heart of the difference between what can and cannot be achieved by authoritarian-minded regimes, depending on the structure of the economy they preside over. Mainly privatized, market economies dissipate economic power. Operating above such an economic base, it is not possible for governments to affect total control over society. They can, therefore, be authoritarian, but they cannot be totalitarian because, by definition, it is impossible to wield total power, if an entire section of society is run according to its own interests rather than those of the state.

The Belarusian Counter-Case

With this last thought in mind, once again the great counter example is, of course, Belarus, where the regime of Alyaksandr Lukashenka successfully prevented revolutionary change at elections in March 2006, and has done so for years. With 80 percent of the economy under state control and a private business elite that was either totally beholden to the regime or too small to be significant, the authorities in Belarus found themselves capable of pushing dissident media outlets right to the fringes of society.

But, the Belarusian case not only illustrates how important state control over the media can be in preventing bad news getting through. It also, of course, shows how total control over the media can be used to purvey regime propaganda in a manner unavailable to the other regimes discussed in this book. And, it was precisely his allegedly successful management of the economy that formed a key pillar of Lukashenka's claim to political legitimacy.

As the Belarusian analyst Vitali Silitski put it in 2005, "Economic performance has become one of the central points of official propaganda. Real positive trends (economic growth, the rise of real incomes, job security) are aggressively promoted by the state controlled media and in the official speeches without reference to the price at which they had been achieved, whereas problem spots (extremely high retail prices, the gap in wages between Belarus and its neighbors such as Lithuania or Poland) are downplayed or ignored (...) propaganda presents Belarus as an 'island of stability in the sea of the storm', working heavily to persuade the population that any change of government would spell chaos and impoverishment".[5]

Of course, it is not simply its ability to control outlets of information that distinguishes a mainly state owned economy from a mainly private economy in what otherwise might be a potentially revolutionary situation. Lukashenka has also directly used economic policy to provide subsidies and handouts to important sections of the population with the explicit aim of turning them into clients loyal to his regime, a task made considerably easier by the fact that most people in Belarus are state employees. If the data are reliable, growth in wages (or rather, in the Belarusian context, state ordered wage hikes) in recent years has been phenomenal. In 2000, gross average monthly earnings rose on an annualized basis by 201 percent (inflation was 169 percent). In 2001, earnings grew by 109 percent (inflation was 61 percent), in 2002 by 54 percent (inflation was 43 percent), in 2003 by 33 percent (inflation was 28 percent), in 2004 by 39 percent (inflation was 18 percent) and 2005 by 35 percent (inflation was 10 percent). The state has, therefore, raised real incomes substantially over a sustained period. Even if there is justified skepticism about the reliability of the figures, most outsiders visiting Belarus do have the impression that living standards have, in fact, been rising in recent years.

Clearly, a serious question mark remains as to whether this sort of blatantly populist economic policymaking is sustainable in the long-term when there is usually a large and painful price to be paid. As the European Bank for Reconstruction and Development said of Belarus in its 2005 Transition Report, " (...) long-term growth prospects remain bleak unless fundamental market-oriented reforms are implemented. (...) Also, excessive dependence on Russia as the main export market and cheap energy supplier is a major source of vulnerability".

But, in the short-term, it is clear that a state controlled economy has the ability to "purchase" substantial public support to a degree that is not possible in economies, which have been largely privatized. Moreover, the key is not simply that people experience a direct rise in real wages. It is also important that they associate the rises in real wages directly with the regime. Lukashenka is not just the president of Belarus, he has effectively made himself the boss of most of the country's workers.

---

5 Vitali Silitski, "Internal Developments in Belarus", in: Changing Belarus, Chaillot Paper no. 85 (EU Institute for Security Studies, Paris, 2005), p. 36.

He calculates that if he treats them well, perhaps a little strictly, but with generosity, they will be loyal to him. It is a calculation that, at least for now, may be paying off.

Belarus is a country to watch for many reasons. But, since the regime has made economic and social stability such a central item in its bid for the people's loyalty, it will be fascinating to watch what happens if there is an economic downturn or an outright crisis. Problems in that regard may be just around the corner. Russia, which currently subsidizes Lukashenka's regime to the tune of billions of dollars a year in cheap gas exports has recently forced Belarus to accept substantial price rises, more than doubling the 2006 price in 2007. Gazprom, Russia's monolithic gas company, has said it will be pushing for further substantial price rises in the coming years. This could have devastating consequences for Lukashenka's popularity base. It may turn out to be a highly illuminating test case.

Conclusion

The central problem of postcommunism was well encapsulated in the early 1990s in the phrase "multiple-transition". Governments were charged with the task of moving away from totalitarian systems, had to build market economies and liberal democracies and, in many cases, had to redefine nationhood. They had to fight on several different fronts at once.

Such governments can be broadly divided into two camps: those that tried and those that did not. The countries surveyed in this book fall into the second category, of which, there are further subdivisions. In one form or another, however, they are rightly described as "neo-authoritarian".

The role of the economy in promoting or restraining change is hard to define, as discussed in the first part of this chapter outlining the broad macro-economic context. The role of some parts of the economy, most obviously the media, is somewhat easier to grasp. It is also clear that the size and strength of the private economy may well be highly relevant, both in terms of the kind of economic ownership issues which separate Belarus from the rest, and also in the more general sense that a largely privatized economy spreads power through society in a manner that even neo-authoritarian governments find difficult to control.

The number of issues up for discussion is almost limitless. One widely talked about issue is the extent to which young, aspiring middle classes, usually based in the capital cities overcame older, more rural citizens to help effect political change. It appears to have been significant in most cases. But, separating the political and cultural ambitions of such young, urban citizens from their economic and social ambitions is difficult. Many young people active in the opposition movements were convinced that their countries should join the European Union. Did they want this because they believed that would help cement democracy or because they thought it would make them richer? In all probability they hoped the answer would be both.

Perhaps the most sensible conclusion borne out by this brief survey is that it is only really possible to asses the role of the economy in association with all the other factors that were also present. Strong analysis is more likely to be multi-disciplinary and focused on individual cases rather than generalities. The economy matters, because in all countries, revolutionary or not, postcommunist or not, the material side of life influences ordinary people's sense of well-being. It also matters because its structure helps define power relations within society. But, anyone looking for simple cases of cause and effect, generalized patterns or unshakeable conclusions about how this or that economic factor led to this or that political outcome, is likely to be disappointed.

COMPARATIVE PERSPECTIVES ON THE FOURTH WAVE OF DEMOCRACY

Taras Kuzio

The democratic breakthroughs that took place from 1998 to 2004 in Slovakia, Croatia, Serbia, Georgia and Ukraine constituted a second and final stage of their transformation as postcommunist states. All five countries experienced national revolutions that prevented them from simultaneously pursuing nation-state building and democratic consolidation in the immediate aftermath of the collapse of communism. After the dissolution of the Czechoslovak state, Slovakia had to come to terms with being independent and with the challenge of co-existing with a large Hungarian minority. Croatia's war of independence monopolized the first half of the 1990s and the threat from Serbia only receded after the retaking of the Krajina in 1995. From 1988 to 1999, Serbia was dominated by Slobodan Milošević and his plans for a greater Serbia that were at the origin of unprecedented war crimes and chaos in the former Yugoslavia, policies that unleashed NATO's bombardment of Serbia in 1999. Georgia entered the post-Soviet era dominated by ethnic nationalism, leading to civil war and the loss of two separatist enclaves. Ukraine was key to the dismantling of the USSR in 1991, with 91 percent of Ukrainians voting for independence in a referendum. But, national independence came without democracy, with the state being hijacked until 2004 by the former "sovereign communists", turned centrists, under Leonid Kravchuk and Leonid Kuchma.

Therefore, the OK '98 campaign was perceived by the Slovak democratic opposition as postcommunist Slovkia's chance to complete the Velvet Revolution and to remove Vladimír Mečiar's populist nationalism that dominated until 1998. The Croatian opposition also sought to distance themselves from the nationalist 1990s in favor of a "return to Europe" through domestic democratic reform. Georgia's opposition sought to overcome the effects of a failed and dismembered state, deeply affected by stagnation under the government of Eduard Shevardnadze. Georgian analyst, Ghia Nodia, believes that, "our revolution in 2003 reminded us of the Eastern European revolution of 1989" when a new generation of non-communist elites came to power.[1] A similar sense of the unfinished permeated Ukraine's Orange Revolution that, for its leaders and supporters, represented the democratic conclusion to the national revolution of 1991.

This chapter is divided into two sections. The first section analyses ten causal factors that contributed to the democratic breakthroughs and revolutions that took place in

---

1 Interview with Ghia Nodia by Robert Parsons in RFE/RL Features, June 15, 2005.

Slovakia, Croatia, Serbia, Georgia and Ukraine. These factors differ in their degree of intensity for each of the five countries. It is noteworthy, however, that the absence of all or some of these factors will prevent successful democratic revolutions from taking place elsewhere in the post-Soviet space. The second section discusses developments in the five countries under consideration in the aftermath of their democratic breakthroughs.

Causal Factors in the Democratic Breakthroughs of the Fourth Wave

Ten factors have been important for the success of the democratic breakthroughs and revolutions that have taken place in postcommunist states. These include a competitive (i.e. semi-) authoritarian state facilitating space for the democratic opposition, "return to Europe" civic nationalism that assists in civil society's mobilization, a preceding political crisis, a pro-democratic capital city, unpopular ruling elites, a charismatic candidate, a united opposition, youth politics, regionalism and foreign intervention. The latter two have both hindered and supported democratic breakthroughs, depending on the country in question and the foreign actor.[2] These causal factors are examined in the following considerations.

A competitive authoritarian regime

The replacement of authoritarian regimes in Slovakia (1998) and Croatia (1999 to 2000), and democratic revolutions in Serbia (2000), Georgia (2003) and Ukraine (2004), occurred in five countries that can be classified as "competitive authoritarian", with hybrid regimes combining elements of both authoritarianism and democracy.[3] As Silitski demonstrates in his contribution to this volume, Slovakia and Croatia exhibited some similarities to Serbia, Georgia and Ukraine, in which civil society mobilized to get out the vote and prevent election fraud.[4]

---

2 McFaul lists seven factors: a semi-authoritarian regime, an unpopular leader and regime, a united opposition, the perception of a falsified election, some degree of independent media, the ability of the opposition to mobilize and divisions in the security forces; see Michael McFaul, "Transitions From Postcommunism", Journal of Democracy, vol. 16, no. 3 (July 2005), pp. 5-19.

3 Steven Levitsky and Lucan A. Way, "The Rise of Competitive Authoritarianism", Journal of Democracy, vol. 13, no. 2 (April 2002), pp. 51-65; Lucan A. Way, "The Sources and Dynamics of Competitive Authoritarianism in Ukraine", Journal of Communist Studies and Transition Politics, vol. 20, no. 1 (March 2004), pp. 143-161.

4 See the special issue of Communist and Post-Communist Studies (guest edited by Taras Kuzio), vol. 39, no. 3 (September 2006) on "Democratic Revolutions in Post-Communist States". On Serbia, see Damjan de Krnjević-Misković, "Serbia's Prudent Revolution", Journal of Democracy, vol. 12, no. 3 (July 2001), pp. 96-110.; on Georgia, see Charles H. Fairbanks, "Georgia's Rose Revolution", Journal of Democracy, vol. 15, no. 2 (April 2004), pp. 110-124; on Ukraine, see Taras Kuzio, "Kuchma to Yushchenko: Ukraine's 2004 Elections and 'Orange Revolution'", Problems of Post-Communism, vol. 52, no. 2 (March-April 2005), pp. 29-44.

But, there were also three crucial differences. First, the Slovak and Croatian regimes did not orchestrate mass election fraud and did not plan to refuse to recognize a victory by the democratic opposition. The absence of these two factors, in turn, meant there was no need for the opposition and civil society to organize street protests, culminating in a revolution. In Serbia, Georgia and Ukraine, these two factors (election fraud and unwillingness to accept opposition victory) were present and instrumental in leading to democratic (or electoral) revolutions. Second, the Slovak and Croatian regimes were thought unlikely to use violence to suppress the opposition or crush street protests. In Slovakia under Vladimír Mečiar, the security forces were certainly involved in illegal activities against the opposition and in Croatia, some elements of the internal security forces may have participated in the war of independence in 1991 to 1995 or in war crimes. But, in Serbia and Ukraine, the bloated internal security forces engaged in serious crimes and violence. In the case of Serbia, the security forces committed war crimes in neighboring territories. In Ukraine, they committed violence against journalists and opposition leaders. In Georgia, Serbia and Ukraine, the ministries of the interior all had strong links to organized crime. In Ukraine, hard-line elements in the security forces may have received encouragement from Russia during crises. Third, external factors played a different role in all five cases, with the EU playing a positive role in Slovakia and Croatia, encouraging a democratic breakthrough with the "carrot" of membership, a factor which was absent in Serbia, Georgia and Ukraine. In Georgia and Ukraine the main external factor was Russia, which played a negative role. In Georgia, Russia's interference served to freeze the conflicts in Abkhazia and South Ossetia. In Ukraine, Russia intervened massively in the 2004 presidential elections.

The presence of competitive authoritarian regimes had profound implications for the potential of success of the democratic opposition in elections in all five cases and of the success of democratic revolutions following rigged elections in Serbia, Georgia and Ukraine. Competitive authoritarian regimes provided space for civil society, a limited number of media outlets and international organizations to freely operate in the country. Further, they provided space for the existence of a democratic opposition and their access to participation in state institutions (i.e. parliament and local government). Such regimes are, nevertheless, vulnerable during elections and succession crises and they can tip towards a democratic breakthrough, as was the case in the five countries treated here.

However, regimes can also shift in the direction of authoritarian consolidation. In this case, the democratic opposition will find it difficult to bring about a democratic breakthrough, and when such a regime commits election fraud, the democratic opposition's efforts to mobilize the protest potential of citizens are likely to be thwarted. Aside from Ukraine, Georgia and Moldova, which Freedom House classified as "transitional governments" or "hybrid regimes", the remaining nine Commonwealth of Independent States (CIS) states are classified as "semi-consolidated authoritarian" or "consolidated authoritarian" regimes[5]. Attempts at launching democratic revolutions in protest at election fraud in Belarus, Azerbaijan, Armenia and Uzbekistan have failed due to the weakness of the democratic opposition and because the regimes in question did not hesitate to use violence and to engage in repression against the opposition, the most notorious case of which took place in Andijan in Uzbekistan in May 2005.

"Return to Europe" civic nationalism

"Return to Europe" civic nationalism mobilized the democratic opposition and civil society in Slovakia, Croatia, Serbia, Georgia and Ukraine, particularly, young people. In Slovakia and, to a lesser extent, in Croatia, the EU actively encouraged democratic breakthroughs by proffering the "carrot" of future membership. The civic nationalism of the democratic opposition in Slovakia and Croatia competed with the regimes' own brand of extreme right or populist nationalism. In Slovakia, the Mečiar leadership built an authoritarian-populist regime whose nationalism was directed not at "returning to Europe", but against the Czechs and the country's Hungarian minority. During the 1990s, Croatia was dominated by the political regime of Franjo Tuđman, built on extreme right nationalism that partially drew its inspiration from the World War II Ustaša Nazi puppet state. A central demand of the EU was for Croatia to cooperate with the International War Crimes Tribunal, a demand that the democratic opposition, once in power, fulfilled to some degree.

In Serbia, the democratic opposition associated the break with the Slobodan Milošević regime as returning Serbia to its rightful European path, to which Yugoslavia had strong connections, as a communist state outside the Soviet empire. Yugoslavs were able to travel and work in Europe and the rest of the outside world, during a period in which this was unthinkable for most of those living inside the Soviet empire. In Georgia and Ukraine, "return to Europe" civic nationalism developed on the basis of the dream of becoming integrated into transatlantic structures and of departing from the vacuous, fluctuating and unclear multivector foreign policies of the Shevardnadze and Kuchma eras.

In the case of these counties, though, the EU was not as generous and membership was not part of the equation. Nevertheless, Viktor Yushchenko's opposition political platform supported a pro-European orientation for Ukraine that built on a national identity situating Ukraine in "Europe" and outside Eurasia. But, in Ukraine "return to Europe" civic nationalism was not uniformly strong across the country, being weaker in Eastern Ukraine, where the Orange Revolution found little support. In Georgia, the ethnic nationalism of the early 1990s, during which Zviad Gamsakhurdia briefly ruled the country, was replaced by Georgian opposition leader Mikheil Saakashvili's civic nationalism. In the meantime, Saakashvili has worked to rebuild trust in the state and its institutions among Georgians and "to inject national pride [in the citizenry]

---

5 See Freedom House, Nations in Transit surveys, available at www.freedomhouse.org.

without making it ethnic pride".[6] He emphasized state symbols such as the national anthem and the state seal, and changed the national flag, a highly popular move.

Different types of nationalism can be used to establish a democratic regime and to promote the country's "return to Europe" or to institutionalize an authoritarian regime and to turn the country's back on Europe. Two other types of nationalism (Soviet and Great Power) are supportive of the establishment of authoritarian regimes that are not interested in returning their countries to Europe. In Belarus, the Soviet nationalism exhibited and institutionalized by Alyaksandr Lukashenka, has a stronger support base than the discourse of "return to Europe" civic nationalism promoted by the democratic opposition led by Alaksandar Milinkievič. In Russia, Vladimír Putin has successfully marginalized the democratic opposition and promoted a Great Power nationalism that combines Soviet, Tsarist and Eurasian symbolism.

A preceding political crisis

The nature of competitive authoritarian regimes inevitably produces an unstable political environment that has the potential to tip either toward a democratic breakthrough or authoritarian consolidation. Prior to the crucial elections there were scandals and crises of varying kinds in Slovakia, Croatia, Serbia, Georgia and Ukraine. The use of violence, kidnapping and murder against citizens led to a growing wave of protest and a real desire to stop the incumbent in Slovakia, Serbia and Ukraine from further consolidating the authoritarian regime. In Croatia, the Tuđman regime was involved in the ethnic cleansing of Serbs and other war crimes during the war of independence. The Milošević regime lost three nationalist wars in Slovenia, Bosnia & Herzegovina and Kosovo, committing untold atrocities. Serbia's intervention in Kosovo in 1999 led NATO to bomb Belgrade, a prelude to the democratic revolution a year later under the opposition slogan *"Gotov je"* (He's finished!).

In Georgia, Shevardnadze's decade in office led to stagnation, with a large part of the economy pushed underground, where organized crime ruled. Two frozen conflicts in South Ossetia and Abkhazia were ignored, while Adjara was granted *de facto* autonomy in exchange for political loyalty. In Ukraine, the "Kuchmagate crisis" of 2000 to 2001, when recordings proved that President Kuchma had authorized violence against opposition journalist Heorhiy Gongadze became the precursor to the Orange Revolution. Although this scandal did not lead to Kuchma's downfall, it triggered the Ukraine Without Kuchma and Arise Ukraine! opposition protests of 2000 to 2003 and severely undermined the legitimacy of the ruling elites, discredited Kuchma, created a hard-core group of opposition activists and awakened young people from their political apathy.

A democratic capital city

Unlike in authoritarian systems, competitive authoritarian regimes do not completely marginalize the democratic opposition. In the time before the democratic

---

6 Interview with Ghia Nodia by Robert Parsons, RFE/RL Features, June 15, 2005, op cit.

breakthrough, the democratic opposition will have been elected to local governments, gained control of mayoral offices and seats in the parliament. These local institutional bases of support were important springboards for launching democratic challenges to competitive authoritarian incumbents in Slovakia, Croatia, Serbia, Georgia and Ukraine. The National Movement-Democratic Front (EM-DP) won control of Tbilisi City Assembly in June 2002 and its leader, Mikheil Saakashvili, became chairman. In Ukraine, Kyiv's Mayor, Oleksandr Omelchenko, had long been sympathetic to Yushchenko, while Kyivites have consistently voted for reformers and the opposition in successive elections since 1994. The sympathetic attitude of Kyiv's residents and its city authorities was crucial to the success of the Orange Revolution. Revolutions traditionally begin in capital cities and a supportive city population and politicians are, therefore, strategically important to their success.

Unpopular ruling elites

The Kuchmagate crisis in Ukraine served to undermine the commonly held view in post-Soviet states that the leader is not at fault, but rather those around him, a syndrome commonly referred to as "good Tsar, bad Boyars". While Kuchma successfully deflected the blame for the 1999 elections, he was unable to following the Kuchmagate crisis. In countries where the "good Tsar, bad Boyars" syndrome still functions, such as Russia and Belarus, the chances for a democratic breakthrough are slim. An unpopular incumbent, unable to deflect blame onto his "Boyars", provides the incentive for a democratic opposition to unite, becoming a target on which the opposition can focus their energy. Putin and Lukashenka remain popular because the populations under their control do not blame them directly for their country's problems and no major scandals have besmirched their reputations. Democratic breakthroughs and revolutions took place in Slovakia, Croatia, Serbia, Georgia and Ukraine where there was an unpopular incumbent and a popular opposition.

The Mečiar regime in Slovakia exhibited similar characteristics to those found in hybrid regimes, such as Croatia, Serbia, Georgia and Ukraine. These included an executive seeking to concentrate its power, statist economic policies, no separation of the ruling party of power from the state, clientelism during privatization, interference in the media and attempts to marginalize the opposition. A sense of urgency developed: the authoritarian entrenchment of the regime had to be avoided. Two fears fuelled this sense of urgency. First, there was fear that if Mečiar's HZDS won the 1998 elections, Slovakia would move towards consolidated authoritarianism. Second, there was fear that such a trend would irrevocably harm Slovakia's chances of joining the EU and NATO.

During the 1990s, Croatia was dominated by the Croatian Democratic Union (HDZ) and Franjo Tuđman. HDZ claimed credit for Croatia's successful war of independence, maintaining the country's territorial integrity and putting paid to the Serbian threat. This nationalist success made it difficult for the democratic opposition to challenge the Tuđman-HDZ regime, which regularly accused it of treason and of being in the pay of the United States. Accusations of being an American puppet were also made against Yushchenko in the 2004 elections in Ukraine. The retaking of the Serb enclave of Krajina in 1995 removed the Serbian minority as a threat that could rally Croatians around the HDZ, in the same way as Mečiar had successfully used the Hungarian minority to bolster support for the HZDS in Slovakia. The death of Tuđman in 1999, on the eve of the January 2000 elections, therefore, proved fortuitous for the democratic opposition. The removal of Tuđman from Croatian politics opened up divisions in the HDZ between hardliners and softliners over the need for continued nationalism versus the acceptance of democratization as a precondition for EU membership. The democratic opposition was also divided over whether to cooperate with, or oppose, HDZ.

Such divisions plagued the democratic oppositions in all five countries. In Ukraine, Yushchenko was loyal to Kuchma until April 2001, when his government was sacked. After that, he created Our Ukraine as a "constructive" (i.e. loyal) opposition force that vacillated between cooperating with the anti-Kuchma opposition (grouped in the Ukraine without Kuchma and Arise Ukraine! movements) and cooperation with pro-Kuchma political forces. Calls to rally around the head of state can attract support on the right of the democratic opposition, often willing to temporarily sacrifice democratization in exchange for nation-state consolidation.

Shevardnadze's For a New Georgia bloc, which had been hastily created after his Union of Citizens of Georgia disintegrated in summer 2001, began to fall apart after the November 2002 elections, thereby, creating a crisis within the Georgian ruling elite. Kuchma's For a United Ukraine bloc, which came second to Our Ukraine in the 2002 elections, disintegrated a month into the newly elected parliament. Georgia and Ukraine are examples of the failure of competitive authoritarian regimes to establish ruling parties of power. On the other hand, in Slovakia and Croatia, HZDS and HDZ failed in their bids to monopolize power.

Ukraine's ruling elites entered the 2004 elections disunited and unsure about the post-Kuchma era with many within the Kuchma camp unsympathetic to Yanukovych. They, therefore, either sat on the fence or unofficially backed the Yushchenko campaign. During the Orange Revolution, parliament issued a resolution refusing to recognize the official central election commission's decision to declare Yanukovych victorious. Parliament also voted no confidence in the Yanukovych government. By contrast, in authoritarian regimes, such as Russia, Belarus and Azerbaijan, the incumbent remains popular, while the democratic opposition is marginalized through what Silitski terms "preemptive strikes" or "preemptive authoritarianism".[7] Democratic breakthroughs and revolutions are impossible in countries with popular incumbents and marginalized oppositions.

7 Vitali Silitski, "Preempting Democracy: The Case of Belarus", Journal of Democracy, vol. 16, no. 4 (October 2005), pp. 83-97.

A charismatic opposition candidate

In Slovakia, Croatia and Georgia, the need for a charismatic opposition leader proved less important, as their democratic breakthroughs occurred during parliamentary elections. In Georgia, presidential elections followed the Rose Revolution and led to the sweeping victory of Saakashvili with 96 percent of the vote. His charisma certainly played an important role in the success of the Rose Revolution, his election and continued popularity. In Serbia, Vojislav Koštunica's popularity lay less in his charisma than in the fact that he could appeal to both camps. On the one hand, he appealed to the opposition because he was not corrupt and was not associated with the Milošević regime. On the other hand, for the softliners in the Milošević regime his moderate nationalist credentials made him a safe candidate. In this manner, Koštunica played a similar role to Yushchenko in Ukraine, whose candidacy assured softliners in the Kuchma regime, a role that the more radical Tymoshenko could not have played.

A charismatic candidate who does not have a past visibly marred by corruption is vital. It provides the opposition with a figure around which to unite. And, it gives hope to voters that not all politicians are "corrupt", a view commonly held in postcommunist states. Opinion polls in postcommunist states regularly show that voters believe that politicians are only interested in self-enrichment, not in voters' rights or the country's national interest. In Ukraine, public opinion polls conducted in 2003 to 2004 pointed to only two politicians with high moral standing, Yushchenko and Socialist leader Oleksandr Moroz. As a moderate and positively received candidate, Yushchenko was assisted by his main opponent, Yanukovych, providing a negative counterpoint. Yanukovych's criminal record, the widespread perception of Donetsk as a "Wild West" where everything goes, his low level of education and rough personality haunted him throughout the 2004 elections. Ukrainian youth NGO's learned from their Slovak, Croatian and Serbian counterparts that using humor and political theatre to satirize leaders with a dubious reputation would help to break down fear of the regime among voters.

A united opposition

A united opposition shows voters that politicians can rise above narrow personal interests and unite around a concrete election platform. The oppositions in all fives states were disunited throughout the 1990s. Only during the political crises on the eve of the democratic breakthroughs did the opposition unite, often after pressure from youth NGOs, civil society and, in the case of Slovakia and Croatia, with the assistance of the EU. This contrasts with authoritarian regimes, in which the democratic opposition is marginalized, imprisoned or in exile and, therefore, unable to mount a serious challenge to the regime.

The Slovak Democratic Coalition (SDK) united in 1997 around four main democratic parties and aligned with the Civic Campaign OK '98 that brought together 35 NGOs. In Croatia, six opposition parties met in September 1998, creating two opposition coalitions to take on HDZ. These were backed by the broad based NGO coalition called GLAS 99, whose strategy drew on the success of the Slovak OK '98 campaign. The Democratic Opposition of Serbia (DOS) united 18 parties and several NGOs which, hitherto, had not cooperated, with the major fault line running between radicals and moderates, a division common to democratic coalitions in postcommunist states who are united more by what they oppose than by what they support. In Georgia, the opposition united around the EM-DP during the Rose Revolution, which merged into the United National Movement. There was little opposition to the EM-DP from pro-Shevardnadze political forces, unlike in Slovakia, Croatia, Serbia and Ukraine.

Youth politics

As discussed by Bunce and Wolchik in their contribution to this book, young people played a strategic role in democratic breakthroughs and revolutions in Slovakia, Croatia, Serbia, Georgia and Ukraine.[8] They provided the human resources in numbers for the NGO civic campaigns in all five cases and encouraged established politicians to overcome their differences and unite into democratic opposition coalitions. These young people are the generation that grew up in the 1980s and 1990s and that were least influenced by communist and Soviet political culture. The 1998 (Slovakia), 2000 (Croatia, Serbia), 2003 (Georgia), 2002 and 2004 (Ukraine) elections were the first occasions when this younger generation emerged as a serious actor in domestic politics.

Young people had already developed their political skills during preceding political crises, during which they learned from mistakes and honed their organizational skills. The mass civic mobilizations in the 1998 Slovak and 2000 Croatian and Serbian campaigns were diffused to Georgia and then Ukraine through shared training, publications and internet discussions, often with the assistance of western foundations and think tanks. Young people were most adept at using modern communication tools, such as the Internet (for email communication, as a source of news and as a discussion platform) and mobile phones (communications, SMS, camera-phones). Besides the Internet, domestic cable and international television played an important role in breaking the state's monopoly on information and in mobilizing voters.

In all five states, youth created movements that took the initiative to mobilize civil society. The most well known are OTPOR, KMARA and PORA in Serbia, Georgia and Ukraine, respectively. In addition to these well known NGOs, others focused on election monitoring, mobilizing students for civil society activities, strikes and monitoring the media. Polls and surveys in the region showed that youth tended to be pro-western and sympathetic to democratic values.

---

8 See also Taras Kuzio, "Civil Society, Youth and Societal Mobilization in Democratic Revolutions", Communist and Post-Communist Studies, vol. 39, no. 3 (September 2006), pp. 365-386.

Regionalism

Regionalism can be both a contributing factor and an inhibitor in democratic breakthroughs and revolutions. Mečiar, Tuđman and Milošević's misplaced use of ethnic nationalism was one factor that the democratic opposition, who espoused an inclusive civic nationalism, opposed. In Georgia, Saakashvili's civic nationalism came after the disastrous ethnic nationalism of Gamsakhurdia that led to defeat and frozen conflict in Abkhazia and South Ossetia. Regionalism in Ukraine is a two edged sword. On the one hand, it inhibited a landslide victory of democratic forces in the Orange Revolution. On the other, it continues to inhibit the monopolization of power by potential autocrats either in power (as in the Kuchma era) or after they return to power (as in the case of Yanukovych in 2006).

Slovakia's Hungarian minority was used by HZDS and its nationalist allies to mobilize nationalist-populist support. The democratic opposition promoted an alternative inclusive civic nationalism that included the Hungarian minority. Ethnic cleansing during the war of independence made Croatia a mono-ethnic state, with the perceived domestic Serb threat being neutralized from 1995. Other than in the region of Vojvodina, Serbia has few national minorities on its territory. Excluding Kosovo, the Serb titular nation comprises 83 percent of the population. Many democratic parties, such as Vuk Drašković's Serbian Renewal Movement and Koštunica's Democratic Party of Serbia were in two minds about supporting the goal of a greater Serbia, backing the inclusion of all Serbs in one state.

The democratic opposition in Georgia inherited a fractured and failed state. Two regions, South Ossetia and Abkhazia, suffer frozen conflicts since the early 1990s. Shevardnadze struck a deal with the leader of the Adjara region (where many Georgian Muslims live), Aslan Abashidze, whereby he would provide political backing for Shevardnadze in return for non-interference in corrupt and autocratic Adjara. Abashidze's supporters were bussed into Tbilisi to back Shevadnadze during the 2003 elections. Shevardnadze further sought to maintain power through mass election fraud in Adjara, where the Democratic Revival Union won 95 per cent of the vote in the 2003 elections. In Ukraine, an unofficial agreement also existed between Kuchma and leaders in Donetsk, such as Renat Akhmetov, Ukraine's wealthiest oligarch. Kyiv would turn a blind eye to how local elites ran their fiefdoms in exchange for political and territorial loyalty. This loyalty was seen in the 2002 elections when the pro-Kuchma For a United Ukraine bloc came first only in Donetsk oblast. In all other Ukrainian oblasts, Our Ukraine or the Communists came first.

Of the five countries where democratic breakthroughs and revolutions took place, Slovakia is the most heterogeneous in ethnic terms and Ukraine is the most divided regionally. Ethnic and regional divisions should not be overestimated, though. Regional divisions, as in Ukraine, can lead to tension in the design of constitutions and power sharing arrangements between the center and periphery, but do not necessarily lead to violence. Ethnic divisions, as those present in Slovakia, however, can lead to conflict. The one evident similarity relates to voting preferences. In Slovakia, only ethnic Hungarians vote for Hungarian parties. In Ukraine, voting patterns in the 2004 and 2006 elections closely followed linguistic cleavages that mirror regional divisions (i.e. Western-Central Ukrainian speaking regions voted Orange, Eastern-Southern Russian speaking regions voted Blue).

Foreign intervention

Foreign intervention can be benign or negative. The former can take the form of the EU intervening in support of the democratic opposition, as was the case in these five democratic breakthroughs and revolutions. The EU's intervention was particularly noticeable in Slovakia and Croatia, where it proffered the "carrot" of membership. In Serbia, NATO played a positive role by "softening up" the regime with the 1999 bombardment. This was followed a year later by U.S. support for the Serbian democratic opposition. The intention of NATO and the U.S. was clear: to remove Milošević from power. Russia and a minority of western newspapers alleged that the democratic revolutions in Georgia and Ukraine were "U.S. conspiracies", but such allegations have never been substantiated.

Of the five countries under consideration, the Russia factor has only played a role in Georgia and Ukraine. Russia did not intervene in Slovakia, Croatia or Serbia, although it tacitly backed the Mečiar and Milošević regimes. Russia also condemned NATO's bombing of Serbia. In Georgia, Russia chose to freeze the conflicts in Abkhazia and South Ossetia, rather than to undertake peacekeeping operations and hold negotiations on reunifying Georgia. The inhabitants of Abkhazia and South Ossetia have been illegally granted Russian citizenship and in December 2006 the Russian State Duma called for the unification of both enclaves with Russia. Russia intervened massively in the Ukrainian elections in 2004, providing political assistance and a reported US$ 300 million to the Yanukovych election campaign. Russia was also allegedly behind two of the three attempts on Yushchenko's life (the September 2004 poisoning and the November 2004 bombing).

After the Democratic Breakthrough: Main Problem Areas

Democratic breakthroughs as described in this book are never the end of the democratization process. Once democratic oppositions enter government, democracy requires further consolidation. In Slovakia and Croatia, the reform process was quicker than in Serbia, Georgia and Ukraine. The speed of the reforms and their success is related to legacies inherited by the new governments in each country, as well as the availability of external incentives to overcome them. Four problem areas have been central to developments following democratic breakthroughs in the countries covered. These are examined in the following considerations.

Dealing with the past

Dealing with the previous regime has proven difficult in many transition countries, whether Spain following Franco, Chile following Pinochet or Greece following the military junta. Most postcommunist states never undertook lustration or condemnations of communism. In most CIS and some Central European states, the former communist elites continued to govern after the collapse of the USSR. Dealing with the inherited past has pre-occupied and divided the democratic opposition in Serbia, Croatia and Ukraine, but not in Slovakia and Georgia. This may be because the crimes and abuses of office committed by Mečiar and Shevardnadze pale in comparison to those committed by Croatian, Serbian and Ukrainian leaders.

Shevardnadze and Kuchma were granted immunity during the democratic revolutions in Georgia and Ukraine. While, as Mason writes about Georgia, "[a]rresting officials of the old regime and their cronies has been a hallmark of Saakashvili's tenure",[9] in Ukraine immunity seems to have been extended to other Kuchma era figures and no senior official has been put on trial. Issues that were particularly divisive for the Orange Coalition after it came to power included the abuses of office that took place under the *ancien regime*, how to deal with those who are known to have been involved in Gongadze's murder, the treatment of the perpetrators of the 2004 election fraud and the reprivatization process involving oligarchs. Many members of Our Ukraine, including Yushchenko, had been loyal to Kuchma for seven of his ten years in office and proved unwilling to back the prosecution of former Kuchma regime officials. The unwillingness to charge the organizers of Gongadze's murder and the election fraud is linked to secret immunity deals made at the round table negotiations during the Orange Revolution. The issue of reprivatization divided Our Ukraine, which opposed the move, and the Tymoshenko bloc, which supported such it. The question of who would be responsible (a corrupt court system or parliament) for identifying cases for reprivatization was highly controversial.[10]

Dealing with war crimes in the case of Serbia, or crimes against opposition politicians and journalists in the case of Ukraine, is a test of the political will of the president and the ability of law enforcement to prosecute. In Serbia and Ukraine, law enforcement has failed the test. Koštunica and Yushchenko differ, however, in that the former denied the crimes took place altogether, while the latter raised them in the 2004 elections and Orange Revolution in his call for "Bandits to Prison", only to completely forget about them after being elected. Not a single criminal case against former senior officials has made any progress in Ukraine. Most of those involved in election fraud in 2004, in fact, were re-elected to parliament for the Party of Regions in 2006.

---

9 Whit Mason, "Trouble in Tbilisi", The National Interest (Spring 2005), p. 140.

10 See Anders Aslund, "The Economic Policy of Ukraine after the Orange Revolution", Eurasian Geography and Economics, vol. 46, no. 1 (July-August 2005), pp. 327-353.

Investigations into the assassination of Đinđić and the three attempts on Yushchenko's life in 2004 have also made little progress. Supporters of a "hard" transition want to see a more radical break with the former regime that would include punishment for crimes committed. On these issues Yushchenko, like Koštunica, has lacked political will and revealed a preference for providing immunity. An opportunity was missed immediately after the Serbian and Ukrainian revolutions to quickly deal with the former regime. Serbia has demonstrated the danger of adopting the "soft" transition, in that it permits the old guard the opportunity to regroup. Those who committed war crimes under Milošević went on to assassinate Đinđić. In Ukraine, the old guard regrouped after the implosion of the Orange camp in September 2005 and used public dissatisfaction and Orange in-fighting to win the 2006 elections.

Divisions in the democratic opposition

Slovakia and Georgia are the record holders for the once opposition-turned government staying in power longest. Divisions between radicals and moderates in these two states did not lead to open splits in the new governing coalitions. The democratic opposition is inevitably split between moderates and radicals. In Ukraine, the Orange Revolution coalition was dissolved by President Yushchenko in September 2005 when he dismissed the Tymoshenko government. Georgia is the only case where the democratic coalition has remained united and the moderate and radical parties in the EM-DP, led by Speaker of the Parliament Nino Burjanadze and President Mikheil Saakashvili, merged into a united party (the United National Movement), an unusual occurrence in postcommunist states.

A major difference between Georgia and Ukraine has been in the type of leader that came to power. While in Georgia, the radical wing of the Rose Revolution won the presidency, in Ukraine a moderate took office. Saakashvili's victory in Georgia has resulted in three post-revolutionary factors that are absent in Ukraine. First, it brought to power an "extremely motivated, extremely impatient" group of young politicians. Nodia points to Saakashvili's "massive energy" in pushing forward reforms, yet the drawback is that Saakashvili, like his Ukrainian equivalent, Yulia Tymoshenko, may have "modernizing authoritarian instincts".[11] Second, Saakashvili defines himself in opposition to his predecessor, Shevardnadze, while the more moderate Yushchenko has never criticized Kuchma after he was elected. The minimum his Orange voters expected was a moral denunciation of the Kuchma regime, which Yushchenko failed to deliver (the maximum would have been his trial for abuse of office). This led to widespread disillusionment among voters and their defection from Yushchenko to Tymoshenko, as clearly seen in the 2006 election results.[12] Third, Saakashvili has

---

11 Interview with Ghia Nodia by Robert Parsons, RFE/RL Features, June 15, 2005, op cit.

12 See the two detailed surveys conducted in Ukraine by the International Foundation for Electoral Systems (IFES) in April and November 2005. Both surveys are available at http://www.ifes.org/publications-detail.html?id=175 and http://www.ifes.org/publications-detail.html?id=270.

self-confidence in his policies and actions domestically and abroad. The same is not true of Yushchenko's dealings with Russia, particularly in the energy sector.

Of the five countries with successful democratic breakthroughs and revolutions, Serbia and Ukraine demonstrate many similarities. Presidents Yushchenko and Koštunica and former Prime Ministers Tymoshenko and Đinđić represent the split between moderates and radicals in the Ukrainian and Serbian oppositions. Gordy classifies Koštunica as supportive of "soft transition", while Đinđić backed the "hard transition" approach,[13] with Yushchenko and Tymoshenko taking comparable approaches to Koštunica and Đinđić, respectively. The difference between "soft" and "hard" transition lies in the attitude taken to dealing and breaking with the *ancien regime*.

Koštunica's Democratic Party of Serbia and Yushchenko's Our Ukraine lost popularity, leading to the return to power of *ancien regime* parties (nationalists and socialists in Serbia and the Party of Regions in Ukraine). President Yushchenko's Our Ukraine came third in the 2006 elections with only 13.95 percent, a major loss in comparison to the 23.57 percent it received in the 2002 elections. Orange voters migrated from Our Ukraine to the Tymoshenko bloc, which increased its support from 7.26 percent in 2002 to 22.29 in 2006, giving it second place. Since the elections, Our Ukraine has continued to decline in popularity, now having only eight percent of support, as a result of negative public reaction to its failure In the coalition negotiations after the 2006 elections. The Tymoshenko bloc's continued popularity has prevented the marginalization of Orange Revolution political forces, unlike in Serbia, where the popularity of Đinđić's Democratic Party has also declined.

The Orange Revolution coalition has not only been divided between the moderate Our Ukraine and radical Tymoshenko bloc. Our Ukraine had always been a "constructive" (i.e. loyal) opposition, with close ties to softliners in the Kuchma regime. The Tymoshenko bloc and Socialists were at the root of the real opposition to Kuchma during the Ukraine Without Kuchma and Arise Ukraine! protests of 2002 to 2003. In Our Ukraine there was also disagreement between national democrats and business centrists. The former refused to consider any relationship with the Party of Regions, while the latter preferred the Party of Regions to Tymoshenko. The dual track negotiating strategy of Our Ukraine following the 2006 elections, therefore, was not only the result of personal distaste for Tymoshenko's return to government, but also a reflection of the existence of two wings inside Our Ukraine: the pro-Tymoshenko national democrats and pro-Regions business centrists. Each wing sought to negotiate its own parliamentary coalition, Our Ukraine-national democrats with Orange allies and Our Ukraine-business centrists with the Party of Regions in a Grand Coalition. Such a duplicitous and fractious strategy opened the space up to allow for the return of the *ancien regime* in form of the anti-crisis coalition.

---

13 Eric Gordy, "Serbia After Djindjic. War Crimes, Organized Crime, and Trust in Public Institutions", Problems of Post-Communism, vol. 51, no. 3 (May-June 2004), pp. 10-17.

The return of former regime parties

Democratic breakthroughs in Slovakia and Croatia and democratic revolutions in Serbia and Ukraine did not completely remove the partisans of the *ancien regime*. This only took place in Georgia, where pro-Shevardnadze forces were routed without the slightest chance of their return to power. In the other four countries, the *ancien regime* retained a considerable base of support that enabled it to return to power in either a reformed format, as in Croatia, or in a wholly unreformed format, as in Serbia. In Slovakia, Mečiar's HZDS and its nationalist allies re-entered government after the 2006 parliamentary elections, albeit as junior partners.

Following a similar pattern, the democratic opposition in Slovakia, Croatia, Serbia and Ukraine saw their coalitions disintegrate once the democratic breakthroughs were achieved and the *ancien regime* was defeated. They were sufficiently weakened for the return of the partisans of the *ancien regime* to become credible candidates in subsequent elections. Often this followed strategic policy mistakes on the part of the democratic opposition and obvious disagreements between moderates and radicals.

In Slovakia, the 2002 elections marked the first time that Mečiar's HZDS received fewer votes than the left or center-right, although it still received considerable support with 29.8 percent. At the same time, the country had consolidated its democracy sufficiently for populist-nationalist forces to be unable to derail the course of reform or accession to NATO and the EU. Comparably, in Croatia, softliners in HDZ supported its transformation into a center-right conservative party, a process similar to reformers from the Franco regime in Spain, who created the Popular Party led by José María Aznar. The reformed HDZ returned to power in 2003, defeating the center-left coalition that had been elected in 2000. Yet, this return to power has not impeded Croatia's democratic progress and its likely acceptance as a member of NATO and the EU.

In Serbia and Ukraine, the *ancien regime* is more worrying. In Serbia, two pillars of the Milošević regime, the Socialist and Radical Parties, continue to command significant popular support. The Radical Party won the December 2003 elections, only nine months after Đinđić's assassination and in spite of the fact that its leader, Vojislav Šešelj, is on trial in The Hague for war crimes. In turn, in Ukraine, the former pro-Kuchma and oligarch Party of Regions won the March 2006 elections with 32.14 percent of the vote. After the parties that had carried the Orange Revolution failed to build a coalition, a so-called Anti-Crisis Coalition emerged with the Socialists and Communists joining the Party of Regions under Prime Minister Yanukovych, whose government has re-instated many senior members of the Kuchma regime.

In both Serbia and Ukraine, the *ancien regime* is a credible threat that could potentially undermine democracy in the years to come. In Serbia, the extreme left and right have a stable 30 to 40 percent of popular support and are more united than the country's fractured democratic parties that led the democratic revolution in 2000. In Ukraine, the Party of Regions is the only former pro-Kuchma party to have entered the 2006 parliament. The SDPUo, the party that provided for the creeping authoritarianism of Kuchma's last years in office, failed to enter parliament. The return of the Party of Regions poses two serious questions to Ukraine.[14] Firstly, can the Party of Regions transform itself into a post-oligarchic and democratic party? Such transformations have taken place in East-Central Europe and the Baltic States, yet there has been no such case in any CIS country. Second, will the return of Yanukovych to government lead to a reversal of the gains of the Orange Revolution? Observers have pointed out, that "it would be wrong to conclude that little has changed. Ukraine today is a different country from the timid nation that existed before the Orange Revolution. There is a greater sense of freedom and a stronger sense of national identity".[15] While a reversal of these gains seems unlikely as the Party of Regions has insufficient nationwide popularity to monopolize power, stagnation in the democratic reform process is possible.

Serbia is facing very similar questions. But, Serbia has one distinct advantage over Ukraine. EU membership, however distant, remains a prospect for Serbia and could encourage democratic progress. Ukraine, in turn, is only being offered a free trade agreement, following its accession to the WTO, and an enhanced agreement to replace the current Partnership and Cooperation Agreement.

Democratization

The victories of the Slovak and Croatian democratic oppositions over competitive authoritarian regimes in 1998 and 1999 to 2000, respectively, constituted real democratic breakthroughs in both countries. Success in Slovakia's democratic reforms and the dismantling of the Mečiar legacy led to membership of NATO in 2002 and the EU in 2004. NATO invited Croatia into the Membership Action Plan in May 2002 and it may be invited to join NATO in 2008. Croatia is also likely to be invited to join the EU any time soon, in contrast to Serbia, Georgia and Ukraine. The latter three countries, those that undertook more fully-fledged democratic revolutions, have more difficult legacies to overcome and are grappling with entrenched remnants of the *ancien regime*.[16]

Basic democratic freedoms, such as support for civil society, media freedom, free elections, support for democracy over the alternative of authoritarianism, are positive outcomes of the democratic breakthroughs and revolutions in all five countries. Serbia, Georgia and Ukraine have poorer records of democratic progress

---

14 See Taras Kuzio, "The Orange Revolution at a Crossroads", Demokratizatsiya, vol. 14, no. 4 (Fall 2006), pp. 477-492.

15 Stefan Wagstyl, "Ukraine: Orange Revolution Gives Way to Reality", Financial Times, December 15, 2006.

16 See Steven Levitsky and Lucan A. Way, "International Linkage and Democratization", Journal of Democracy, vol. 16, no. 3 (July 2005), pp. 20-34.

than Slovakia and Croatia, though. Slovakia is classified in Freedom House's 2006 Nations in Transit report as a "consolidated democracy", whereas Croatia and Serbia are defined as "semi-consolidated democracies". Georgia and Ukraine are considered to be "transitional" or "hybrid" regimes. Freedom House's 2006 Freedom in the World survey upgraded Ukraine to "Free", joining Slovakia, Croatia and Serbia, while Georgia is classified as "Partly Free".[17]

Democratization in Georgia and Ukraine has improved following their democratic revolutions. Both countries hold free elections and enjoy free media. The interior ministries in both countries, which had ties to organized crime and were involved in illegal violence against regime opponents and journalists, have been cleaned up. Freedom House's 2006 Nations in Transit survey gives credit to Georgia for enhancing local government capacity, launching a struggle against corruption and improving the protection of human rights, but registered no change in Georgia's election administration, civil society, media and national governance. According to Ghia Nodia, one of the reasons for the decline in civil society activity following the Rose Revolution is that "half" of civil society moved into government. In Ukraine, Freedom House registered a vastly improved media environment with an end to censorship, greater transparency in government and state activities and policies and a free election environment. Nevertheless, problem areas remain. Georgia lacks a strong opposition, partly because of the high threshold to enter parliament (seven percent) and the judiciary is subject to political interference. Political parties in Georgia and Ukraine remain weak and tied to personality politics, rather than to ideologies. This is especially true of the radical wing of democratic oppositions that came to power in 2003 to 2004, including Saakashvili and Tymoshenko.

Democratization has proceeded faster in postcommunist states, which have introduced parliamentary systems, commonplace in East Central Europe and the three Baltic States. During postcommunist transitions, abuse of office, election fraud and corruption has tended to occur around the executive. Of the twelve CIS states, ten have super presidential systems with emasculated parliaments. The exceptions are a parliamentary-presidential system in Ukraine and a fully parliamentary system in Moldova.

The victory of democratic oppositions in Slovakia and Croatia convinced their leaders of the need to temper executive power, because it had been abused during the Mečiar and Tuđman competitive authoritarian regimes. In 2000, Croatia moved from a semi-presidential to a parliamentary system and from a bicameral into a unicameral parliament. Round table negotiations during the Orange Revolution led to a political compromise in the ruling elite that included three elements: an unwritten agreement on immunity from prosecution, reform of the election law and constitutional reform in 2006. The constitutional reforms transformed Ukraine from

---

17 See Freedom House Nations in Transit surveys, available at www.freedomhouse.org.

the 1996 semi-presidential system to a parliamentary-presidential republic, reducing presidential powers, transferring them to the prime minister and introducing control of government by parliamentary majorities, rather than by the executive.

Conclusion

Slovakia rejoined "Europe" relatively quickly after the 1998 democratic breakthrough. This, in itself, demonstrated that Mečiar's populist nationalism was more of an aberration than a factor that could permanently derail Slovakia's democratization. Croatia has also quickly moved forward in capitalizing on its 1999 to 2000 democratic breakthrough and is likely to accede to NATO and the EU within a few years.

Serbia, Georgia and Ukraine's records are very mixed, though. EU membership, which could be encouraging to democratic political forces in the face of still significant domestic support for the *ancien regime*, is only a real, even if distant, prospect for Serbia. But, Serbia will not overcome the Milošević legacy quickly, as the extreme left and nationalist right continue to have a strong base of support in the country. In Georgia and Ukraine, democratization will be complicated by the absence of any offer of EU membership and, in the case of Ukraine, by the return to power of the Party of Regions, strongly associated with the *ancien regime*. Democratic freedoms, free elections, independent media and political competition have all improved in Georgia and Ukraine since their democratic revolutions, but both countries still face major hurdles, especially in asserting the rule of law and in effectively eradicating corruption.

Internationally, Serbia is located in a neighborhood where most states are consolidated democracies, a factor that could lead to democratic diffusion. Geography does not comparably favor Georgia, which borders three authoritarian states, including a large and threatening neighbor, Russia, that controls its two separatist enclaves and opposes its integration into transatlantic structures and only one democracy, that being Turkey. In fact, Georgia's geography is its Achilles' heel, making NATO membership likely, although not EU membership. Ukraine, in turn, borders four NATO and EU member states, semi-democratic Moldova and authoritarian Belarus and Russia. Thus, although not in the most advantageous position, the democratic revolutions that took place in Georgia and Ukraine are, nevertheless, testament to their desire to establish democratic societies that are firmly embedded in Euroatlantic institutions.

WHERE NEXT OR WHAT NEXT?

Ivan Krastev

The beginning of the 21st century was marked by an explosion of electoral revolutions in Eastern Europe. A "bulldozer" revolution put an end to the criminal regime of Slobodan Milošević in Serbia. The Rose Revolution changed the color of the political regime in Georgia and the Orange Revolution brought an end to kleptocratic rule in Kyiv.[1] All three revolutions were nonviolent, liberal and pro-western. They looked like the second coming of 1989.

The color revolutions captured the imagination of the West with the promise that liberal democratic revolutions can even be successful in countries with troubled pasts, post-conflict presents and where institutions are weak and incomes low. At the very moment the idea of liberal democratic revolution was both defeated and discredited in the Middle East, true-believers of universal democracy found their hopes fulfilled and spirits lifted by events in Georgia and Ukraine. Georgia and Ukraine were viewed as leaders of a new wave of democratic change in the world. The anti-Syrian electoral revolution in Lebanon further strengthened this impression.

In the view of many democracy activists the only relevant questions were how many more weeks in power Alyaksandr Lukashenka in Minsk would survive and where the next color revolution would take place. Political theorists and democracy activists were convinced that color revolutions were a pattern for democratic change that would spread all over Eastern Europe and Central Asia. Replicating color revolutions was the winning strategy for the future.

At the time, these color revolutions were varyingly conceptualized as a) liberal revolutions, b) EU inspired revolutions, c) NGO revolutions and d) a model for the next generation of democratic revolutions. Two years on, all these ideas about color revolutions require profound rethinking.

It could turn out that, in their nature, these color revolutions have more in common with the recent populist revolutions in Latin America, than with the liberal revolutions in Central and Eastern Europe of 1989. NGO-centric interpretations of the color revolutions have so far tended to be a marriage of ideological convenience and institutional self-interest, more than a fair reflection on the real strength of the civil society actors involved. And, the notion that color revolutions represent a model of democratic change that can be replicated might not only be incorrect, but even dangerous, if considering how to develop strategies for assisting democracy in the post-Soviet space.

---

1 The "Tulip Revolution" in Kyrgyzstan has suspiciously disappeared from the list of color revolutions in the literature on the subject.

In accepting color revolutions as the new paradigm for democratic change, one runs the risk of making the same mistake as when one universalizes Central European political experience. It took the democratic community the failure in Iraq, Hamas' victory in Palestine and the wave of populist revolutions in Latin America to see the obvious. The end of the Cold War and the emergence of pro-western liberal democracies and market economies in Central Europe are events that cannot simply be "replicated" in regions like the Middle East or Central Asia. As Francis Fukuyama, the disillusioned prophet of "the end of history" bitterly remarked in his latest book, "(...) the democratization of Central Europe was a miracle. And, one can react to a miracle either by dramatically raising expectations for a repeat-effect or by being grateful, pocketing one's luck, and reflecting on the uniqueness of circumstance. Unfortunately, the democracy promotion community shared the first reaction, and tried to turn the miracle into a natural law".[2]

Is this mistake to be repeated? Is it not wiser to pocket one's luck and to reflect on the uniqueness of circumstance when it comes to drawing lessons from the color revolutions that have already taken place, instead of raising expectations of repeat-effects? Has the music stopped playing, without the dancers realizing?

The central argument of this chapter is that in their nature color revolutions are not liberal democratic revolutions. What has been witnessed in the post-Soviet space was not a new wave of democratic revolutions, but the collapse of the hybrid regimes that emerged out of the ruins of the partial democratization of the 1990s. This collapse took the form of democratic breakthroughs in Georgia and Ukraine, but it led to the consolidation of authoritarian trends in Russia and Central Asia. The failure of the revolutionary strategy in the case of Belarus was just the first warning signal for the limits of the color revolution as a model for breaking authoritarian regimes and promoting democracy.

In the view of this author, therefore, the real question is not where the next color revolution will take place, but how the new post-revolutionary strategy for democracy promotion in Eastern Europe should be articulated.

Liberal Revolutions?

What most political observers registered, but failed to emphasize sufficiently, was that color revolutions were revolts against semi-autocratic and not autocratic regimes. In 1989 the people on the streets of Budapest and Prague demanded free multi-party elections, freedom of speech and a free market economy. The slogans on the streets of Tbilisi and Kyiv were different. They protested against regimes that called themselves democracies, looked like democracies, but were

---

2 Francis Fukuyama, America at the Crossroads: Democracy, Power, and the Neoconservative Legacy (Yale University Press, New Haven, 2006), p. 67.

anti-democratic in their nature. These were regimes where citizens had the right to vote, but the governments reserved for themselves the privilege of counting the votes and announcing the results. Ukrainians and Georgians protested, not against totalitarian regimes, but "democracy's doubles".[3] Disappointment and disillusionment with postcommunist democratization from above was the major underlying cause for the eruption of the protests.

Color revolutions had more in common with the wave of populist revolutions that took place in Latin America than with the velvet revolutions of Eastern Europe. The color revolutions expressed a strong desire for change, but not necessarily a desire for more democracy, let alone more capitalism. The people on the streets of Kyiv, unlike the people on the streets of Central Europe in 1989 (but, like populist voters in Latin America today), were asking for the revision of the privatization process, not for more privatization. They were fighting corruption, not communism. Democratic ideals played only a limited role in mobilizing support for the color revolutions, whose victors won power as opposition movements rather than as democratic movements. As Michael McFaul has observed, their "main message was a cry of 'Enough!' hurled in the face of the incumbent power-holders".[4]

Surprisingly, the similarities between Eurasia's color revolutions and the recent dramatic changes in Latin America have remained largely unnoticed or neglected. Observers have been blinded by the fact that the Orange Revolution was led by a free-market liberal like Yushchenko, while Latin America's electoral revolutions have been led by leftists sympathetic to Fidel Castro. The similarities between Ukraine and Latin America were also obscured by the fact that anti-elite rhetoric in Ukraine spoke in anti-Russian tones, while in Latin America anti-elitism speaks the language of anti-Americanism.

But, regardless of these and many other differences, the color revolutions stand closer to their Latin American relatives than to their Central European forebears. Claims about fraud and not about the future were at the core of political discourse. Ukrainian voters contested the fraudulent elections and, therefore, took to the streets during the Orange Revolution. The angry electorates in Latin America protested not only against the neo-liberals and their policies, but against the fraud and the "violin politics" of the establishment. As José María Aznar, former Prime Minister of Spain once said, exercising power in Latin America during the last decade and a half has been like playing a violin. One takes the violin with one's left hand, but one plays it with one's right.[5]

3 Ivan Krastev, "Democracy's 'Doubles'", Journal of Democracy, vol. 17, no. 2 (April 2006), pp. 52-62.
4 Michael McFaul, "Transitions from Postcommunism", Journal of Democracy, vol. 16, no. 3 (July 2005), p. 16.
5 José María Aznar, "(...) leftist politics of Latin America is like playing the violin. You grab it [the violin/power] with your left hand (...) and play it with your right". See http://www.rgemonitor.com/blog/roubini/91201.

The distinctive feature of the new politics is that the new populist majorities do not have a clear project for transforming society. They are inspired, not so much by hope as by a sense of betrayal. They are moralistic, not programmatic. They represent the crisis of traditional political identities. In their view, social and political change is possible only through a sea change in the elite. The absence of new ideas and of a new vision for society has resulted in rising pressure to put new people into power. The war cry of the new protest politics is Hugo Chavez's electoral slogan: "Get rid of them all!".

The color revolutions, unlike the velvet revolutions, are not manifestations of the victory of liberal ideas, but are symptomatic of the emerging tension between the concept of people power and the representative institutions of liberal democracy. Like the Latin American revolutions, the color revolutions represent protest against the disempowerment of the people, but in a democratic context. They were revolutions demanding democracy, at the same time as rejecting "the real-life democracy" they experienced in the last decade. The populist nature of the color revolutions is at least part of the explanation for the difficulty the new leaders have had to consolidate the revolutionary gains in the post-revolutionary period.

Today, two years after the Orange Revolution in Kyiv and seven years after the anti-Milošević "bulldozer" revolution in Serbia, the time has come to face the reality of post-Orange society. It is, of course, fair to say that Ukraine today is more democratic than it was two years ago. There is a free and lively media environment, the government is more accountable than ever before and the separation of powers functions better than previously, but the euphoria that accompanied the revolution and the hopes that it raised have dissipated. The popular mood ranges from despair, anger and cynicism among the revolution's supporters to confusion, disappointment and disillusionment among the revolution's opponents. Increasingly, Ukrainians are giving up on all their leaders and treating their promises as empty. In geopolitical terms, Kyiv is creeping back into Russia's sphere of influence, while the reformist momentum has slowed to a crawl.

Georgia, in contrast, is firmly anchored in the West and its government strives for NATO and EU membership. But, the authoritarian tendencies in the Georgian government are too obvious to be neglected and some NGO leaders claim that the new government is less open to criticism than the "authoritarian regime" it has overthrown. Serbia, for its part, has failed to reconcile its nationalistic past, and while competitive political processes exist, illiberalism is on the rise.

Meanwhile, contrary to the colorful logic of revolutionary-minded democracy promoters, Lukashenka in Minsk continues to survive, while Moscow has undergone regime change in the opposite direction to that expected. As Jean Cocteau once remarked, "Every revolution begins standing and ends seated".[6]

The Myth of the NGO Revolution

It is hard to understand what makes revolutions so engaging. The story unfolding has been witnessed so many times before: excited crowds, vague slogans and charismatic leaders flicker on the television screen, in a familiar sort of heroic (melo) drama. But, no one is ever prepared for the disappointment that follows. And, it is always tempting to believe that what is being witnessed is a new kind of revolution. The color revolutions were believed to be a new phenomenon, the "NGO revolution". Wikipedia, the bible of the information society, insists that color revolutions "are notable for the important role of nongovernmental organizations (NGOs) and particularly student activist organizations in organizing creative nonviolent resistance".[7] The concept of civil society was as fundamental to the color revolutions as the concept of the "third estate" was for the French revolution. The role played by NGOs was deemed as important for the success of the color revolutions as that played by the Bolshevik party in the success of the 1917 revolution in Russia.

"NGO revolutions are revolutions in the age of globalization and information. It is meaningless to protest against this reality", wrote Kremlin political technologist, Sergei Markov, "(...) everybody who wants to take part in the politics of the 21st century has to create his own networks of NGOs and supply them with ideology, money and people".[8] NGOs have been conceptualized as the major protagonists of political change in the new century. They are viewed as more important than political parties, trade unions or charismatic political leaders. The question, however, is how well-founded this NGO-centric interpretation of the color revolutions actually is.

The birth of the NGO-centric interpretation of the color revolutions was a happy accidental encounter between ideological convenience and institutional self-promotion. If one wants to be written about in history textbooks, it is necessary to ensure that one has something to do with writing them. This is what the NGO leaders did. They were not only among the leaders of the color revolutions, but more importantly, they have been the most active interpreters of the events. They were the ones fluent in English and in democracy-speak. The anti-political mood, prevailing in both East and West, has contributed to the success of this NGO-centric interpretation. Political parties have been labeled as representatives of special interests, whereas, the NGOs were the voice of civil society. And, in one of

---

6 Jeanne Fuchs, "George Sand: Notorious Woman, Celebrated Writer", The Coast of Utopia, no. 43 (Fall 2006).

7 See http://en.wikipedia.org/wiki/Color_revolutions, accessed on January 23, 2007.

8 Steve Gutterman, "Russia wants its NGOs to play stronger role in world affairs", AP, March 13, 2006.

those ironic twists of fate so dear to historians, the prominence of the NGO-centric interpretation of the color revolution was achieved by the inadvertent collaboration of democracy activists and Kremlin political technologists.

Western pro-democracy foundations were the salesmen of the NGO-centric interpretation of the color revolution. For them, public acceptance of the critical role played by the NGOs was also recognition of the critical role played by agencies and foundations engaged in democracy assistance in bringing about democratic change. In other words, western foundations cannot be considered disinterested parties, when it comes to the interpretation of the color revolutions. This is also true for the academic centers affiliated to them.

The packaging of the color revolutions as NGO revolutions was also ideologically convenient. The western-funded NGOs were the only openly liberal, pro-democratic and pro-capitalist constituency in the revolution. NGO-centric interpretations of the revolutions made it easy to argue for the primacy of the liberal nature of the political change. The emphasis on the role and the potential of the NGOs as leading actors in the democratic revolutions also drew attention to the transnational nature of the political change in the context of color revolutions. It is no accident that political theorists have devoted much more attention to the role played by the Serbian activists that turned out in Georgia, or the Georgian activists that turned out in Ukraine, than to the social inequality and ethnic tensions these societies demonstrated in the run-up to their democratic breakthroughs. Marketing has overtaken Marxism when it comes to defining the meaning of revolution. But, the revolutionary handbook that was written on the basis of the experience of the color revolutions encourages the democracy promotion community to seize the opportunity for change in places where they lack local knowledge and genuine democratic movements are not available. The existence of an unpopular semi-autocratic regime, splits among the "guys with the guns", an independent media, a unified opposition, a civic sector skillful in the art of popular mobilization and election monitoring capacities were all classified as factors sufficient for the success of a liberal revolution. The new mantra of democratic change has become "all we need is NGOs".

Kremlin political strategists were the other fervent advocates of the view that color revolutions were NGO revolutions. This version of events justified their claims that what the West called revolution, was, in fact, an electoral coup, a covert operation designed and implemented by the western intelligence agencies and their NGO based infrastructure behind the backs of postcommunist societies. NGO-centric interpretations of the color revolutions perfectly fitted the deep belief of the Kremlin's strategists in the primacy of political technologies over political representation.

The pages of this book provide a thorough analysis of NGO activity in each of the countries in the run-up to and during their color revolutions. The case studies provided document what the NGOs did, how they did it and why what they did was important in the course of the revolutions. Nobody can credibly cast doubt on the fact that NGOs were critical in articulating an alternative view of their societies, in mobilizing the people, especially young people, and international solidarity for the protestors on the streets of Eastern Europe. Their role in election monitoring was also critical. The purpose of this chapter is not to cast aspersions on these analyses. It would be a grave mistake to ignore the role of the NGOs in the success of the color revolutions. But, the intention of this author is to question the belief that NGOs are the central actor in opening up societies. It is this author's conviction that there is a clear tendency to overestimate the role of NGOs as agents of democratic change and to overlook the limits of their influence. The strategy of overselling NGOs can easily backfire, by creating expectations that cannot be fulfilled. Moreover, there seems to exist a shared conviction that the importance of the role of NGOs as actors in democracy promotion shall inevitably grow. This, however, contradicts increasingly obvious signs that the NGO moment in democratic politics is in the process of passing.

In the case of Eastern Europe, most of the politically active NGOs are not membership-based organizations. As a rule, most of their funding comes from abroad and they are much more liberal and pro-western than the mainstream of society. The attempt by OTPOR and PORA to enter national politics in the aftermath of the color revolutions in their countries ended in fiasco. These failures demonstrated the limits of NGO influence. NGOs were important, but they were not the major protagonist of change. What was consciously or unconsciously underestimated by the NGO-friendly analysts was the power of nationalist and populist sentiments in any of these revolutions and the importance of the role played by their political leaders.

The anti-elite and anti-political language that was critical for the popularity of NGOs in the "long 1990s" has been captured by the populists. In other words, the rise and success of populist parties and the populist agenda presents a direct challenge to the public role of the civil society sector. Liberal ideas were very attractive to societies that were fighting totalitarianism. But, in the age of failed democratization, liberal NGOs are less attractive than the populist alternative. What liberals promise is institutional change. What populists promise is revenge on incumbent political elites. NGOs promote civic participation and deliberation as correction mechanisms for the failures of democracy, while populists promise strong leadership and an unmediated relationship between the leaders and the people.

The other factor contributing to the new context, in which pro-democracy NGOs are forced to work, is the strategy of non-democratic forces adopting democracy promotion rhetoric and creating their own NGOs as an instrument for promoting their foreign policy agendas. The creation of Russia-dominated NGO networks, including think tanks, media organizations and development centers, on the territory of the post-Soviet republics, is an essential element of Russia's new policy of domination in the region.

Rethinking Color Revolutions

Color revolutions were critical events in postcommunist Europe, but they were part of a broader trend. What the advocates of "the new wave of democratic revolutions" thesis have failed to grasp is that the common factor in Eastern Europe was not a new wave of democratization, but the collapse of the hybrid regimes that emerged from the only partial democratization of the 1990s. The color revolutions led to the opening-up of the hybrid regimes in Ukraine and Georgia, but the further consolidation of anti-democratic tendencies of the regimes in Russia and the countries of Central Asia is part of the same process. The preventive counter-revolution designed by Moscow's political strategists, is an essential part of the legacy of the color revolution.

The Kremlin basically "agreed" with democracy theorists that hybrid regimes are structurally unstable and are doomed to collapse. In Moscow's view the color revolutions embodied the ultimate threat: long-distance controlled popular revolt. Putin's preventive counter-revolution following the democratic breakthrough in Ukraine marked a profound transformation in the managed democratic regime in Russia. The change in Russia's policy thinking as a result of the Orange Revolution can only be compared to the change that occurred in American policy thinking as a result of 9/11. Moscow's immediate response to the "orange threat" was to exert total control over the media in Russia. At present, there is no single live political talk show on the major TV channels in Russia.

The Kremlin also "agreed" with the democracy theorists' analysis that splits in the elite were a critical factor for the success of the revolution. In Russia, therefore, the response has been the wholesale nationalization of the elite. The oil and gas industries have been put under total government control. And, the Kremlin has made it clear that flirting with the opposition will not be tolerated. The new NGO law adopted by the Kremlin and the creation of the Citizens' Chamber were aimed at establishing control over civil society. The receipt of "political money" from abroad has been criminalized. More importantly, Russia has rejected the idea of the legitimacy of international involvement in the protection of basic human rights. At the same time, the Kremlin has made an effort to bring the NGO sector under control by increasing the state money available to the third sector domestically and by drawing a clear line between desirable and undesirable NGOs. Scared by the efficiency of the street protests and especially the political potential of student movements, the Kremlin has shifted away from the politics of de-polarization and has created youth groups trained to supply active support to the government (these include *Nashi* and the *Molodaya Gvardia*). The development of the ideology of sovereign democracy is the last element of Moscow's preventive counter-revolution. Sovereign democracy is meant to be the ideological justification of the new regime that has been established in Russia.

The last and most convincing argument for the "change of weather" in Russia is the renewed taste for open repression of the more radical groups challenging the regime that the government seems to have developed. Activists of "The Other Russia" have been beaten and arrested. The message was unambiguous. The time of nonviolent revolutions is over. The Kremlin has shown its readiness to use violence against its enemies. The violent suppression of the pro-democracy riots in Uzbekistan was the most powerful demonstration of this new trend.

Conclusion

The central argument of this chapter is that color revolutions, as important as they were and as inspiring as they were, cannot serve as a model for further democratic breakthroughs in Eastern Europe. The promotion of democracy in the region has entered a new post-revolutionary stage. So, the real question is not "where next?", but rather "what next?". A profound change in the geopolitical, ideological and institutional contexts in which democratization efforts will take place is underway.

The war in Iraq and the rise of anti-Americanism has become a major obstacle for the promotion of democracy. U.S. foreign policy is shifting towards "realism". What now matters for U.S. foreign policy are the foreign policies of other countries, rather than their domestic policies. The famous visit of Dick Cheney to Eastern Europe, during which he sharply criticized Russia's backlash against democracy on one day, and on the next, praised the democratic achievements of the even more authoritarian regime in Kazakhstan, is representative of the new reality. "Double standards" will no longer be just an "accusation" against the U.S. administration's approach to such issues. It will be the reality of its approach. This approach will fuel anti-American sentiment and will make U.S.-supported democracy assistance much more vulnerable to criticism and denunciation. At the same time, anti-Americanism will be cynically used by non-democratic governments to discredit pro-democracy groups. These groups will be less and less inclined to accept financial support from abroad for fear of losing their public legitimacy.

The emergence of the post-enlargement European Union is the other important factor that will negatively affect not only the chances for the new wave of democratic breakthroughs in Eastern Europe, but also the chances for the consolidation of the post-revolutionary regimes. The color revolutions were the most powerful demonstration of the European Union's "soft power". The democratic breakthrough in Ukraine, particularly, has revealed an extraordinary paradox: that the European Union is a revolutionary power with transformative power sufficient to overthrow non-democratic regimes at the same time as the majority of its member-states is committed to preserving the *status quo*. But, at the same time the color revolutions have shown that the EU's soft power, its ability to mobilize and empower people, to inspire their imagination, to affect change via civic example not superior physical force, itself derives from its soft, shifting, borders. The EU's soft power lies in the promise that "if you are *like* us, you could *become* one of us". At the moment when soft borders are replaced by hard borders the ability of the EU to inspire will dramatically decline.

Further, the ideological context has changed. The anti-totalitarian liberalism advocating for human rights, free market and the rule of law that was the ideological hegemon of the 1990s is on the retreat. Societies in both Central and in Eastern Europe are in an anti-transition mood. Nationalist and populist ideologies have become worryingly popular among the voting publics. One can observe severe attacks on liberalism and on representative democracy in some of the countries of the region.

The institutional context has also changed. The war on terror has raised fears over the power of non-state actors. Funding of civil society from abroad now meets resistance in different parts of the world. And, the rise of populist parties directly affects the legitimacy of NGOs. Populism, as a worldview, considers society to be ultimately divided into two homogeneous and antagonistic groups, "the pure people" versus "the corrupt elite", and argues that politics is the expression of the general will of the people and that social change is possible only as a radical change of elite. And, ironically enough in this case, liberal NGOs are widely viewed as members of such elites, no matter how reluctant.

The western-supported NGO sector has lost its monopoly on "representing" civil society. In Russia and other countries, a well-coordinated effort on the part of the government to criminalize pro-democracy NGOs, on the one hand, and to promote and finance a government friendly third sector, on the other, is underway. Both the legitimacy and the room for maneuver of the pro-democracy civic sector have shrunk.

"Nothing seems harder to understand about a great revolution than when it is over",[9] wrote Stephen Sestanovic. In the view of this author, his observation is particularly true about the recent wave of color revolutions in Europe. The expectation that color revolutions are a model of political change that can be replicated is false. These historic upheavals signaled not a new wave of democratic revolution but the exhaustion of the "liberal moment" in democratic politics. This does not suggest that the democratization agenda is obsolete or that people will not go out onto the streets demanding their rights. It does, however, suggest that the role of international actors will decline and that the next protagonists of democratic revolutions will probably not be liberal-minded and western-sponsored NGOs. Democratization will not be what it used to be and it is time to face up to it.

---

9 Stephen Sestanovich, "Force, Money, and Pluralism", Journal of Democracy, vol. 15, no. 3 (July 2004), pp. 32-42.

ABOUT THE AUTHORS

Biljana Bijelić is a Ph.D. student of history at the University of Toronto in Canada, where she researches the impact of memories of World War II in Croatia. She completed her M.A. degree in Russian, East European and Central Asian studies at the University of Washington (United States). During the 1990s she was an activist with the Women's Human Rights Group B.a.B.e. and the Human Rights Center in Zagreb (Croatia). As a volunteer, she took part in many public campaigns organized by civil society groups in Croatia, including GLAS 99.

Valerie J. Bunce is Professor of Government, Chair of the Government Department and the Aaron Binenkorb Chair of International Studies at Cornell University in the United States. Since receiving her doctorate in Political Science at the University of Michigan (United States), she has taught at Northwestern University (United States), the University of Zagreb (Croatia) and at Central European University in Budapest (Hungary). Her research has concentrated on four sets of issues, all from a comparative perspective: democratization, economic reform, nationalism and state dissolution. Her current work (with Sharon L. Wolchik) focuses on American democracy promotion and electoral change in postcommunist Europe and Eurasia.

Martin Bútora is Honorary President of the Institute for Public Affairs, an independent public policy think tank in Bratislava, Slovakia. A sociologist by training, he was one of the founders of the Public against Violence Movement in Slovakia in November 1989 and served as Human Rights Advisor to President Václav Havel of Czechoslovakia (1990 to 1992). He taught at Charles University in Prague (Czech Republic) and at Trnava University (Slovakia) before co-founding the Institute for Public Affairs in 1997. Between 1999 and 2003, he served as Ambassador of the Slovak Republic to the United States. Martin Bútora writes on civil society, foreign policy and democratic transformation and is the author of three works of prose.

Iryna Chupryna is a graduate of the National University Kyiv-Mohyla Academy in Kyiv (Ukraine) and of the European University Viadrina in Frankfurt/Oder (Germany). In 2004, she served as deputy head of secretariat at the Freedom of Choice Coalition and was responsible for monitoring projects and fundraising. She assisted the head of the PORA coordination center with external contacts and organized the day-to-day work of the coordination center. She is one of the founders of the Civic Party PORA and received the memorial award "for outstanding participation in the Orange Revolution".

Pavol Demeš is Director for Central and Eastern Europe at the German Marshall Fund of the United States, based in Bratislava, Slovakia. Previously, he was Executive Director of the Slovak Academic Information Agency – Service Center for the Third Sector and acted as spokesperson for the Gremium of the Third Sector from 1994 to 1999. In these capacities, Pavol Demeš was actively involved in the OK '98 campaign. He served as Foreign Policy Advisor to the President of the Slovak Republic between 1993 and 1997, as Minister of International Relations in 1991 to 1992 and as Director of the Department of Foreign Relations in the Ministry of Education in 1990 to 1991. Pavol Demeš has published widely on issues of democracy and civil society, most recently the book *Prospects for Democracy in Belarus* (2006), and he has extensively trained civic activists across Central and Eastern Europe.

Miljenko Dereta is Executive Director of Civic Initiatives, a Serbian NGO he founded in 1996 to involve people in local communities in democratic change. He also serves on the council of the Federation of Serbian NGOs, the largest platform of civil society organizations in the country. Originally a freelance director of TV programs and movies, Miljenko Dereta was barred from working in his profession when he took a public position against Milošević, war and nationalism in 1989. In 1992, he became President of the Executive Board of the Civic Alliance and engaged with the Center for Antiwar Action and the Belgrade Circle.

Sharon Fisher is a Central European and Balkan specialist at Global Insight in Washington, DC, in the United States, where she conducts economic and political analysis, risk assessment and forecasting on a number of countries. She spent six months in Croatia while doing her Ph.D. studies at the London-based School of Slavonic and East European Studies (United Kingdom) and was in Zagreb for the month prior to the January 2000 parliamentary elections, allowing her to witness the campaign first hand. Sharon Fisher wrote her doctoral thesis on national identity in Slovakia and Croatia during the 1990s and is the author of *Political Change in Post-Communist Slovakia and Croatia: From Nationalist to Europeanist* (2006).

Joerg Forbrig is Program Officer for Central and Eastern Europe at the German Marshall Fund of the United States, based in Bratislava, Slovakia. Prior to assuming this position in 2002, Joerg Forbrig worked as a Robert Bosch Foundation Fellow at the Center for International Relations in Warsaw (Poland) and conducted doctoral research at the European University Institute in Florence (Italy). As a scholar and practitioner, he has worked extensively on democracy, civil society and Central and Eastern European affairs and has published widely on these issues, most recently the books *Prospects for Democracy in Belarus* (2006), *Revisiting Youth Political Participation* (2005) and *Ukraine after the Orange Revolution* (2005).

Václav Havel is a renowned Czech writer and dramatist, dissident and politician. He established himself as a playwright in the 1960s, with plays including "The Garden Party" (1963), "The Memorandum" (1965) and "The Increased Difficulty of Concentration" (1968). He was one of the first spokespersons for Charter 77 and a leading figure in the Velvet Revolution in Czechoslovakia in 1989. He was President of Czechoslovakia from 1989 to 1992 and of the Czech Republic from 1993 to

2003. For his literary and dramatic works, for his lifelong efforts and opinions and for his unyielding position in defense of human rights, Václav Havel has received numerous state decorations, international awards and honorary doctorates.

Giorgi Kandelaki was elected to the first student self-government at Tbilisi State University, Georgia, in 2001. In this capacity, he contributed to a high-profile campaign against corruption and for reform in higher education. In April 2003, he co-founded the youth movement KMARA, which played an instrumental role in Georgia's November 2003 Rose Revolution. More recently, he has trained young activists to organize for nonviolent change in Kazakhstan, Ukraine, Moldova and Belarus, where he and a colleague were detained for eleven days in August 2005. Since June 2005, Giorgi Kandelaki has been an advisor in the administration of President Mikheil Saakashvili.

Vladyslav Kaskiv is a civic activist hailing from the Ukrainian student movement of the 1990s. He served on the Presidium of the All Ukrainian Public Resistance Committee *Za Pravdu!* (For Truth) in 2000 and 2001. Between 1999 and 2004, he was coordinator of the Freedom of Choice Coalition, which implemented monitoring projects during the 1999 and 2004 presidential elections. Author of the PORA strategy, he was a member of the PORA council and head of its coordination center. After the Orange Revolution, he headed a working group on the transformation of PORA into various civil society organizations. Since April 2005, he has been an advisor to the president of Ukraine. Currently, he heads the political council of the Civic Party PORA.

Ivan Krastev is a Political Scientist. He is chair of the board of the Center for Liberal Strategies in Sofia, Bulgaria. He also serves as Executive Director of the International Commission on the Balkans and as Director of the Open Century Project of Central European University in Budapest (Hungary). In 2006, Ivan Krastev was awarded membership in the Forum of Young Global Leaders, a partner organization of the World Economic Forum. Ivan Krastev is Editor-in-Chief of the Bulgarian edition of *Foreign Policy* and a regular contributor to the *Journal of Democracy, openDemocracy* and *Europe's World.* His recent books include *Shifting Obsessions: Three Essays on the Politics of Anticorruption* (2004) and *The Anti-American Century* (co-edited with Alan McPherson, 2006).

Taras Kuzio is an Adjunct Professor at the Institute for European, Russian and Eurasian Studies of the Elliott School of International Relations at George Washington University in the United States where he previously worked as a visiting professor. In prior appointments, Taras Kuzio was a Resident Fellow at the Center for Russian and East European Studies of the University of Toronto (Canada), a Post-Doctoral Fellow at Yale University (United States), a Senior Research Fellow at the University of Birmingham (United Kingdom) and Head of Mission of NATO's Information and

Documentation Center in Kyiv (Ukraine). He contributes regularly to a variety of international media and academic publications.

Giorgi Meladze is Program Director of the Liberty Institute, a Georgia-based liberal public policy institute. He joined the Institute in 2001 and has served as its Rule of Law Director since September 2004. Giorgi Meladze holds a law degree from Tbilisi State University in Georgia and was a Public Interest Law Initiative visiting scholar at Columbia University Law School in the United States in 2002 and 2003.

Jelica Minić is a leading Serbian NGO activist and expert on European integration, currently serving as a Senior Scientific Advisor at the Institute of Economic Sciences in Belgrade, Serbia. From 1992 to 2000, she was Vice President and subsequently Secretary General of the European Movement in Serbia. She served as Deputy Minister of Foreign Affairs from 2000 to 2004, in charge of economic relations, EU affairs and regional integration. She has been a consultant for think tanks and NGOs, the Stability Pact for South Eastern Europe, international donors, European Union projects and the United Nations Development Program. Jelica Minić has lectured at various academic and professional institutions in Serbia and is the author of more than 150 publications.

Robin Shepherd is a Senior Transatlantic Fellow with the German Marshall Fund of the United States. His work focuses on global integration issues in Central and Eastern Europe and the relationship between economic development and democratization. Formerly a Public Policy Scholar at the Woodrow Wilson International Center for Scholars and since 2003 an adjunct fellow of the Center for Strategic and International Studies, Robin Shepherd was the Moscow Bureau Chief for the *Times* of London and held positions with Reuters in Central and Eastern Europe and London. He is the author of *Czechoslovakia: The Velvet Revolution and Beyond* (2000) and regularly contributes op-eds and articles to a variety of international media and publications.

Vitali Silitski, a Minsk-based political analyst, graduated in 1994 from the Belarusian State University and received his Ph.D. in Political Science from Rutgers University in the United States in 1999. He returned to Belarus to work as an associate professor at the European Humanities University in Minsk (Belarus), a position he was forced to leave in 2003 after publicly criticizing the government of President Alyaksandar Lukashenka. Since then, he has been a freelance author and analyst for the Freedom House *Nations in Transit* Report and Radio Free Europe/Radio Liberty. In 2004 to 2005, he was a Reagan-Fascell Fellow at the National Endowment for Democracy (United States). In 2006, he joined Stanford University (United States) as a visiting scholar at the Center for Democracy, Development, and the Rule of Law.

Sharon L. Wolchik is Professor of Political Science and International Affairs at George Washington University in the United States. She is the author of *Czechoslovakia in Transition: Politics, Economics, and Society,* and co-editor of

Women and Democracy: Latin America and Central and Eastern Europe; Domestic and Foreign Policy in Eastern Europe in the 1980s; Ukraine: In Search of a National Identity; The Social Legacies of Communism; and *Women, State and Party in Eastern Europe.* She is currently conducting research on the role of women in the transition to postcommunist rule in Central and Eastern Europe, on ethnic issues in postcommunist societies and the development of party systems and other aspects of politics in the Czech and Slovak Republics.

Yevhen Zolotariov holds a degree in history from Kharkiv State Pedagogical University in Ukraine. In 2000 to 2001, he headed the Kharkiv branch of the All Ukrainian Public Resistance Committee *Za Pravdu!* (For Truth). In 2004, he served on the PORA council and headed the department for special operations at the PORA coordination center. He coordinated street actions and civic resistance during the presidential campaign and the Orange Revolution. He is the head of the all-Ukrainian NGO *Nova PORA* and one of the founders of the Civic Party PORA that emerged from the transformation of the PORA civic campaign. He has received the memorial award "for outstanding participation in the Orange Revolution".

SELECTED BIBLIOGRAPHY

Aslund, Anders, "The Economic Policy of Ukraine after the Orange Revolution", Eurasian Geography and Economics, vol. 46, no. 1 (July-August 2005), pp. 327-353.

Aslund, Anders, and Michael McFaul (eds.), Revolution in Orange: the Origins of Ukraine's Democratic Breakthrough (Carnegie Endowment for International Peace, Washington DC, 2006).

Berecká, Oľga, Natália Kušnieriková, and Dušan Ondrušek, NGO Campaign for Free and Fair Elections. OK '98 – Lessons Learned (Partners for Democratic Change, Bratislava, 1999).

Bieber, Florian, "The Serbian Transition and Civil Society: Roots of the Delayed Transition in Serbia", International Journal of Politics, Culture and Society, vol. 17, no. 1 (Fall 2003), pp. 73-90.

Birch, Sarah, "The 2000 Elections in Yugoslavia: The 'Bulldozer' Revolution", Electoral Studies, vol. 21, no. 3 (September 2002), pp. 499-511.

Bunce, Valerie J., and Sharon L. Wolchik, "Electoral Breakthroughs in Postcommunist Europe and Eurasia: How Do We Explain Successes and Failures?", unpublished manuscript.

Bunce, Valerie J., and Sharon L. Wolchik, "Favorable Conditions and Electoral Revolutions", Journal of Democracy, vol. 17, no. 4 (October 2006), pp. 5-18.

Bunce, Valerie J., and Sharon L. Wolchik, "International Diffusion and Postcommunist Electoral Revolutions", Communist and Post-Communist Studies, vol. 39, no. 3 (September 2006), pp. 283-304.

Bunce, Valerie J., and Sharon L. Wolchik, "Youth and Electoral Revolutions in Slovakia, Serbia and Georgia", SAIS Review, vol. 26, no. 2 (Summer-Fall 2006), pp. 55-65.

Bútora, Martin, and Zora Bútorová, "Slovakia's Democratic Awakening", Journal of Democracy vol. 10, no. 1 (January 1999), pp. 80-95.

Bútora, Martin, Grigorij Mesežnikov, Zora Bútorová, and Sharon Fisher (eds.), The 1998 Parliamentary Elections and Democratic Rebirth in Slovakia (Institute for Public Affairs, Bratislava, 1999).

Bútorová, Zora (ed.), Democracy and Discontent in Slovakia: A Public Opinion Profile of a Country in Transition (Institute for Public Affairs, Bratislava, 1998).

D'Anieri, Paul, "Explaining the Success and Failure of Post-Communist Revolutions", Communist and Post-Communist Studies, vol. 39, no. 3 (September 2006), pp. 331-350.

Demeš, Pavol, OK '98 Campaign of Slovak NGOs for Free and Fair Elections: A Case Study (Slovak Academic Information Agency, Bratislava, 1998).

Fairbanks, Charles H., "Georgia's Rose Revolution", Journal of Democracy, vol. 15, no. 2 (April 2004), pp. 110-124.

Fisher, Sharon, Political Change in Post-Communist Slovakia and Croatia: From Nationalist to Europeanist (Palgrave Macmillan, New York, 2006).

Hale, Henry E., "Democracy or Autocracy on the March? The Colored Revolutions as Normal Dynamics of Patronal Presidentialism", Communist and Post-Communist Studies, vol. 39, no. 3 (September 2006), pp. 305-329.

Ilic, Vladimir, Otpor: In or Beyond Politics (Helsinki Committee for Human Rights in Serbia, Belgrade, 2001).

Kandelaki, Giorgi, Rose Revolution: A Participant's Story, Special Report (U.S. Institute of Peace, Washington DC, 2005).

Kapusta, Marek, Rock volieb '98 Campaign-Report on Activities and Results: A Case Study (Foundation for a Civil Society, Bratislava, 1998).

Karatnycky, Adrian, "Ukraine's Orange Revolution", Foreign Affairs, vol. 84, no. 2 (March-April 2005), pp. 35-52.

Karumidze, Zurab, and James V. Wertsch (eds.), Enough: The Rose Revolution in the Republic of Georgia 2003 (Nova Science Publications, New York, 2005).

Kaskiv, Vladyslav, Iryna Chupryna, Anastasiya Bezverkha, and Yevhen Zolotariov, PORA – Vanguard of Democracy (PORA, Kiev, 2005).

Krastev, Ivan, "Democracy's 'Doubles'", Journal of Democracy, vol. 17, no. 2 (April 2006), pp. 52-62.

Krnjević-Misković, Damjan, "Serbia's Prudent Revolution", Journal of Democracy, vol. 12, no. 3 (July 2001), pp. 96-110.

Kužel, Rastislav, and Marek Mračka, Project MEMO '98: A Case Study (Helsinki Citizens' Committee and Association for the Support of Local Democracy, Bratislava, 1998).

Kuzio, Taras, "Civil Society, Youth and Societal Mobilization in Democratic Revolutions", Communist and Post-Communist Studies, vol. 39, no. 3 (September 2006), pp. 365-386.

Kuzio, Taras, "From Kuchma to Yushchenko: Ukraine's 2004 Elections and 'Orange Revolution'", Problems of Post-Communism, vol. 52, no. 2 (March-April 2005), pp. 29-44.

Kuzio, Taras, "The Orange Revolution at a Crossroads", Demokratizatsiya, vol. 14, no. 4 (Fall 2006), pp. 477–492.

Lazić, Mladen (ed.), Protest in Belgrade: Winter of Discontent (Central European University Press, Budapest, 1999).

Levitsky, Steven, and Lucan A. Way, "International Linkage and Democratization", Journal of Democracy, vol. 16, no. 3 (July 2005), pp. 20-34.

Levitsky, Steven, and Lucan A. Way, "The Rise of Competitive Authoritarianism", Journal of Democracy, vol. 13, no. 2 (April 2002), pp. 51-65

Locke-Binnendijk, Anika, and Ivan Marović, "Power and Persuasion: Nonviolent Strategies to Influence State Security Forces in Serbia (2000) and Ukraine (2004)", Communist and Post-Communist Studies, vol. 39, no. 3 (September 2006), pp. 411-429.

Marples, David R., "Color Revolutions: The Belarus Case", Communist and Post-Communist Studies, vol. 39, no. 3 (September 2006), pp. 351-364.

McFaul, Michael, "The Fourth Wave of Democracy and Dictatorship: Compromise and Noncooperative Transitions in the Postcommunist World," World Politics, vol. 54, no. 2 (January 2002), pp. 212-244.

McFaul, Michael, "Transitions from Postcommunism", Journal of Democracy, vol. 16, no. 3 (July 2005), pp. 5-19.

Paunović, Žarko et al. (eds.), Exit 2000 – Non-governmental Organizations for Democratic and Fair Elections (Center for Democracy Foundation, Center for Development of the Non-Profit Sector and Civil Initiatives, Belgrade, 2001).

Silitski, Vitali, "Belarus: Learning from Defeat", Journal of Democracy, vol. 17, no. 4 (October 2006), pp. 138-152.

Silitski, Vitali, "Preempting Democracy: The Case of Belarus", Journal of Democracy, vol. 16, no. 4 (October 2005), pp. 83-97.

Spasić, Ivana, and Milan Subotić, (eds.), Revolution and Order: Serbia after October 2000 (Institute for Philosophy and Sociology, Belgrade, 2001).

Szomolányi, Soňa, and John A. Gould (eds.), Slovakia: Problems of Democratic Consolidation and the Struggle for the Rules of the Game (Slovak Political Science Association and Friedrich Ebert Stiftung, Bratislava, 1997).

Way, Lucan A., "The Dynamics of Autocratic Coercion after the Cold War", Communist and Post-Communist Studies, vol. 39, no. 3 (September 2006), pp. 387-410.

Way, Lucan A., "The Sources and Dynamics of Competitive Authoritarianism in Ukraine", Journal of Communist Studies and Transition Politics, vol. 20, no. 1 (March 2004), pp. 143-161.

Way, Lucan A., "Ukraine's Orange Revolution: Kuchma's Failed Authoritarianism", Journal of Democracy vol. 16, no. 2 (April 2005), pp. 131-145.

Wheatley, Jonathan, Georgia from National Awakening to Rose Revolution: Delayed Transition in the Former Soviet Union (Ashgate, New York, 2005).

G | M | F The German Marshall Fund
of the United States

STRENGTHENING TRANSATLANTIC COOPERATION

The German Marshall Fund of the United States (GMF) is a nonpartisan American public policy and grant making institution dedicated to promoting greater cooperation and understanding between the United States and Europe.

GMF does this by supporting individuals and institutions working on transatlantic issues, by convening leaders to discuss the most pressing transatlantic themes, and by examining ways in which transatlantic cooperation can address a variety of global policy challenges. In addition, GMF supports a number of initiatives to strengthen democracies.

Founded in 1972 through a gift from Germany as a permanent memorial to Marshall Plan assistance, GMF maintains a strong presence on both sides of the Atlantic. In addition to its headquarters in Washington, DC, GMF has six offices in Europe: Berlin, Paris, Bratislava, Brussels, Belgrade and Ankara.

The German Marshall Fund of the United States
1744 R St. N.W.
Washington, D.C. 20009
T: (+1) 202 745 3950
F: (+1) 202 265 1662

The German Marshall Fund of the United States
Transatlantic Center for Central and Eastern Europe
Sturova 3, 811 02 Bratislava, Slovak Republic
T: (+421) 2 5931 1522
F: (+421) 2 5931 1405

ERSTE Foundation

DIE ERSTE österreichische Spar-Casse Privatstiftung is the direct successor to the savings association bank Erste Oesterreichische Spar-Casse, founded in Vienna in 1819. ERSTE Foundation draws its mandate from the tradition of the savings banks, which were founded more than 180 years ago as non-profit organizations. As the main shareholder of Erste Bank, ERSTE Foundation ensures the bank's independent future. It is one of the largest foundations in Europe and dedicates parts of its profits to the common good of the region in which the Erste Bank Group operates.

DIE ERSTE österreichische Spar-Casse Privatstiftung is active in the entire Central and South Eastern European region. It commenced its activities in 2005, focusing its work on three programs in the areas of Social Responsibility, Culture and Europe. Through the interaction between these programs, a platform will develop which promotes dialogue and a transfer of knowledge in Central and South Eastern Europe.

ERSTE Foundation collaborates as directly as possible with local partners that identify and initiate local requirements and needs. In the medium term, ERSTE Foundation will build up a network of such partners in Central and South Eastern Europe.

DIE ERSTE österreichische Spar-Casse Privatstiftung
Graben 21, 1010 Vienna, Austria
T: (+43) 50100 15430